The Leaderless Economy

The Leaderless Economy

Why the World Economic System Fell Apart and How to Fix It

PETER TEMIN and **DAVID VINES**

PRINCETON UNIVERSITY PRESS

Princeton and Oxford

Published by Princeton University Press, 41 William Street, Princeton, New Jersey 08540
In the United Kingdom: Princeton University Press, 6 Oxford Street, Woodstock, Oxfordshire
OX20 1TW
press.princeton.edu

Library of Congress Cataloging-in-Publication Data

Temin, Peter.
    The leaderless economy : why the world economic system fell apart and
  how to fix it / Peter Temin and David Vines.
        pages   cm
    Includes bibliographical references and index.
    ISBN 978-0-691-15743-6 (alk. paper)
    1. Economic policy.   2. International economic relations.   3. Global
  Financial Crisis, 2008–2009—Government policy.   I. Vines, David.   II. Title.
  HD87.T416   2013
  320.6–dc23   2012032589

British Library Cataloging-in-Publication Data is available

This book has been composed in Minion Pro with ITC Franklin Gothic display
by Princeton Editorial Associates Inc., Scottsdale, Arizona

Printed on acid-free paper. ∞
Printed in the United States of America

10   9   8   7   6   5   4   3   2   1

For our children and grandchildren
in the hope that they will soon see a return to prosperity

For Peter: Elizabeth, Melanie, Colin, Zachary, and Elijah

For David: Sam, Alexander, Louis, Luke, and Tom

CONTENTS

THE DISCUSSIONS THAT LED TO THIS BOOK began after the eruption of the unpronounceable Icelandic volcano, Eyjafjallajökull, stranded Peter in London after a 2010 conference. David invited him to wait for the skies to clear in Oxford, leading to four days of discussion about the topics of this book. We transformed our clear agreement on the issues into a book outline during Peter's week in Oxford in the spring of 2011, and we worked on it while David visited MIT in the fall of 2011 under the MIT-Balliol Program. (We first met two decades earlier, when David hosted Peter at Balliol College under this same program, and have been in touch since.)

We have been giving talks and writing papers on these themes over the past few years, and we decided that a full-length presentation of our thesis and its historical background would help current policy deliberations. We offer this volume to all who are interested in the world economy and distressed at the lack of understanding often shown in the popular press. As we describe in the text, we use only simple economic models and reserve discussion of the models—as opposed to the history and analysis—to an Appendix.

For their feedback we thank the audiences at the American Academy of Arts and Sciences; the Asia Europe Economic Forum in Paris, Seoul, and Tokyo; the Australian National University; the Fundación Ramón Areces (Madrid); MIT; Oxford University; the Reserve Bank of Australia; Swarthmore College; the University of California at Berkeley; and Wake Forest University. And we thank Christopher Adam, Christopher Allsopp, Ross Garnaut, and Max Watson for their insights along the way.

We thank Balliol and Nuffield Colleges for accommodation while meeting in Oxford and Balliol College and MIT for accommodations while meeting in Cambridge, Massachusetts.

The Leaderless Economy

ONE The World Economy Is Broken

I T IS CLEAR THAT THE WORLD ECONOMY is in a mess. Since its collapse in the autumn of 2008, the world economy has gone through three distinct phases. It contracted by 6 percent between 2007 and 2009. A bounceback took place in 2009–10, which did not amount to a full recovery because output rose by only 4 percent. Then the recovery paused, and some countries have experienced another downturn, albeit one much shallower than that in 2008–9.

The resulting damage over the past four years has been immense. The world economy is 10 percent poorer than it would have been had economic growth continued smoothly after 2007, and unemployment has risen sharply. In many advanced countries the level of activity has even now not yet returned to what it was in 2007. And the pain is not yet over. However much national economies pick up, unemployment is set to fall only very slowly in the United States and Europe. For unemployment to drop significantly, we need a resumption of global growth. That does not seem likely based on current policies. Five years after the collapse, even economic growth in China and India is falling.

Instead we live in a world in which risks to global growth appear great. The risk of a European crisis is real, as indicated by newspaper coverage that looks like *The Perils of Pauline*. Both consumers and the financial system are anxious to deleverage—that is, to pay down debt. The public sectors are under pressure to reduce government deficits and pay down public debt. Concern is mounting about international trade imbalances like those between Germany and Southern European countries, and many observers are alarmed by the magnitude of government debt in Southern Europe. The imbalances between the United States and East Asia, including China, are troubling, and some are concerned about the stability of US debt held in the form of Chinese foreign exchange reserves. In the face of this uncertainty, productive investors are holding back from making large-scale investments. At a time of great uncertainty, many producers deem it unwise to invest, just as consumers find it prudent to save.

How can policymakers get growth to recover and unemployment to fall when there are so many troubling signs? Depending on whom you talk with, the unnatural magnitude of either unemployment or debt is a major sign of disarray. These symptoms of economic distress can be observed in many countries in America and Europe, but they are only parts of the problem that need to be addressed. For these national problems are all aspects of an international problem, in fact a global one.

We contend that that the multitudinous national problems can be solved only in the context of straightening out the international economy. We argue that domestic (internal) economic problems cannot be solved without also resolving international (external) problems. Unless the trade of major countries can be made more balanced and the debts of some unfortunate countries can become more acceptable to investors, it will not be possible to restore prosperity within nations. This holds both in Europe and for global trade among industrialized countries.

We argue further in the following pages that the modern world economy falls apart occasionally from lack of international leadership. A hegemonic country has the power to help countries cooperate with one another for the maintenance and, when needed, the restoration of prosperity. When no country can or will act as hegemon, a world crisis erupts. The Great Depression was the result of Great Britain's loss of hegemonic power and the failure of the United States to pick up the mantle. The weakness of the recovery from the Global Financial Crisis, of 2008, and the future risks to this recovery, is the result of the United States' diminished influence and the lack of a successor on the world stage.[1]

We can learn how to understand our current troubles by comparing the current crisis with the Great Depression. The parallels are a bit frightening, and we hope that the lessons learned from the comparison can speed the resumption of prosperity. One lesson is that large international crises are hard to understand; it took many years for John Maynard Keynes and others to understand what was happening in the 1930s. If this book can help current politicians and economists frame the right questions, perhaps we can help speed the journey out of the present troubled economic woods.

This book explains how domestic and foreign problems, which we generally refer to here as internal and external problems, respectively, are related and how economic policies can be constructed to make progress in both areas. We call on history to show how ignoring one or the other problem has led to economic disaster, and we use simple economic tools to explain how to view these problems in concert. It is sad that few people recall this history and remember the simple tools used to grapple with such situations, and we hope to raise the awareness of these tools in our readers.

All countries are part of the world economy. Some are more active than others, but few of them can exist without contact and commerce with other countries. This need for external contacts imposes obligations on each country to participate in the general patterns of the common world economy. When something goes wrong either domestically or abroad, a country needs to make internal adjustments to adapt to the new situation. The adjustments then will alter the external relations of that country, forcing other nations to adapt as well. In other words, domestic and international aspects of economic health are intertwined.

We focus on the problems of fixed exchange rates: the gold standard, the euro, and the dollar-renminbi peg. The basic theory of the relations between countries on the gold standard was formulated by David Hume over two centuries ago. The price-specie-flow mechanism has been taught to generations of students, but insufficient thought has been given to how this mechanism works (or does not work) in an industrial world. Keynes tried to unravel this problem when he testified before a government committee of enquiry in 1930, known as the Macmillan Committee. But he was confused and failed to convince anyone of his views. He subsequently tried to address the questions he failed to answer in front of the committee, and we follow him in this effort. We argue that today's policymakers have forgotten the progress made in understanding how fixed exchange rates worked in the past, lessons which Keynes learned, with painful consequences. We use a mixture of history and theory to explain what is required to dig ourselves out of the deep hole into which the world economy has fallen.

This complicated project requires explanation. We provide background in this chapter, starting with national problems and progressing to those of the world economy. The description of contemporary conditions occupies this chapter; the historical background needed to understand the role of international imbalances fills later chapters. We argue that the international imbalances are fundamental to the world economic problems we face today, even though these imbalances are not immediately apparent. Only by examining arcane data, such as the balance of payments, do observers sense the dynamics of the global economy—except of course in times of crisis like the one we have been living through.

The principal source of current distress is the waste of resources evident in the lack of employment for those seeking work. The most obvious way to gauge unemployment is to examine the unemployment rate. The rate in the United States is around 8 percent and only declining slowly. It rose dramatically in 2008 and 2009 and has stayed high since then (see Figure 1.1). This rate remains far higher than the 5 or 6 percent that economists previously thought was enough to account for labor-market frictions (that is, the processes of looking for good work and changing jobs when conditions change). The rate represents an increase of about 5 million workers who would be happy to work if there were jobs. There are 5 million or so additional workers who say they are underemployed.

However, unemployment rates include only those workers looking actively for jobs. As the recession drags on, more and more unemployed people become discouraged and stop looking. They will disappear from the lists of unemployed, but not into work. One way to avoid this bias in the rate is to examine the ratio of employment to the population. This ratio fell 5 percentage points from a narrow band close to 63 percent in 2008 and 2009. As with unemployment, the change appears to be durable; we certainly hope it will not be permanent. These data are shown in Figure 1.2.

There are many things wrong with this new "normal." First is the waste of resources stemming from the forgone labor of the millions of unemployed workers. We do not have data on the unutilized and underutilized capital to go with them, but idle labor is a good indicator that we are leaving dollar bills on the sidewalk. There is no good reason to ignore millions of workers seeking work. Work is a defining characteristic of life, as witnessed by the number of names that echo employment, from Millers to Masons, Coopers, Taylors (tailors), and Weavers. It is worth recalling Orwell's observations from England during the long spell of unemployment in the 1930s: "The peculiar evil is this, that the less money you have, the less inclined you feel to spend it on wholesome food. . . . There is always some cheaply pleasant thing

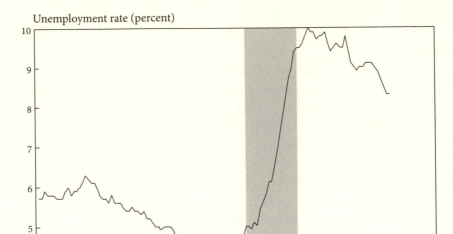

FIGURE 1.1 US unemployment rate

Source: US Department of Labor, Bureau of Labor Statistics. Available at http://research.stlouisfed
.org/fred2/.

Note: Shaded area indicates US recession.

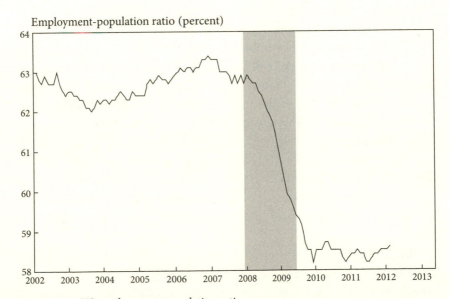

FIGURE 1.2 US employment-population ratio

Source: US Department of Labor, Bureau of Labor Statistics. Available at http://research.stlouisfed
.org/fred2/.

Note: Shaded area indicates US recession.

to tempt you. . . . Unemployment is an endless misery that has got to be constantly palliated, and especially with tea, the Englishman's opium."[2]

In addition to becoming depressed, unemployed workers lose their skills. They are like ice cubes that melt or evaporate when stored. They become harder and harder to employ again as their skills decline and their socialization into a working environment disintegrates. This is particularly hard on young people just entering the labor force. If they cannot find a good job to launch a career, they may miss out on this opportunity for the rest of their working lives as younger cohorts seize subsequent opportunities. In the United States, where health care typically is linked to employment, people may actually die from unemployment. By allowing unemployment to continue, we risk eroding the reservoirs of knowledge and skills that are key resources for economic growth in the long run.

Finally, depressed and unemployed workers take out their frustrations in politics. They are angry and prone to voting against anyone who has been in office without fixing the economy. They may be receptive to extreme views and to politicians who propose simple solutions to complex problems. The Nazi vote in Germany grew dramatically as unemployment increased in 1931 and 1932; riots in Greece during the autumn of 2011 and election patterns in 2012 showed the appeal of extreme positions today. We can only hope that such enthusiasms will not be embodied in national policies.

Unemployment is similarly rife in Europe, but there are differences that are important to our story. There is no United States of Europe. While Europe is roughly the same size as the United States, it is composed of about 30 independent countries. They are associated in a variety of mutual organizations, but they have not given up central issues of sovereignty to these entities. The European Union (EU) contains 27 member countries, and the European Monetary Union (EMU) has 17. Countries in EMU of course share a common currency—the euro. We describe these organizations more fully in Chapter 5, but the primary contrast with the United States can be stated here.

The United States was formed in 1789 when the separate states realized that they were vulnerable in their poorly organized confederation. The new constitution gave the federal government the ability to tax citizens of the previously sovereign states. George Washington's Secretary of the Treasury, Alexander Hamilton, had the federal treasury purchase all state debts at par—that is, for their face value—in 1790. In the short run, he was accused of rewarding speculators who had bought highly depreciated state bonds. In the long run, he is credited with establishing the credit of the United States, a critical component of economic prosperity. The existence of the union was challenged only once, in the Civil War of the 1860s, and it has survived conflicts about the nature and extent of taxation for more than two hundred years.

The act of creating EMU established a uniform currency, the euro, but individual countries within the Eurozone maintained their own sovereignty. Monetary policy was centralized in a new European Central Bank, but fiscal policy was left to individual states—subject to guidelines that were stated but not enforced. Because member nations issued their own bonds, they were subject to country risks. EMU, in other words, adopted a single currency without also adopting centralized fiscal control.

Unemployment in the EU, and in the Eurozone, jumped in 2009 with the American rate. The picture is not as clear there as in the United States, due to both pervasive unemployment before the crisis of 2008 and great differences in the records of individual member countries. Economic policies since the crash have been contractionary in most European countries, and unemployment has continued to increase as a result. Unemployment rates for a few European countries are shown in Figure 1.3, where the contrast between Germany and Spain can be seen clearly. We analyze this divergence in Chapter 5.

The imbalance in the supply of and demand for labor is echoed in the financial markets. There appears to be money available everywhere, as indexed by the essentially zero return on securities of the US government and the variety of assets that ordinary citizens can buy at their local banks. But if an individual tries to borrow money for personal use or for her business, she discovers that she can borrow only with difficulty and by paying a large premium over the government rate. The difference partly comes from the risk that she or her business will fail to repay the loan (known as a risk premium). Large debts are common, and the cost of financing them varies by the perceived risk of default. Potential borrowers from banks who had assets of their own now find that their resources, and therefore their collateral, have been reduced. In these uncertain times with so many unemployed resources, it is hard for banks to evaluate the risks of individual enterprises. Banks therefore lend to only the safest customers and take a long time to decide who is worthy; many interest rates are above zero as a result.

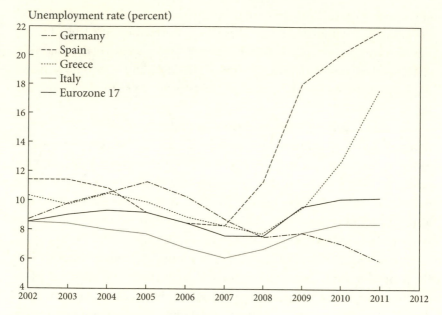

FIGURE 1.3 Selected European unemployment rates

Source: "Unemployment rate, annual average, by sex and age groups (%)" under the dataset "Employment and unemployment (Labour Force Survey)." Eurostat, updated April 2, 2012. Available at http://appsso.eurostat.ec.europa.eu/nui/show.do.

There are two other, more worrying, reasons why some interest rates on borrowing have remained high three years after the Global Financial Crisis of 2008. The first is that bank assets lost value in the crisis. Bonds of various sorts that seemed worth close to their face value before the crash are salable at prices far lower, if they are salable at all. Banks have been reluctant to admit that their balance sheets are less solid than they appear, and regulators have been loath to press them. Banks, whatever they say in public, are acting as if they lack adequate capital. They are restricting loans and charging high interest rates to rebuild their capital at their customers' expense.

The second reason is that public bonds have come under fire as well as private assets. The credit of the United States is good and is viewed as such around the world, even though the US government lost its triple-A rating from Standard & Poor's in the summer of 2011. The value of US government bonds has stayed high, and the interest rate on them hovers near zero. By contrast, the value of various European bonds has fallen as investors fear that they will not be redeemed at par. The decline in the value of these bonds, held by banks in both Europe and the United States, has put additional pressure on bank balance sheets.

There are of course many kinds of debts, and they are all lumped together in the preceding paragraphs. One way to understand the relations among them is to invoke the most elementary truth of macroeconomics: investment equals savings. The latter gives rise to financial assets and liabilities, and it can be divided into three parts. Personal savings result in retirement accounts if they accumulate or in personal debts if people consume more than they earn and have negative savings. Governments save when they run a government surplus and have negative savings, which increases government debt, when they run a budgetary deficit. Foreign countries contribute their savings when a country imports more from foreigners than it sells to foreigners in exports. And foreign savings decrease when the foreign country buys more exports from a country than they provide to it by way of imports. Domestic investment then is equal to the sum of personal, government, and foreign savings.

This is simply an explanation of the elementary equation of macroeconomics. It acquires more life if one thinks about the movement of these quantities over time. Assume for simplicity at this stage that investment stays constant, so we can look at various kinds of savings. Then changes in one kind of savings need to be offset by changes in another to keep the two sides of the equation equal. For example, if a government dis-saves by running a large deficit, either domestic savings must rise or foreign savings must rise (in which case the country will run an increased foreign deficit). For most countries, this offset comes from foreign savings, giving rise to the story of this book. The example of Japan, where government deficits have been offset by domestic savings, reminds us that outcomes can vary with three kinds of savings. We expand this thought to the world in Chapter 6.

We argue that the world economy at the moment is unbalanced. This is revealed by the large and destabilizing capital flows among countries. The problem is not the flows themselves, as capital inflows have promoted economic development all over the world. But when capital inflows are used for consumption instead of investment, the receiving country does not create the capacity to repay the loans it received. Investors get scared, and a crisis can ensue.

Of all nations, China has the largest surplus on current account by far—more than $300 billion in 2011. The runners-up are Germany and Japan, with less than $200 billion apiece. The only other countries with more than $100 billion are oil exporters Saudi Arabia and Russia. The largest deficit country is the United States, with a current account deficit of close to $500 billion. No other country comes close; they all have deficits under $100 billion. In Europe, Germany again is the largest surplus country by far, joined by the Netherlands on a smaller scale; Italy, France, and Spain have the largest deficits. These imbalances have endured long enough to result in large assets and debts in surplus and deficit countries, respectively. The United States has about $16 trillion of foreign debt, rivaled only by the total EU debt. China has the largest foreign reserves of any country, amounting to more than $3 trillion in 2012.[3]

There is nothing wrong with international borrowing, but large debts can lurch out of control. If the borrowed resources are consumed instead of invested, borrowing countries may not generate enough surplus to repay the loans. Domestic housing should be considered as a consumer durable rather than investment in this discussion because houses are not traded on international markets. The three most important characteristics of housing are location, location, location, and an increase in domestic housing does not add to a country's ability to pay its foreign debt. If lenders suspect that deficit countries have consumed the resources acquired by borrowing, they may charge more for renewing loans from the consuming countries. As the costs of outstanding loans increase, the burden on the borrowing countries rises. In the limit, as we will see, the burden is regarded as unsustainable. The risk premium for countries—just as for individuals—rises, and trouble follows.

This kind of crisis can be seen in the events in the autumn of 2008, when Lehman Brothers failed. As we discuss further in Chapter 4, private debt in the United States had been subdivided into tranches that were supposed to represent different degrees of risk. When calculating these risks, no one anticipated the Lehman failure. When it did fail, all previous risk calculations were called into question. Because the accepted value of many assets depended on these calculations, investors instantly became suspicious of asset values. There were many sellers and few buyers of what became toxic assets.

Before the failure, only the bottom tranches with high risks were known as toxic assets. The effect of the Lehman failure was to make all assets look alike; they were all toxic waste. With sellers far outnumbering buyers, prices fell precipitately in a kind of fire sale. Markets became deranged when appropriate buyers could not be found , and asset trading ground to a halt. Only after prices had crashed and investors had recovered from their initial panic did markets regain their normal relations—albeit at far different prices than before the Lehman bankruptcy.

Europe flirted with the same kind of panic in the autumn of 2011. It all started with a realization that the Greek national debt was larger than had been thought and larger than Greece could easily pay. As in the United States in the summer of 2008, nothing was done in Europe to allay investor fears until much later. Investors normally distinguish among European countries, but the monetary union led them to believe that many countries are like Greece. Greece did not go bankrupt, and there was no cataclysmic signal like the Lehman bankruptcy, but panic began to spread. More investors wanted to sell the bonds of European countries than to buy them, and their prices fell.

Fortunately, conditions did not develop into a fire sale. In early 2012, the European Central Bank offered to lend euros to banks using national bonds as collateral. To investors, this policy looked like the proverbial bag of gold in a bank window, a signal that the bonds would not default. Prices rose, and interest rates fell. Calm returned to the euro region. But the problems that had induced the panic have not been resolved. Greece still has an unsupportable debt, and other countries have large debts as well. The complexities of this story are described in Chapter 5; here we assert that abundant debts—domestic and foreign—are signals of world disorder, just as extensive unemployment is.

Now that we have seen both indicators of our current distress—unemployment and excess debts—we might ask whether there is any relationship between them. The answer of course is yes. Unhappily, they are cousins rather than siblings, so it will take a little explanation to show how they are related. We need to take you into the kitchen to show how the world economy is made. Like all kitchens, this intellectual one is filled with bright lights, sharp corners, and hot items. We implore you to bear with these possible discomforts long enough to get a first look at how the separate episodes to follow fit together into a unified narrative.

Unemployment and financial crises are both signs of macroeconomic dysfunction. They are the results of breakdowns in economies, and they are not normally considered in economists' models of well-functioning economies. To understand how they are related, we need to consult an older train of economic thinking that specialized in the analysis of these breakdowns. This body of thought is typically called Keynesian, because it answers questions Keynes raised in the course of the previous end-of-regime crisis, the Great Depression. The important role of this theory is to suggest policies when normal conditions are absent. (See the final section of the Appendix for more details.)

Start with unemployment. We consider a country with full employment and stable prices to be in equilibrium. We call this *internal* equilibrium because it is concerned with conditions inside a country. If the demand for labor is less than its supply, then there will be people who cannot find jobs. Unemployment typically is measured by the number of workers actively seeking work who cannot find it. When unemployment is high, we speak of involuntary unemployment to distinguish workers looking for jobs from those who are not—whether they are retired, discouraged, or simply happy to be idle.

If the demand for workers is larger than the supply, then we expect employers to raise wages to attract workers out of other jobs and to compete actively with other employers to get workers. Wages will rise under these conditions, and prices will follow, resulting in inflation. Just as unemployment is a measure of disequilibrium on one side, so inflation is an indication of disequilibrium on the other. Taking our cue from the labor market, we see the former gap as having insufficient demand and the latter gap as having excess demand.

When many countries have insufficient demand, we speak of a world depression. This does not mean that all countries suffer to the same extent—some may even prosper. But many countries suffered in the Great Depression of the 1930s, even some we do not regard as active participants in the world economy. By contrast, worldwide inflations have also occurred, particularly in the second half of the twentieth century, which affected all countries as well. Small countries can have their own difficulties, but large countries affect others whether they intend to or not.

The causes of debts appear to be quite different from those which cause demand to be too high or too low, but they are really rather similar. The debts that interest us here are national ones, that is, debts that one country owes another. These debts are distinguished from private debts of households and business firms and public debts of governments. These various kinds of debt are all important, and we will discuss the relations among them later, but foreign debts are the focus of interest here.

A country falls into debt with other countries if the value of its exports is smaller than that of its imports. In balanced trade, a country pays for its imports by its exports. If the exports fall short, there has to be another way to pay for some of the imports. One option—the most popular one in the modern world—is to export paper IOUs. These IOUs are foreign debts, and we will refer to them now by this more formal term. In the short run, every country would prefer to pay for imports with debts, because debts are so easily produced. In the long run, however, these debts will have to be paid, and most countries curb their appetites to limit the magnitude of their outstanding debt.

Who buys these debts? By symmetry, countries whose exports are larger than their imports trade some of their exports for debt from other countries. As these surplus countries accumulate foreign debts, they accumulate foreign assets. In the short run, countries may want to increase their exports to promote economic growth; they may value growth more than they value current consumption, composed partly of imports. In the long run, these countries have to decide what they are going to do with all their foreign assets. The British exported goods to their empire and accumulated massive foreign assets in the nineteenth century, as we discuss in Chapter 2, and then spent all these assets fighting the First World War. That history, however, is unusual; the more general case is when countries promoting economic growth through exports find themselves with lots of foreign assets and nothing to do with them. We discuss this problem further in Chapters 5 and 6.

We define a country to be in *external* balance when it does not increase or decrease its foreign debts—its IOUs to foreign countries—faster than its national income is growing. We speak of a country as being in deficit when it is acquiring more foreign debt and in surplus when it is reducing its foreign debt or increasing its foreign assets. Countries for which the ratio of foreign debt or assets to national income stays constant are thus considered to be in external balance.

A simple example may make this concept clear. Under the gold standard that was the framework for international trade and investment before the First World War, deficit countries paid for excess imports with gold. In other words, countries with abundant gold reserves could afford to import more goods and services than they could pay for with their exports. But countries that used up their gold reserves this way could find themselves in trouble. If they ran out of gold, or if investors thought they might soon do so, investors might try to sell their currency for gold to get what they could before the country ran out of gold. This sounds like a traditional banking panic, and currency crises share the dynamics of bank panics. During a currency crisis, countries might have to abandon the gold standard in one way or another, as described in Chapter 2.

Adam Smith's friend David Hume explained in his essay "Of the Balance of Trade" how a country on a specie standard maintained external balance (Hume referred to coins of gold and silver collectively as specie). In a very modern form of economic thinking, Hume stated his "general argument":

> Suppose four fifths of all the money in Britain to be annihilated in one night, and the nation reduced to the same conditions with regard to specie as in the reigns of Harrys and Edwards; what would be the consequence? Must not the price of all labor and commodities sink in proportion, and every thing be sold as cheap as they were in those ages? What nation could then dispute with us in any foreign market or . . . sell manufactures at the same price which to us would afford sufficient profit? In how little time, therefore, must this bring back the money which we had lost and raise us to the level of all the neighboring nations? Where, after we have arrived, we immediately lose the advantages of the cheapness of labor and commodities, and the farther flowing in of money is stopped by our fullness and repletion.
>
> Again, suppose that all the money in Britain were multiplied fivefold in a night, must not the contrary effect follow? . . . Now 'tis evident that the same causes which would correct these exorbitant inequalities, were they to happen miraculously, must prevent their happening in the common course of nature and must for ever in all neighboring nations preserve money nearly proportioned to the art and industry of each nation.[4]

We can reframe Hume's model in a more modern guise. Assume that a country in external balance suffers a decline in its exports, so that they no longer pay for its imports. Needing something to use instead, it uses its specie (that is, gold and silver coins) to pay for its imports. Because the domestic money supply consists largely of coins, this international transaction decreases the domestic money stock. As there is less money, people do not have enough cash to pay for all the goods and services being produced at the old prices. Prices have to fall to adjust to the lower monetary stock. Even though the exchange rate with other countries, set by the amount of gold and silver in their specie, has not changed, what economists call the *real* exchange rate has changed. The prices of domestic goods are lower relative to foreign goods than they were before, not because the exchange rate has changed but because prices have changed. (The real exchange rate measures the exchange rate after allowing for any change in prices.) Exports are cheaper for potential foreign buyers, and imports are more expensive for potential domestic consumers. Exports rise; imports fall. The balance between exports and imports can be regained, and the outward flow of specie halted. This simple process is known as the price-specie-flow model.

Although this model is very simple, its insights stimulated economists and governed policies for two and a half centuries, until the early twentieth century. It was elaborated by many people to take account of changed circumstances, leaving the main insights intact. We discuss the mechanism by which prices are raised or lowered in the presence of financial assets and interest rates in later chapters. But before we get to its modern analogues and extensions, we can reveal a few of this model's insights here.

The first insight is that the price-specie-flow model connects internal and external balances. The beginning of the process can be described as an external imbalance, because it is the result of a change of exports without a corresponding change in imports. The outcome of the process, however, can be described as an internal imbalance, because the reduction of the money stock results in deflation. The connection between external and internal imbalances is one of the central topics of this book. In fact, the point of our analysis is precisely to explain the connections between external and internal balances. Some analysts focus on the need for internal balance within isolated economies; others consider the need to balance international trade: they consider external balance. We contend that this separation of analyses prevents economists and others from understanding the true complexity of the world's problems today. Keynes spent the 1930s trying to understand these linkages in the midst of the Great Depression. He did not understand them in 1930, but he had a clear grasp of them a decade later.

The second insight is tied up in an important asymmetry in the discussion so far. We have measured internal imbalances by inflation on the one hand and unemployment on the other. But in Hume's narrative, the imbalance in the price-specie-flow mechanism caused deflation of prices instead of causing unemployment. When considering internal imbalance, why did we distinguish between inflation and unemployment (our asymmetry),

whereas Hume thought symmetrically, with a rise in demand causing inflation and a fall in demand causing deflation? What happened since 1750 to
destroy Hume's symmetry? The answer is that the Industrial Revolution
came between his time and ours. Hume lived in an agricultural society,
while we live in an industrial or even a postindustrial one. Agricultural
prices and wages move up and down in responses to changes in the supply of
and demand for workers, crops, and animals. But industrial prices move
upward far more easily than downward. The problem is that it is hard to
lower wages in industrial economies.

This transformation to an asymmetric response came about halfway
between Hume's time and ours, in the late nineteenth century. The growth of
large firms (described in Chapter 4) led to large concentrations of workers in
factories and cities. Industrial workers resist wage cuts, although they cheer-
fully accept wage increases. This asymmetry was true before unions became
strong and continues unabated even where unions have declined. It certainly was present in the Great Depression, and economists and policymakers alike dealt with its consequences at that time.

The price-specie-flow model can be easily altered to take account of this
change. When exports fall relative to imports in this more modern version,
employment falls. The decline in the money stock leads—by mechanisms we
detail later—to a reduction in the quantity of work instead of a reduction in
the pay for work. Unemployment instead of deflation is the path to the
recovery of external balance. Economists today refer to this asymmetry as
Keynesian because Keynes emphasized it in his work, but he described it as
an empirical fact well before he wrote his most famous book, *The General
Theory*, in 1936. When Keynes wrote *A Treatise on Money*, published in 1930,
he assumed full employment and appealed to the symmetrical form of the
price-specie-flow mechanism in his analysis. It was precisely this disconnect
between his evidence and his theory that produced Keynes' problems before
the Macmillan Committee in 1930 and led him to write *The General Theory*
thereafter. Having straightened out his assumptions to describe more accurately the twentieth-century world in which he lived, Keynes could use his
new understanding to return to questions of international balance he originally had raised in *The Economic Consequences of the Peace*, published in
1919, just after the First World War. This intellectual journey and its lessons
for today are the topics of Chapter 3, although, as we will see, they were not
fully understood until presented in a book by James Meade in 1951 and in a

paper by Trevor Swan in 1955. These lessons are explained more fully with the aid of what is called the Swan diagram in the Appendix.[5]

We begin our journey to this understanding with an account of how the world got into the Great Depression, a mess even worse than the current one. Worldwide imbalances prevailed both internally and externally. It took a great set of shocks to shatter the world economy in this way. As we show in Chapter 2, these shocks, and their outcome in the form of the Great Depression, can fairly be called an end-of-regime crisis. We recall that crisis because of the obvious parallels with the problems we now face. That crisis also provides the setting for our view of Keynes' intellectual odyssey (recounted in Chapter 3) that foreshadows our own in the final chapters of this book. The path to the end-of-regime crisis we are now experiencing is described in Chapter 4. We chronicle recent events and ask how this history can inform decisions now in Chapters 5 and 6.

We are hardly the first to survey the damage from the Global Financial Crisis of 2008. Reinhart and Rogoff surveyed the data for many crises under the ironic title *This Time Is Different*. Their point is that all crises are alike; this time is never different. They document this similarity largely by calculating averages of various measures related to crises. They infer from their work that it normally takes years to recover from a financial crash—a salutary warning. Their work carries the implication that there is nothing to do but wait. However, averages cannot by themselves indicate whether crashes can be separated usefully into different types. In fact, Reinhart and Rogoff broke their own rules and distinguished between domestic banking crises and currency crises. But is this the proper taxonomy? And might not different kinds of crises have different sorts of outcomes and call for different policy responses?[6]

Koo divided crashes into two kinds in his modestly titled book *The Holy Grail of Macroeconomics*. Ordinary recessions have little effect on the value of assets, but balance-sheet recessions are big enough to affect asset values, as described earlier. In what Koo calls balance-sheet recessions, banks and nonfinancial corporations restrict spending in the recovery as they deleverage. In other words, there are big and small recessions, depending on the effect of a crash on asset values. This is a useful reminder that asset values are important, but it does not provide a way to tell how much change in asset values is needed to cross the line into a balance-sheet recession.[7]

We also argue that there are two kinds of financial crises. Almost all of them are what we think of as ordinary crises, where the work of Reinhart and Rogoff is invaluable. But there are occasional crises that throw the world economy into disorder. We argue in this book that these are end-of-regime crises, ones that occur infrequently and only when the regime that governs the world economy is unable to provide the needed leadership. We argue that the industrial world economy is stable when there is a hegemonic power. In fact, we define a *hegemon* as an economically powerful country that can promote cooperation among nations. Hegemons endure for generations, and we speak of Britain as the hegemon of the nineteenth century and the United States as that of the twentieth. Changing hegemons is difficult: a new hegemon often takes a while to emerge after the old one declines. The result is a major recession—often classified as a depression—that marks (in retrospect) the end of a hegemonic power. The Great Depression was one end-of-regime recession; the current world crisis is another.

Britain ruled the waves in the nineteenth century. It set an example for all nations in the midcentury Crystal Palace exhibition of manufactures, and it promoted industrialization in many countries. The Bank of England was the custodian of the gold standard in the late nineteenth century, and adherence to the gold standard became a goal of all nations active in the growing international trade stimulated by industrialization and cheap ocean transport. Keynes referred to London as the conductor of the international orchestra. After the First World War, however, Britain lost its ability to foster cooperation among nations that is the hallmark of a hegemon. Relations among the warring nations were poisonous after the war, and Britain was either unable or unwilling to promote a cooperative world order. Britain was powerless to affect the punitive French occupation of the Ruhr in the early 1920s and to convince countries outside the British Empire to go off gold in the early 1930s. Without a conductor, the international orchestra descended into cacophony, and the world economy collapsed into the Great Depression.[8]

The United States was hegemonic in the twentieth century. Its late entry into both world wars made the difference between stalemate (or worse) and Allied victory. Its postwar leadership promoted cooperation among the warring parties that contrasted sharply with the aftermath of the First World War. Its economic prowess had no rival and became the standard against which all other economies were measured. Its educational accomplishments set the standard to which other countries aspired. But, as with Britain nearly a century earlier, American uniqueness diminished as other nations progressed toward the end of the twentieth century. After the boom and bust of the first decade of the current century, the United States found itself demoralized and in debt as its financial leadership collapsed. In the international discussions that now are considering policies to alleviate the problems described earlier, the United States is hardly the conductor—and may not even be a leading orchestra member. There is no hegemonic power around today to lead the world economy toward prosperity and balance.

We therefore begin our narrative with an account of the British century: the period when Britain was a world hegemonic power. Britain lost this status in the turmoil of the early twentieth century, and the Great Depression was the result. This is the story of Chapter 2, which sets the stage for all that follows. In Chapter 3, we trace Keynes' efforts to understand this process as it unfolded. We argue that he was concerned with the interaction of internal and external balances from *The Economic Consequences of the Peace* in 1919 to his work at Bretton Woods in the early 1940s. Keynes' first popular book showed his intuitive understanding of the issues, but he could not convince others of his approach solely by intuition. It took the combined efforts of Keynes and many others to provide a convincing version of his conclusions about the Versailles Treaty ending the First World War, and to see how to apply this after the Second World War.

We continue the story through the period of American hegemony in Chapter 4. The American century began before the Great Depression and continued for the rest of the twentieth century. The United States developed and changed in this time, recently bringing its hegemonic status into question. Like the Great Depression, the current economic distress has exposed the limits of the assumed hegemon. We analyze current imbalances in EMU —the euro area—in Chapter 5. And we expand this story to the imbalances between China and the United States and then to those of the world as a whole in Chapter 6. The interaction between internal and external balances that we introduced here and develop further in Chapters 5 and 6 guides our analysis.

The world now faces choices that will determine how the imbalances analyzed in these chapters can be corrected. If a cooperative solution can be found, then the task will be feasible, although it will take several years to unwind all the positions that have developed over the past decade. This kind of cooperation will be encouraged if a hegemon emerges to stimulate and guide it. If nations cannot cooperate, then the world may be subject to the perils of a noncooperative default that will be distinctly unpleasant. We describe the choice of cooperation in terms of the Prisoner's Dilemma game, explained in the Appendix. It is hard to predict how bad the situation will become, but the example of the Great Depression as described in Chapter 2 is hardly encouraging.

We argue throughout that history provides a useful guide for current decisions. It seems as if Marx was right: history repeats itself, first as tragedy, then as farce. We are not yet in another Great Depression, largely because of safety nets that have been constructed since the 1930s. However, the collective memory appears to have forgotten the lessons of the previous end-of-regime crisis. And policies at the moment seem to risk allowing the world to stumble into another Great Depression, rather than resolutely leading us away from it. We hope that our book will help people to remember the relevant history and use it to put the world economy back together again.[9]

TWO The British Century and the Great Depression

W̲E BEGIN THE PROCESS OF UNDERSTANDING how to rebalance the
world economy after the recent end-of-regime crisis and work toward
solving the problems described in the last chapter by analyzing the previous
end-of-regime crisis. The Great Depression marked the end of the British
century, just as the recent crisis signals the end of the American century.
Expanding our number of observations from one to two provides an enormous gain of information. We might wish for more observations, but we
also must be grateful that history does not provide more examples of these
rare and severe events.

Preparation for the British century began in the eighteenth century with
two peaceful revolutions. The Financial Revolution of the first half of the
eighteenth century allowed the British government to tax its citizens reliably
enough to borrow vast sums of money to fight its many continental wars.
The growing government revenue also supported the English navy, which
ruled the oceans in the nineteenth century and led in the conversion from
sail to steam. British primacy in steam power came from the Industrial Revolution, which began in the second half of the century with the application
of inanimate power to industrial activities. The contrast between the origins
of British hegemony and the waning of American hegemony—where war
was waged and taxes lowered—is in contrast all too clear.[1]

The Industrial Revolution began with innovations in cotton textiles, iron,
and steam engines in the late eighteenth century. The innovations came
from the unique British combination of high wages from Britain's pivotal
role in the expanding Atlantic trade and low fuel costs from the country's
large endowment of coal. Several innovations mechanized the spinning of

cotton thread with the use of water and then steam power. Ironmongers learned to use coke (made from coal) in place of charcoal to smelt iron ore, reducing the price and expanding the output of iron. James Watt patented the separate condenser that made the steam engine into a versatile power source in 1776. Joined by many smaller innovations, these productive advances propelled the British economy into international leadership based on cotton, coal, and steam.[2]

All subsequent industrializations were accomplished by a massive shift of labor from agriculture to industry. Britain was the first to industrialize because it had already made much of the transition away from agriculture. London was the largest city in the world in its role as the center of a vast network of trade and colonization. Rural families had left agriculture for manufactures in the old sense of the word, making cloth for export. The share of the labor force in agriculture at the start of British industrialization was around one-third, a share for an agrarian economy that was "astonishingly low."[3]

The British century began with the defeat of Napoleon at Waterloo in 1815, leading to a century of peace in Europe, albeit with several interruptions by limited wars. By the middle of the century and the Great Exhibition of 1851, Britain was the workshop of the world. British ships circled the globe and were leading the change from sail to steam. British engineers were ubiquitous, introducing standard screw threads—so that nuts and bolts could be mass produced—and building railroads in America and Asia. Following the British example, aspiring countries began their industrializing with the mechanization of cotton textile production.

Britain was the first industrialized country to prosper by an export-led strategy. The British concentrated on exporting manufactures and achieved great success, as they had industrialized first. Cotton textiles initially were their largest export, but these textiles were joined by woolen goods, iron and steel, coal, and machinery. If importing countries could not pay for these goods, Britain lent them the funds. This pattern of exports paid for by balance-of-payments surpluses allowed Britain to continue its exports throughout the nineteenth century. It also allowed the country to accumulate an enormous portfolio of foreign assets. This in turn enabled the City of London to dominate international finance and become the conductor of the international orchestra.[4]

Britain's dominance of international financial markets came from its positive balance of payments, that is, the excess of exports over imports, which lasted through most of the nineteenth century. In the language of Chapter 1, Britain was willing to accept IOUs from other countries so that it could send goods and services to them. It accumulated an enormous sum of foreign assets by the end of the century. Britain was able to reach this favorable position because it was exporting its manufactures to the rest of the world. In modern terms, it was using an export-led program of industrialization. This is not to say that British leaders or industrialists perceived the situation in this way. They thought that there was a worldwide demand for cotton thread and cloth, an insatiable demand for railroads in a growing number of countries, and demand as well for industrial goods and engineering services that British entrepreneurs profitably could supply.

Britain was the first country to follow this export-led development strategy, and many other countries, small and large, have followed its lead. Britain had an advantage in many markets, and its firms prospered, because it was the first country to industrialize. By continually running a positive balance on its current account, Britain accumulated foreign assets. Investing some of these assets in local projects led to British earnings that accentuated the positive balance. Once started, this process flourished, leading to massive British holdings on the eve of the First World War. Britain had foreign assets of £4 billion in 1913.[5]

Other countries were catching up to Britain as the century progressed, and steel production in the United States and Germany surpassed that in Britain by the end of the century. It was noted at the time as the "crossing of the courses" of national steel output. Britain held to free trade, while the Americans and Germans promoted their industries behind high tariff walls. This forced Britain to emphasize exports of its traditional products to less industrialized countries. It was not that Britain fell behind in every industry, but rather that the British economy did not move into new industries. Britain's economic problem was not so much in what it did and how well it did it, but rather in what it did not do as other industrial giants grew.[6]

The growth of two economic rivals raised the question—only dimly apparent at the end of the nineteenth century—of which one would be the next hegemon. However, there was only one military rival. The British and Germans started an arms race that was destined to end in war. Germany stepped up its naval construction project after some diplomatic reversals in the early twentieth century. Admiral Alfred von Tirpitz wanted to bring the German navy from half to two-thirds of the size of the British navy. The British launched the *Dreadnought* in 1906, a large battleship powered by steam turbines and mounted with large guns. Trying vainly to keep up, Tirpitz got authorization for three new battleships in 1912, financed by taxes on sugar and distilleries. This highly visible naval arms race inflamed public opinion in both Britain and Germany, setting the stage for the war to come.

German troops poured into Belgium on their way to France in August 1914. Britain could not stand by while a bid for hegemony from its economic, military, and diplomatic rival began with an attack on France. However unprepared, Britain had to fight. A revisionist historian has argued that Britain should have sat out the war—because Germany ultimately became hegemonic in Europe after the Second World War—and saved itself the trauma of the Great War.[7] Abdicating its worldwide hegemony was not a choice that Britain could be expected to have made—instead the country was trying to maintain this supremacy. In addition, Germany lost its bid to become the next hegemon, as we all know. We discuss the important difference between Europe and the rest of the world in Chapter 5.

The First World War descended into a stalemate. Germany had tried to exert its power in Europe and been thwarted by Britain and France. But they were unable to defeat Germany, and it was only the entry into the war of the United States in 1917 that moved the war to its conclusion. The United States showed its power at this time, but it was not yet ready to assume international hegemony. President Wilson came to the Versailles negotiations with his plan for the League of Nations, but he was unable to convince his opponents in the United States of its merits. He suffered a debilitating stroke just after the negotiations, and the League opened without American participation.

Article 231 of the Versailles Treaty held Germany responsible for the war, establishing legal grounds for reparations. These were supposed to cover war-related material damages. The definition of damages was ambiguous; whereas the cost of reconstruction undoubtedly was included, controversy developed over the inclusion of compensation for personal losses (mainly pensions to widows and disabled men). An official of the British Foreign Office who later became a leading historian remarked later that "the important difference between the Versailles Treaty and the previous peace treaties providing for payment to the victors by the defeated Power was that, on this occasion, no sum was fixed by the treaty itself."[8] Soon after the Armistice, Germany was stripped of its gold reserves, most of its merchant navy, and whatever equipment (such as rolling stock) that might be of use to the victors. Deliveries of coal were also required. In the following months, preliminary reparation payments were required, pending a final settlement.

It is here that John Maynard Keynes enters our story. At the end of the First World War he held a key post at the British Treasury in charge of all international aspects of Britain's war policy, even though he was then only in his mid-thirties. He was sent to Paris after the war as the chief representative of the British delegation at the negotiations that led to the Versailles Treaty. But Keynes resigned at the end of June 1919 in quiet fury at what was happening in these negotiations. Returning to Britain, he slipped away to a country house that was the rural retreat of artistic friends from the Bloomsbury group. There, in two short months, he wrote *The Economic Consequences of the Peace* in protest at what had happened at Versailles.

Keynes condemned reparations as economically irrational and politically unwise. He argued that the treaty was not sensible—indeed, that it was against the best interests of the victorious powers to cripple Germany economically, because much of Europe's pre-1914 welfare had depended on German economic growth. Moreover, Keynes envisaged difficulties in transferring real resources across borders, given the uncertainty about how the postwar international capital market would work. His overall view was that reparations were vindictive, insane, and ultimately unworkable. They would lead to continued conflict, not peace. *The Economic Consequences of the Peace* was a best seller that established Keynes as a global public intellectual. It also set the agenda for Keynes' subsequent research, as we describe in Chapter 3.[9]

Keynes phrased his conclusion in two ways. He began with dry economics:

> It is certain that an annual payment can only be made by Germany over a series of years by diminishing her imports and increasing her exports, thus enlarging the balance in her favour which is available for effecting payments abroad. Germany can pay in the long-run in goods, and in goods only, whether these goods are furnished direct to the Allies, or whether they are sold to neutrals and the neutral credits so arising are then made over the Allies.[10]

He concluded with a strong statement of his opinion:

> The policy of reducing Germany to servitude for a generation, of degrading the lives of millions of human beings, and of depriving a whole nation of hap-

piness should be abhorrent and detestable—abhorrent and detestable, even if
it were possible, even if it enriched ourselves, even if [it] did not sow the
decay of the whole civilised life of Europe.[11]

These statements present what economists now call the transfer problem.
How does one country pay a debt—whether reparations or sovereign debt—
to another? Only by transferring goods, that is, only by forgoing consumption of the goods it produces. Forced savings, for that is what they are,
degrade the quality of life in the debtor country, as Keynes noted so force-
fully. His clear statement of the problem shows that Keynes already had conceptualized one of the difficult problems of international economic relations;
he would continue to work on this problem for the next quarter century. It
also anticipates problems in today's world that have their origins in the
architecture of the European Monetary Union and the export-led growth
strategy of Japan and China. Today's problems did not arise in a military
conquest, but that does not mean that the solution of the transfer problem is
any easier than the problems of the 1920s, as we discuss in Chapters 5 and 6.

Reparations became Germany's foreign debt. No explicit bond had been
issued by Germans or the German government to non-Germans, but there
was a schedule of payments that had the same characteristics as debt service.
It was as if Germany's consumption spree was war, and the demand for reparations can be seen as a claim on Germany by those countries who involun-
tarily had been forced to use their production to make war—some of which
was sent toward the German army. The analogy works the other way, as current calls for Greece to pay its debts without requesting any contribution
from its bond holders smack of the reparations arrangements in the 1920s.

Keynes predicted continued hostility and opposition to the treaty and
reparations. He did not foresee any cooperative movements by the previous
combatants:

All these influences . . . favour a continuation of the present conditions instead
of a recovery from them. An inefficient, unemployed, disorganized Europe
faces us, torn by internal strife and international hate, fighting, starving, pil-
laging, and lying. What warrant is there for a picture of less somber colors?[12]

The tragedy foreseen by Keynes proceeded in three acts. We can think of
these three acts in terms of our simple model presented in Chapter 1, which

described the need for an economy to have both internal balance and external balance. The first act was characterized by continuing conflicts within
and among countries, conflicts that prevented internal balance from being
re-established within countries for many years.

However bad the Versailles Treaty was, internal politics in Weimar Germany were worse. The German high command refused to acknowledge its
responsibility for losing the war. The generals instead tried to blame others
for their failings. They argued that Germany had been stabbed in the back
by republicans who had deserted the monarchy. These republicans were
termed November Criminals for signing the Versailles Treaty. The *Dolchstosslegende* (stab-in-the-back legend) became a rallying cry for the right-
wing extremists of the Weimar Republic.

The legend echoes the epic poem *Nibelungenlied* in which the dragon-
slaying hero Siegfried is stabbed in the back. The association of myth and
history was made at the highest levels of the German high command. It fell
on fertile ground, as the war had been fought mostly on French soil. Berlin
was far from the Western Front, and Germany still had a large agricultural
sector despite its impressive recent industrialization. From Berlin and the
German countryside, it was hard to believe that the German army had been
defeated.

The *Dolchstosslegende* had important effects on German politics and economics. Some of the republican leaders were Jewish, and the legend quickly
became an anti-Semitic slogan. Well before the Nazis came to power, virulent anti-Semitism could be seen in a wave of assassinations of progressive
German politicians. Matthias Erzberger, who signed the Versailles Treaty for
Germany, was assassinated in 1921. Walter Rathenau, Foreign Minister of the
Weimar Republic, was assassinated in 1922. These high-profile murders kept
the *Dolchstosslegende* alive and legitimated less severe anti-Semitic acts.[13]

The *Dolchstosslegende* was created by General Erich Friedrich Wilhelm
Ludendorff, assistant to General Paul von Hindenburg, who had been called
from retirement to head the German high command. It was the official line
of the German military, coming from the top of the command. Hindenburg
was elected President of the Weimar Republic in 1925; he was very popular
even though the war had been lost, as the legend perpetuated the idea that
he had been stabbed in the back. He was persuaded to run for reelection
against the newly popular Hitler in 1932, even though he was 84. He won,
but it was a Pyrrhic victory for the opponents of Hitler. Hindenburg dis-

solved the Reichstag almost immediately and appointed Hitler as chancellor at the start of 1933. There was a straight line from the German defeat in the First World War to the Nazi aims that led to the Second World War.

Weimar economics followed the political line. Policy was designed to oppose the British and French and reduce or eliminate reparations. We cannot know how far this negative aim went and whether the German economic policies were adopted in good faith. However, it is clear that German leaders put the termination of reparations ahead of domestic prosperity in making their plans.

British prices doubled after Britain's suspension of the gold standard at the start of the war. This created a problem for the country's position under the gold standard. The British Treasury appointed a commission on the currency and foreign exchange after the war under the direction of Lord Cunliffe, Governor of the Bank of England, to consider the options in this situation and report back to the government. The commission's 1918 report foreshadowed the economic history of the interwar years. It argued that the best defense against instability was the gold standard and invoked the stability of the past to predict that similar arrangements would guarantee stability in the future. The most important of these arrangements guaranteed the free purchase and sale of gold at prewar parities. "In our opinion," wrote Cunliffe, "it is imperative that after the war the conditions necessary to the maintenance of an effective gold standard should be restored without delay. We are glad to find there was no difference of opinion among the witnesses who appeared before us as to the vital importance of these matters."[14]

But even though Cunliffe wrote that the gold standard should be restored without delay, he recognized that this was not possible. Given inflation, it was not possible to simply revert to gold at prewar parity once the war ended. Cunliffe therefore recommended a delay of several years. This tension between the immediate need and the distant implementation reveals the ambiguous position of Britain in the world economy. On the one hand, it was still the leader of the world economy and of the gold standard on which international economic affairs were based. On the other hand, it was unable to pick up the baton as conductor of the international orchestra immediately —or, as it turned out, for long. Just as Britain had not been able to defeat Germany by itself, it could not sustain peace by itself.

This discussion reveals the importance of the short run. The relevant short run can last for several years, as Cunliffe noted. Long-run equilibrium and current conditions were far apart. The only way to get from here to there in the early 1920s appeared to be in a straight line. We assert that consideration of the short run provides a way to consider other alternatives and avoid the predictable strains of proceeding in a straight line. Implementation in the 1920s of policies designed for the long run led to strains on the international economy that eventually led to crisis rather than to the long-run goal.

Cunliffe set the model for current discussions of national debts deriving from the crisis of 2008. But even though it is important to think of the long run and long-run institutions, it also is necessary to consider policy in the short run. The unanimity of Cunliffe's statement of policy forecasts the unanimity of central bankers and national governments that preach austerity today. It contrasts with the Marshall Plan after the Second World War and the bilateral effort in the Bretton Woods negotiation that set the terms for the resumption of international economic relations that we discuss in Chapter 4.

Widespread explosions of working-class struggles and protests after the war complicated economic policies in the early 1920s. Workers had formed increasingly successful unions in the years before the war in Britain, where they dated back several decades, and on the continent. The war provided a tremendous boost to these organizations. Maintaining the discipline and morale of huge armies raised through compulsory conscription entailed both pressures and concessions, and the latter included promises of a better life for the masses as soon as hostilities were over. Life in the trenches also proved to be a tremendous catalyst for the emerging mass society: workers from various areas and occupations got to know one another's needs and local strengths, and at the same time socialist propaganda could be much more effective in such huge concentrations of working-class people. At home, the urgent need to increase production of military supplies and overcome traditional restrictive practices required recognition of, and concessions to, the trade unions. From 1916 on, trade union membership increased steeply in Britain, Germany, and France. The Russian Revolution also exercised considerable influence on working-class movements, even though this influence was ambiguous: it was a model for a militant minority but at the same time a highly divisive factor for those who did not share this ideology.

The economic impact of social developments differed according to the relative weakness of the economies and of the governments that emerged from the war. Thus, in Weimar Germany, the social democratic government undertook a number of social reforms, certainly out of its own political conviction, but also to undermine working-class support for the revolutionary movement. Mines and metal-making were socialized; that is, trade unions were fully recognized and the eight-hour week was introduced. Deficit spending by the state followed, partly feeding into the price spiral. As a result, however, social unrest diminished considerably; by early 1920, hours lost in strikes were already half the number counted one year earlier.

The Italians sought to emulate Britain and deflate to establish their claim to membership in the first rank of financial and economic powers. Monetary expansion during the war had led to inflation. Italy's prime minister in 1920–21 prescribed the classic gold-standard medicine to deal with Italy's postwar problem: deflation and reduced government services. He assigned "higher priority to financial and monetary stabilization than to cultivating the political support of the mass parties."[15] But as creating conditions to restore the gold standard was reviving the flow of capital into Italy, Benito Mussolini was exploiting the domestic strains needed to achieve this result. Workers took over the management of a number of companies during the so-called red biennium, and the working-class movement was weakened by the division resulting from the creation of a Communist Party in 1921. The political fabric in Italy did not prove strong enough to withstand the fiscal retrenchment, which intensified the forces leading to the 1922 March on Rome that inaugurated twenty years of fascist dictatorship.

In France and Britain, the enormous number of strikes during 1919 affected both industrial output and investors' expectations. Governments in both countries regained control of the situation during 1920, often by rather harsh repressive measures. Although the trade union movement suffered a serious setback in France, the circumstances and the results of the social conflict were different in Britain, because the trade unions had already developed strong roots and the 1918 elections brought in a relatively sympathetic government.

The French hesitated to cut public spending and balance the budget, policies that were preconditions for returning to gold. Eliminating the fiscal deficit would have undermined their claim that German reparations were needed to defray the costs of reconstructing the French economy. Insistence that "the Boche" should pay, based on memories of the French indemnity paid to Germany in 1871, encouraged successive governments to postpone the decision of how to distribute reconstruction costs and more generally the costs of putting the national finances on a stable footing.[16]

Germany represented the other side of the French coin. Balancing the budget and stabilizing the currency might be seen as admissions that the government's obligations did not exceed its financial capacity—that the Reich could afford to make reparations after all. The motives of the Weimar government are not clear, but the budgetary policies seem to support the views of the many Germans who thought that their country should not have lost the war and was still destined to replace Britain as the hegemonic power. The internal economic decisions led to conflicts and strife throughout the 1920s. They were a kind of guerrilla war against the victors.

The German failure to fulfil part of the preliminary reparations requests prompted occupation by French and Belgian troops in March 1921 of the towns of Düsseldorf, Duisburg, and Ruhrort on the east side of the river Rhine. Needless to say, this move did not contribute to a stable international environment. Only one month later, the London Schedule of Payments for the first time formally established Germany's reparation obligations. Germany continued to drag its feet, and France and Belgium again entered its territory in 1923, this time occupying the mining district of the Ruhr.

The incentive for the Germans to inflate preceded France and Belgium's invasion of the Ruhr due to the open-ended reparations imposed by the Versailles Treaty, but foreign occupation of Germany's industrial heartland was ample justification for running the printing presses full out. Hyperinflation, though an effective weapon in the country's diplomatic battle with Paris, grew increasingly disruptive of the operation of the German economy as relative prices failed to indicate what to purchase. Money creation, which as late as 1922 still stimulated the demand for the products of the German economy, grew increasingly disruptive in 1923. Previously respectable people on fixed incomes were impoverished, and those who lived on the edge of the economy were enriched. The reversal of economic rewards traumatized German thought and culture; Germans today refer more often to the hyperinflation of 1923 than to the Nazi takeover of 1933.[17]

As inflation ran out of control, its main effects came to be aggravating uncertainty and demoralizing consumers. Industrial production went into steady decline, and the opinion of influential industrialists swung toward compromise, accommodation, and exchange-rate stabilization. In 1924 these shifts in sentiment allowed stability to be reestablished under the Dawes

Plan, named for the American negotiator of the plan, a critical component of which was restoring the mark to its prewar parity with the aid of a massive loan from the United States.

The economic and occasionally military chaos of the early 1920s showed the limits of Britain's tattered hegemony. The First World War had dealt British overseas trade a blow from which it never recovered. The volume of exports of all kinds that the United Kingdom was able to sell abroad in 1920 was about 30 percent less than it had been in 1913. Even in 1929, export volumes still languished almost 20 percent below their prewar level. UK exports of manufactures suffered devastating losses of market share in all types of products and in all markets.

Britain had exported a larger proportion of its output of manufactures than any other country in Europe before the war. The forced withdrawal from the market during the war accelerated the growth of import substitutions and compelled importers to look elsewhere for the cotton cloth, machinery, shipping, and other goods and services they needed. Nonbelligerents had been able to expand their output in ideal conditions and compressed what might otherwise have been a long, drawn-out process of change into a few years, making it difficult or impossible for British industry to find a satisfactory answer to the challenge.[18]

Economic growth in Britain had begun to flag in the late nineteenth century, a movement known as the British climacteric. Although Britain had led all other countries in moving its labor force from agriculture and the countryside into industrial cities, it lagged in the late nineteenth century in the introduction of new techniques and products. Large managerial firms dominated American industry far more than they did in Britain. The Germans pioneered the development of the chemical industry, an offshoot of coke production that was ignored by the British. While the Americans and Germans emphasized new products like steel and chemicals, Britain continued its reliance on cotton and coal. Recent analyses of time series have cast doubt on an actual fall in the national growth rate, but there is little doubt that Britain's leadership of industrial societies was slipping.[19]

The British cotton industry was the flagship of its industrialization; it flourished and exported in the late nineteenth century. It was based on the traditional mule technology, despite the switch in other countries to the newer ring technology. British cotton workers were the most skilled, and they could compete in the late nineteenth century with workers in other countries. Less-skilled cotton workers around the world earned lower wages, largely reflecting their labor productivity as these other countries developed. British workers enjoyed the rewards of great skill, but the traditional mule technology was losing out to the newer ring technology. The war marked a transition from mules to rings even if the actual process took many years. The cotton industry in postwar Britain was no longer competitive, although this future had not been obvious to industry participants before the war.[20]

Unable to return to the gold standard immediately, Britain was powerless as the struggle with Germany continued after the cessation of the war. Britain remained a capital exporter, but it no longer dominated international capital flows. It had sold much of its overseas capital to fight the war, and the Americans emerged as a potential hegemon. It was not until 1924 that the Dawes Loan from the United States created a reasonably stable system of international payments that allowed private capital to flow into Germany. This made it possible for reparations to be transferred peacefully to France (which was due to receive more than half of them), the British Empire, Italy, Belgium, and the minor Allies. The Allies in turn used reparations to repay their war debts to the United States. The Dawes Loan was only the most visible of the ways in which America completed the circle by lending money to Weimar Germany.

Debate over how to apportion the costs of stabilization continued in Britain, becoming acrimonious after Labour's defeat in 1924. The Labour Party had adopted a program of socialism, including a minimum wage and state-provided family allowances legitimated by the workers' contribution to the war effort. The wage issue was particularly contentious in the coal industry, a hotbed of labor activism. The demand for coal received a boost in 1923–24, when Ruhr supplies were disrupted by the French occupation. These circumstances were favorable for the miners, and they negotiated a guaranteed minimum wage. But when the conflict on the continent went into remission, the demand for British coal fell, and the agreement collapsed.

A Royal Commission on the Coal Industry insisted that wages had to be lowered. The result was not just a coal strike, but a general strike in 1926. The general strike ended in defeat for labor, which only hardened the unions' opposition to the constraints of the gold standard. Ultimately, that opposition would weaken both the Tory government, which was defeated in 1929, and Britain's commitment to the gold standard, abandoned in 1931. The

Treasury tried to defuse this conflict in the late 1920s by asserting that the rationalization of industry, rather than wage reductions, was a better way of cutting labor costs, but the gold-standard imperative of lowering costs remained strong.[21]

The second act of Keynes' tragedy of the 1920s had the appearance of stability and prosperity. Internal balance had been reestablished in Germany, and in the United States the economy was growing strongly. France had consolidated its budgetary position, devalued its currency, and was recovering through a growth in exports. Britain had significant unemployment, but it had deliberately chosen to forgo internal balance in the interests of submitting to the corrective discipline of the gold standard,

The tensions evident in act one of the tragedy had only gone underground. Although prosperity was the watchword in the United States, Weimar Germany, and France, international finance was still unsettled. There were external imbalances throughout Europe, and between the United States and Europe, which gave rise to large international flows of capital. The appearance of calm by observers who were not sensitive to the international imbalances and the resulting accumulation of debts and assets is very reminiscent of recent experience during the first decade of the euro. In Chapter 5 we describe the havoc that emerged in the recent crisis that should have reminded people of the 1920s.

The massive flows of capital that emerged from the sequence of postwar financial developments and policies destabilized the apparent equilibrium. The process started early in the 1920s with the flight from currencies, such as the German mark, the French franc, and the Italian lira, as those who could transferred their financial assets to what they perceived to be safer currencies. Because of the high interest rates necessary to defend the pound, London was a favored haven. Once confidence in the stability of the French and other continental currencies and in their underlying public finances was restored, speculative funds flowed back again in eager anticipation of capital gains when the new parities were legally established. Italy was the recipient of considerable capital inflow in the year preceding the de jure stabilization of the lira in December 1927.

The loss of gold as flight capital rushed to France after the stabilization of the franc was always mentioned and often resented as a major cause of the weakening in Britain's external financial position. France had elected to stabilize the franc at one-fifth of its prewar value, whereas Britain had subjected itself to the discipline necessary to restore sterling at its prewar parity. This was seen as a major source of the balance-of-payments disequilibrium among nations. Despite the dramatic increase in French reserves, accumulated at first in foreign exchange and later in gold, the authorities did not respond to this by inducing a corresponding increase in the money supply. To do so would have stimulated a rise in prices that would have helped restore equilibrium.

In June 1928 French gold reserves were only 29 billion francs; by the end of 1932 they had increased by 53 billion, but the increase in the note circulation over the same period was only 26 billion francs. The returning French capital was mainly used for the purchase of government securities, either directly by the private sector or by the commercial banks as their deposits increased. The government in turn was able to repay a substantial part of its debts to the Bank of France. As a result, the large increase in the central bank's holdings of gold and foreign currency was to a considerable extent sterilized.[22]

The gold standard was not operated according to the rules in France, and the necessary adjustment process was frustrated. The very low level of French foreign investment exacerbated the situation. With their pre-1913 assets largely wiped out by the war and the Russian revolution, French rentiers had become extremely reluctant to trust any more of their capital to foreign governments and enterprises. Had they been prepared to do so, it would have returned gold to the rest of the world and helped restore spending there, which was being diverted to cheap French goods. Treasury and central bank officials in Paris and London argued bitterly over the reasons for the movement of gold to France, what actions should or could be taken to reverse the flow, and whose responsibility it was to take corrective measures. Even when it was recognized that the final outcome was not the result of a French policy designed to sterilize the inflow of gold, it was still regarded as a failing in the system leading to a serious misdistribution in international holdings of gold.

Similar issues were raised about policies in the United States, the other country to show a substantial increase in its gold holdings during the 1920s. Gold convertibility of the dollar was restored as early as 1919. American banking authorities considered that gold inflow into the United States in the early part of the following decade was the result of the abnormal postwar conditions in Europe. They expected that most of the gold would in due course return to

Europe and, therefore, should not be used as the basis for domestic credit creation in the United States. Neutralization was thus a deliberate policy, for which there were thought to be "sound and compelling reasons."[23]

In the subsequent period, 1925–29, the United States continued to neutralize any changes in the stock of gold, though on a less extensive scale. In 1928 and 1929, the Federal Reserve Board initiated a progressive increase in interest rates to prevent what it saw as an alarming rise in speculation on the stock exchange, regardless of its implications for the requirements of international stability. Such countries as Britain, which were running balance-of-payments deficits at this time, might well have preferred a more aggressive policy of credit expansion in the United States, which would have led to a higher level of prices and money incomes there. This inflation would have helped meet the foreign demand for dollars and relieve the strain on foreign exchanges and the general deflationary pressure that developed in the latter part of the twenties. Even though the United States had far more gold than France, the inflows of gold to the two countries were almost the same, and the effect of sterilization in both countries was highly deflationary for the world as a whole.[24]

The diminution of the previous hegemon can be seen in balance-of-payments statistics for the individual European borrowers and lenders for 1924–30, shown in Table 2.1. The records of the debtors show an immense net inflow of some $7.8 billion, an average rate of over $1.0 billion per year. The movement of capital was dominated by foreign lending to Germany, which received more than $4 billion, over 50 percent of the gross flow to Europe. Most of this capital came from the United States, and for a while it seemed that there was no limit to the appetite of American issuing houses and their investors for German bonds, regardless of the purposes for which the loans were raised, or for the interest to be earned from placing money on short-term deposit with German banks. The next largest destinations, a long way behind, were Austria and Italy, which together obtained about $1.8 billion. Roughly $1.3 billion was invested in Eastern Europe, especially Romania, Poland, and Hungary. These sums were quite large relative to their recipients' national economies, giving foreign capital a significant role in their interwar economic and political history.

The United States had backed into a position of hegemon. If the measure of a hegemon is to ensure that nations cooperate in their economic policies, the United States failed miserably. It did not even try. During this inter-

TABLE 2.1 Balances on current account, gold and foreign currency, for
European creditors and debtors, 1924–30 and 1931–37 (millions of dollars)

	1924–30 (1)	1931–37 (2)	1924–37 (3)
Europe: creditors			
Britain	1,300	−4,000	−2,700
France[a]	1,340	−690	650
Netherlands	380	−290	90
Switzerland	370	−340	30
Sweden	180	−20	160
Europe: debtors			
Germany	−4,190	1,010	−3,180
France[a]	—	2,190	2,190
Austria	−860	−150	−1,010
Italy	−710	−50	−760
Other countries	−2,030	180	−1,850
Total Europe	−3,970	−2,070	−6,040

Source: Feinstein and Watson (1995).

Notes: Values are to the nearest $10 million. A positive value indicates net capital export; a negative value indicates net capital import.

[a] France is included with the creditors for 1924–32 and with the debtors for 1933–37; the estimates cover the French overseas territories, except Indochina for 1924–30.

regnum, the Germans reprised their bid for hegemonic status. But instead of cooperation, they continued their opposition to the Versailles Treaty: Germany had lost the war because of that famous and mythical stab in the back. American support for restoration of the gold standard through the over-subscribed Dawes Loan in 1924 enabled Germany to pursue its aims. It was comforting for outside observers to note the apparent economic calm of late Weimar Germany, but they ignored the underlying ferment for a greater Germany that resurfaced even before the Nazis took power.

The peak year of capital inflow into Germany was 1928, when it reached $1 billion; it then dropped sharply. Wall Street stock prices, which had started to climb in 1927, surged upward in 1928, luring more American investors away from foreign lending in the hope of a quick fortune at home. There also were growing doubts in the United States about the rapid expansion of Germany's external obligations and the unproductive purposes for which some of the foreign capital had been raised—doubts partly stimulated from within Germany by those concerned about the increase in the country's indebtedness. The accession of Chancellor Heinrich Brüning in 1930 and the adoption of deflationary policies intensified the economic depression. The gains by the National Socialists in the general elections in September of that year enhanced the sense of an impending political crisis—providing a major deterrent to further foreign investment.

Germany went into a slump of unparalleled severity at the end of the 1920s. Real domestic product fell by 16 percent between 1929 and 1932, industrial production fell by over 40 percent, and the value of exports fell by almost 60 percent. Unemployment raced from 1.3 million in 1927 (less than 4 percent of the labor force) to 5.6 million in 1932 (over 17 percent). The sudden contraction of capital imports from the United States initially was cited as the critical factor that precipitated this catastrophe. However, recent scholarship has revealed that the source of Germany's economic troubles was primarily domestic in origin.[25]

The domestic story is supported by the path of nominal short-term interest rates. They were stable through the second half of 1928, fell in the first quarter of 1929, and only moved up in the second quarter. If the view of the depression as coming from abroad had been correct, they would have risen sharply as soon as the foreign inflow was cut off. The observed pattern is easily explained if the German economy was already moving into recession before the influx of capital from the United States dried up.

German industrial production recovered strongly in 1927 after the recession of 1925–26 but then showed virtually no further growth in 1928 or 1929. Similarly, unemployment dropped in the winter of 1927 and then increased sharply in the corresponding period of 1928. The same pattern is evident in the investment data. Gross fixed investment at current prices in the public sector (government and railways) expanded until 1927, and in other sectors the rise continued for a further year, though even at its peak in 1928 the investment ratio was low compared to the prewar period. Moreover, information on investment intentions shows that both nonresidential building permits and new domestic orders for machinery had already turned down in late 1927 or early 1928, well before the cessation of foreign lending.

One view attributed the low level and early decline in investment primarily to an acute and persistent shortage of domestic capital. It claimed that this provided an endogenous explanation for the decline in fixed invest-ment. Another view also found a domestic explanation for the German depression but argued that the root of the trouble was an excessive increase in wages relative to the growth of productivity. The distributional conflicts that emerged in the aftermath of the Great War were the focus of this analysis.[26]

Even if the virtual cessation of capital imports from the United States and the subsequent net outflow did not initiate the depression, they added to the problems facing German policymakers and contributed to the adoption of measures that exacerbated the initial decline in activity. In principle, their options were either to abandon the gold standard, boosting activity by allow-ing the mark to depreciate, or to follow the orthodox policies of retrench-ment, reducing imports, and expanding exports by deflating the economy, as had been done in Britain.

Long-term American capital exports were no longer available to sustain German budget deficits after 1929, despite the Young Plan loan in 1930 that was designed to regain the stability generated by the Dawes Plan loan in 1924. German investors, with the inflationary experience of 1922–23 still deeply etched in their memories, displayed great reluctance to purchase long-term government bonds. As a result, the government and the Reichs-bank were driven to resort to short-term borrowing that led to a downward spiral, foreshadowing that of Greece in 2011. As the short-term debt in-creased, the perceived threat to stability grew, and domestic and foreign asset holders became more energetic in their efforts to withdraw their capi-tal from Germany. The deterioration in the political situation provoked by the steadily deepening depression and the opposition to tax increases bol-stered distrust of the currency.

The first of a succession of waves of capital flight from Germany occurred in the spring of 1929, and there were further massive losses of gold and for-eign exchange in late 1930 and, on an even bigger scale, in 1931. The authori-ties were forced to adopt restrictive policies at precisely the point when the economy was in urgent need of countercyclical measures to stimulate revival. Short-term interest rates were raised in the second quarter of 1929, and the federal government, cities, and states initiated a succession of increasingly desperate efforts to raise revenues and restrict spending. From the end of 1930 and through 1931, Brüning introduced a succession of austerity decrees imposing progressively harsher increases in direct and indirect taxation accompanied by reductions in civil service pay and in state welfare benefits. The descent was cumulative and catastrophic.

The United States ceased to supply capital for Europe on the previous lavish scale after 1929 and was actually a net recipient of long-term capital after 1931. The only other country in a strong financial position was France, which attracted ever larger quantities of gold and foreign exchange. Both the American and French authorities refused to take any steps to relieve the mounting crisis of confidence and liquidity in the rest of the industrial world. In Europe, France was the only possible source of funds for the beleaguered German government. National currencies and banking systems were drawn inexorably into the gathering storm.

Germany clearly was unable to act as a hegemonic power; it was basically on life support at the end of the 1920s. It had not given up its dreams of hegemonic power, but they were postponed. The United States had the resources to exert hegemonic power, but it was reluctant to do so. Cooperation was limited as central bankers consulted one another and wondered what to do. If we contrast the development of this emergency with the Marshall Plan (to be discussed in Chapter 4), it is painfully clear that there was no hegemon in the earlier crisis. "No longer London, not yet New York," as Kindleberger pithily expressed it.[27]

The third act of the tragedy foreseen by Keynes in 1919 began in 1931 as the accumulation of international imbalances and international debts led to a series of currency crises. The crises that ultimately undermined currencies and economies of across central Europe began in Vienna in 1929 with the failure of the Bodencreditanstalt, the second largest Austrian bank. Under pressure from the government, the Rothschilds' Credit Anstalt agreed to a merger, but the rescuing bank was itself in a very weak position, and the enlarged institution could not provide a lasting solution. The Credit Anstalt, Austria's largest bank, had unwisely operated during the 1920s as if the Habsburg Empire had not been broken up. The Viennese banks had been cut off from a good share of their original industrial base, especially in Czechoslovakia. There was never a sound basis for their business in the 1920s, and their heavy commitment to unprofitable industries meant that failures and losses were inevitable.

In May 1931, after an auditor's report revealed the bank's true condition, the Credit Anstalt was forced to reorganize with the help of international credit and a partial standstill agreement with its foreign creditors. This collapse set off a run on the bank that spread to the Austrian schilling. The government quickly ran through its foreign exchange reserves in a vain attempt to adhere to the gold standard and only belatedly imposed foreign-exchange controls.

Although the Austrian crisis was the first in 1931, it did not actually cause the subsequent German crisis and, through it, the others that followed. Instead, the German crisis of July 1931 stemmed exclusively from German causes; the Austrian crisis foreshadowed—but did not cause—the more important German collapse. Both the German banks and the German mark collapsed in the summer of 1931, eventually setting off runs on the British pound and the American dollar. A conventional view of the German crisis perceives it as similar to the preceding Austrian event: a crisis caused by banking problems, resulting from overextended lending, which then brought down the currency. However, the budgetary problems of the Weimar Republic brought down the currency and with it the German banks.[28]

There were no German bank runs in May. Deposits available in a week or less in the Danatbank stayed constant in June, despite the failure of Nordwolle, a major textile firm, which is often seen as the source of bank failures. Banks were not calling in loans, there was no run on demand deposits, and only time deposits were decreasing in June. Acceptances, including many held by London acceptance houses and other foreigners, were rising. Table 2.2 distinguishes deposits that were available immediately from those that were not. "Demand deposits" were accessible in a week or less; "time deposits" were accessible in a week to three months. Demand deposits did not fall at all in the crisis, indicating that there was no panic among depositors at the major banks even in June. Time deposits also did not fall significantly before the end of May.

The Weimar budget was severely out of balance by 1931. Tax revenues had fallen, and unemployment expenses had risen. It proved impossible to agree on a budget, and Chancellor Brüning governed by decree. Loans from the United States and France covered the deficit in early 1931. But Brüning then championed a customs union with Austria and cast doubt on his commitment to pay reparations. His statements exacerbated tensions left over from the First World War and dried up French loans to Germany. Gold reserves at the Reichsbank and deposits at the large German banks held up until Brüning stated he might no longer pay reparations in early June. They then quickly evaporated.

TABLE 2.2 Grossbank deposits by speed of access (millions of Reichmarks)

	Date (1931)					
	February 28	March 31	April 30	May 31	June 30	July 31
Selected liabilities						
Demand deposits[a]	3,756	3,819	3,657	3,626	3,626	3,891
Time deposits[b]	4,627	4,666	4,801	4,632	3,519	2,370
Selected assets						
Schecks, Wechsel	2,497	2,530	2,528	2,547	1,914	1,280
Remboursekredite	2,006	1,894	1,828	1,781	1,748	1,599
Total short-term credits	5,896	5,890	5,834	5,734	5,668	5,484

Source: Ferguson and Temin (2003), tables 5 and 6.

[a]Available in less than a week.

[b]Available in a week or more.

The daily prices of Young Plan bonds in Paris and the weekly gold reserves of the Reichsbank from April 7 though June 30, 1931, are shown in Figure 2.1.[29] They provide a good index of investor sentiment in the spring and summer of 1931. After rallying early in the year, the bond price stayed remarkably constant from March to May, and then fell sharply during the week of May 27. Gold reserves at the Reichsbank also stayed remarkably constant until the beginning of June, when they too fell, as shown in Figure 2.1. There was no news about German banks in late May, but on May 25 German newspapers began to discuss the rumor that Brüning was likely to ask for some sort of relief with regard to reparations, as he did in early June. This, not phantom withdrawals from banks, was the beginning of the fatal run on the currency that paralyzed the Reichsbank precisely at the moment it needed reserves to foster domestic stability. This was a case of how external imbalance —allowed to fester for many years in the form of both reparations debt and excessive loans from abroad—finally brought down the ability to preserve internal balance.[30]

Banks appealed to the Reichsbank for help, particularly the Danatbank, which was heavily invested in Nordwolle. But the Reichsbank ran out of assets with which to monetize the banks' reserves as its gold reserves shrank. Despite credits from other central banks, the Reichsbank had fallen below its statutory requirement of 40 percent reserves by the beginning of July, and

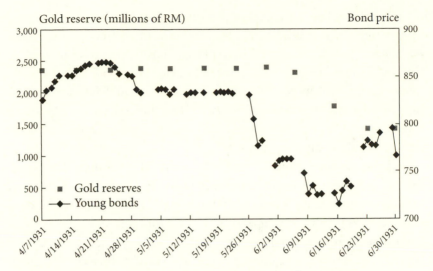

FIGURE 2.1   Reichsbank gold reserves and Young Plan bond prices in Paris,
April 1–June 30, 1931

Source: Ferguson and Temin (2003, 2004).

Notes: Bond prices are discounts from the par value. Breaks in price series indicate no quotation available (for example, weekends).

it was unable to borrow more. By mid-July, the Reichsbank could no longer purchase the Berlin banks' bills.

The Reichsbank tried to replenish its reserves with an international loan, but Brüning's attempts to shore up his domestic support had dried up international capital flows. The French tied political strings to their offer of help that were unacceptable to the Germans, while the Americans tried to isolate the German banking crisis from any long-run considerations. President Hoover proposed a one-year moratorium on war debts in June 1931. The absence of international cooperation was all too evident: no international loan was forthcoming. There was no hegemonic lender of last resort. Britain could not lead—nor could anyone else. This was an end-of-regime crisis.

Germany abandoned the gold standard in July and August 1931. A series of decrees and negotiations preserved the value of the mark but eliminated the free flow of both gold and marks. This was one way of going off gold, in the sense of breaking the constraints imposed by the free purchase and sale of gold at a stated rate. Like devaluation, currency controls resuscitate domestic monetary policy. In one of the great ironies of history, Chancellor

Brüning did not take advantage of this independence of international constraints and expand the economy. He continued to contract as if Germany
was still on the gold standard. It is vivid testimony to the power of ideology
that leaders like Brüning were induced to cling to orthodoxy even as the
world economy collapsed. He continued to advocate gold-standard policies
after abandoning the gold standard itself. He ruined the German economy
and destroyed German democracy in the effort to show once and for all that
Germany could not pay reparations.[31]

As a consequence of the German moratorium, the withdrawal of foreign
deposits was prohibited, and huge sums in foreign short-term credits were
frozen. As other countries realized that they would be unable to realize these
assets, they in turn were compelled to restrict withdrawals of their credits.
Many other European countries suffered bank runs and currency crises in
July, with especially severe crises in Hungary, where the banks were closely
tied to those in Austria. British commercial banks were largely unscathed,
finding strength in their branch structure and security in their traditionally
cautious policy toward involvement in industry.

However, London merchant banks were seriously affected by the German
crisis. They held many of the acceptances in the Berlin banks that were
increasing in the spring of 1931. These acceptances were part of the web of
bills of exchange that financed British trade; they provided insurance for
bills and therefore did not require extensive reserves. When the German
acceptances became illiquid, the English merchant banks were in serious
trouble. The Bank of England stepped in to support the merchant banks by
taking German acceptances as collateral for loans to the banks. Observers
saw this and concluded that the pound was no longer sound. Sales of sterling
increased steadily after July 14, and the Bank of England raised Bank rate on
July 22. British troubles were accentuated when the standstill agreements of
September 1931 froze some £70 million of loans from British bankers and
acceptance houses to Germany. The credit default swaps held by AIG in
2008 were exactly analogous to the acceptances of 1931.[32]

Although the currency crises on the continent added to Britain's problems by simultaneously provoking a flight from sterling and freezing British
foreign short-term assets, the extremely weak balance-of-payments position
on both current and capital account was a more fundamental cause of its
inability to sustain the gold standard. Britain's external financial position
had been undermined by the abrupt postwar collapse of export markets for

coal, cotton, and other staple products. The forced sale of a substantial fraction of its overseas investments to help meet the costs of the First World War reduced Britain's options, as did the adverse impact on Britain's traditional empire and Latin American markets of the calamitous fall in primary product prices in the late 1920s.

Britain had attempted to maintain its pre-1914 role as an exporter of long-term capital to the developing countries, but it could no longer achieve this in the 1920s by means of a surplus on current account and had to finance it by substantial borrowing from abroad. Much of the capital attracted to London was short term, leaving Britain vulnerable to any loss of confidence in sterling. The increasing deficits on the current accounts of Australia and other primary producers who normally held a large part of their reserves in London compelled them to draw on these balances in adverse times, and this further weakened Britain's position. Britain had turned itself into a bank, borrowing short and lending long, a dangerous maturity mismatch.

Britain's gold and foreign exchange reserves amounted to some £175 million by mid-1930, and other liquid assets were approximately £150 million. Because the corresponding short-term liabilities amounted to some £750 million, this was only an adequate defence against withdrawals as long as confidence in the pound remained high. When confidence drained away in the summer of 1931, British authorities realized that sterling's parity could no longer be sustained. After borrowing reserves from France and the United States in July and August, Britain abandoned the gold standard on September 20.

As so often in financial developments during the interwar period, the influence of history was of critical importance. Foreign concern about the scale of Britain's budget deficit increased markedly with the publication of the Report of the May Committee in July 1931 and was the proximate reason for the final collapse of confidence in sterling. It is difficult in hindsight to understand this obsession with the deficit given the relatively trifling sums under discussion:

> The explanation lies . . . in memories of the currency disorders of the early twenties, which were, after all, less than ten years behind. In those troublesome times it had become accepted doctrine that an uncorrected budget deficit is the root of forced increase in the supply of money and depreciation of the currency, and that such depreciations become almost if not quite unmanage-

able. This view was not a mere academic fetish: it permeated the atmosphere in all financial markets. . . . The Bank [of England] itself, in all the advice it tendered to the struggling central bankers of recovering Europe, year after year preached the gospel. It was not to be wondered at, that in 1931 the physician should be expected to heal himself—and that when he seemed unwilling to set about it, his life should be despaired of.[33]

The Bank of England, after an initial delay to rebuild its gold reserves, sharply reduced interest rates in 1932. As in Germany, British monetary authorities continued for a time to advocate gold-standard policies even after they had been driven off the gold standard. They cried "Fire, Fire in Noah's Flood," as Hawtrey phrased it. Although the grip of this ideology was strong in the immediate aftermath of devaluation in Britain as well as in Germany, it wore off within six months in the face of public criticism by James Meade and others. British economic policy was freed by devaluation, and monetary policy turned expansive early in 1932.[34]

The British devaluation was hardly the basis for international cooperation. The British did not seek international leadership; they did not champion their policies as hegemonic activity. Instead they backed into devaluation, arguing they had no alternative; Montagu Norman, long-time governor of the Bank of England, had a nervous breakdown. And while many smaller countries followed the British lead, the other major financial centers sought instead to protect themselves from British policy. The British devaluation was a good policy—it broke the suffocating grip of the gold standard on economic policy—but it did not point the way toward international cooperation.

The British government relinquished its prewar role as steward of the international gold standard. More properly, it acknowledged in 1931, however backhandedly, that this leadership role could no longer be sustained. The domestic cost had become too great relative to Britain's diminished resources. If the international economic orchestra needed a conductor, it would have to be found outside London, presumably in America. The world order based on British hegemony was in shambles.

The financial panic spread from Britain to the United States, jumping rapidly over the Atlantic Ocean in September 1931. Bank failures rose, and the Federal Reserve banks lost gold. There were both internal and external drains. In one of the most vivid acts of poor monetary policy in history, the

Federal Reserve raised interest rates sharply in October to protect the dollar in the midst of the greatest depression the world has ever known. This was not a technical mistake or simple stupidity; the response was standard for central banks under the gold standard. It shows how the ideology of the gold standard transmitted and intensified the Great Depression.

US Treasury Secretary Andrew Mellon advised President Herbert Hoover that the only way to restore the economy to a sustainable footing was to "liquidate labor, liquidate stocks, liquidate the farmers, liquidate real estate . . . purge the rottenness out of the system." "People will work harder," Mellon insisted, and "live a more moral life."[35] Those espousing the puritanical strand of gold-standard dogma grew more strident as unemployment mounted. Hoover regarded the gold standard as little short of a sacred formula. French economist Charles Rist saw the slump as resulting directly from the artificiality of the preceding boom:

> The increased production would have provoked a general decline in the price level earlier if efforts had not been made from all sides to stimulate consumption artificially and to maintain it at a level superior to that corresponding to real income. It is there, in our view, that it is necessary to seek the specific origin of the present crisis.[36]

Prices and costs had to fall to reconcile growing domestic and international transactions with an inelastic supply of monetary gold. Thrift, that intrinsic Victorian predicate of the gold standard, would bring this about if central banks did not manipulate interest rates to unnaturally stimulate consumption. Echoes of this view still can be found in the United States and Europe as the economic problems described in Chapter 1 persevere.

This contractionary policy in the midst of rapid economic decline was the classic central bank reaction to a gold-standard crisis. Friedman and Schwartz acknowledged the power of the gold standard in this action in their account of the American contraction:

> The Federal Reserve System reacted vigorously and promptly to the external drain, as it had not to the previous internal drain. On October 9, the Reserve Bank of New York raised its rediscount rate to 2½ per cent and on October 16, to 3½ per cent—the sharpest rise within so brief a period in the whole history of the System, before or since. . . . The maintenance of the gold standard was

accepted as an objective in support of which men of a broad range of views were ready to rally.[37]

None of the national leaders appear to have escaped their inherited mindset even under the most intense pressure. Brüning and Hoover maintained their deflationary policies for as long as they were in office and continued to champion them after they lost power. Even after losing the 1932 election, Hoover kept trying to enlist the president-elect in support of the gold standard. As late as February 1933, he attempted to chide Franklin D. Roosevelt into a commitment to support the gold price of the dollar, arguing that devaluation would lead to "a world economic war, with the certainty that it leads to complete destruction, both at home and abroad."[38] Twenty years later Hoover repeated approvingly his 1932 claim that maintaining the gold standard had been good for the United States. When Brüning said he had fallen 100 meters from the goal, he meant the end of reparations, not the recovery of employment, and he betrayed no doubt that the proper policy had been to stay within the rhetoric and framework of the gold standard even after abandoning convertibility itself.

The pressure against the dollar eased, but the American economy accelerated its decline in a tragic illustration of the link between external and internal imbalances. The Federal Reserve Bank had chosen international stability over domestic prosperity, a choice the Bank of England had not made. The result was intensified deflation and accelerated economic decline. Unlike Britain, which arrested the decline in 1932, the United States had to wait an additional painful year. This delay was not only costly for America; it also added to the deflationary forces in Europe, delaying European recovery and putting pressure on the fragile Weimar political system as well. If there was one decision that turned a bad recession in the early 1930s into the Great Depression, it was the decision by the US Federal Reserve Bank to preserve the gold value of the dollar instead of promoting domestic prosperity.

The mentality of the gold standard developed during the long boom of the nineteenth and early twentieth centuries. It survived the First World War and promised a safe haven for ships of state buffeted by stormy social, political, and economic seas. But once those ships began taking on water, gold was a heavy cargo. Rather than keeping their economies afloat, gold helped to sink them. The world economy, most observers agree, is well endowed with self-correcting powers. When activity turns down, it tends to bounce back. Only sustained bad policies can drive it so far from this path that it loses its capacity to recover. And only a dominant ideology can convince leaders to persist in such counterproductive policies.

The gold standard provided just such an ideology, supported by references to morality and rectitude. Its rhetoric dominated discussions of public policy in the years leading up to the Great Depression, and it sustained central bankers and political leaders as they imposed ever greater costs on ordinary people. The mentality of the gold standard proved resistant to change even under the most pressing economic circumstances. "What is astonishing," observed a contemporary analyst, "is the extraordinary hold which what is called the gold mentality has obtained, especially among the high authorities of the world's Central Banks. The gold standard has become a religion for some of the Boards of Central Banks in Continental Europe, believed in with an emotional fervor which makes them incapable of an unprejudiced and objective examination of possible alternatives."[39]

The gold standard that had been generally accepted as the best guarantee of international stability, trade, growth, and prosperity had been completely shattered by the middle of 1932. Only the United States and, in Europe, only France, Belgium, the Netherlands, Switzerland, Italy, Poland, and Lithuania remained on the gold standard. Only the first four of these European countries were truly committed to its spirit, refraining from the imposition of exchange controls and allowing relatively free movement of gold. The inability to make the gold standard function successfully in the interwar era was widely regarded as a symbol of failure, even though the actual consequences of devaluation for the real economy were highly favorable. Those countries that remained committed to gold did much less well subsequently than those that abandoned it. Only countries on the gold standard experienced banking crises in the early 1930s.[40]

Unemployment remained high throughout the 1930s despite the growth of incomes. Official unemployment rates in European countries averaged about 20 percent from 1930 to 1938, ranging from 15 to 25 percent. The official rates of course miss many unemployed workers in less industrialized countries, and they do not deal with withdrawals from the labor force. George Orwell was commissioned to report on the condition of workers in northern England in the mid-1930s and went to the small town of Wigan, near Manchester. He reported that everything was poorer and shabbier than in London, although there were fewer beggars and derelicts than in the metropolis. The communal nature of life in the smaller communities enabled unemployed workers to pool their resources and scrape by, but single unemployed men lived in depressing furnished rooms in which they could not stay all day. Their main concern in the winter was to keep warm when out of their rooms. The cinema, the library, or even a lecture offered refuge from the cold. Orwell said he was taken to hear the "silliest and worst-delivered lecture I have ever heard or ever expect to hear." But while he fled in the middle, the hall remained full of unemployed men.[41]

More recent authors have amplified these observations and provided details of unemployment in other countries. The general patterns are similar to those described here. Unskilled workers suffered more than did the skilled. Idleness and discouragement abounded. Unemployment relief often provided the margin between some semblance of the previous life and disruptive poverty.

There are two reasons why the unemployment received such overwhelming attention in the 1930s. To be sure, the slump in output, investment, and prices was of a magnitude never seen before. None of the nineteenth-century depressions produced such numbers of "out of work" persons. At the same time, however, labor markets in the most advanced industrialized countries had considerably changed over the previous fifty-odd years, most changes taking place after 1914. A brief survey of the new labor market conditions allows us to understand the impact of unemployment on the daily life of the most affected individuals and communities as well as to intuitively perceive what difference it made being unemployed in Western Europe and North America rather than in less developed, predominantly agrarian, societies.

At different times in the nineteenth century, various countries made their transition from an agrarian to an industrial society. Labor markets were also affected. The demand for labor maintained a relatively high, if declining over time, seasonal component. A good number of workers were hired and laid off according to the ebb and flow of agricultural activity, which remained of paramount importance. When idle, workers would typically consider themselves as "out of work" rather than "unemployed." The difference between the two terms was sociological and psychological rather than just semantic. Workers, particularly unskilled ones, expected to be out of work for a certain number of weeks every year, but they equally expected be hired again sometime in the future.

During the downward phase of the business cycle, spells of involuntary inactivity were longer than at times of cyclical expansion, but expectations of getting back to work remained. People's lives adjusted accordingly, particularly by using savings to cover out-of-work periods and relying on inter- and intrafamily mutual support (which may be considered as informal insurance). The most enterprising people would travel long distances to find a job when out of normal, close-to-home, work. Southern Italian peasants went as far as taking advantage of the different harvest seasons to temporarily emigrate to Argentina for the winter harvest. The word "underemployment" would later be coined for those who could not work full time over the year or even the life cycle.

There were indeed in the nineteenth century errantly unemployed people. However, these individuals were looked down on with a mix of pity and that moral stigma that is attached to the lazy, vicious, or utterly inept. It was for churches and charitable institutions rather than the government to take care of such hopeless cases of long-term unemployment. Things began to change in the last decades of the century with changing employment patterns as well as the emerging class struggle leading to organized labor (in the form of both trade unions and socialist parties). Both these developments were accelerated by the war. Large factories became common for the mass production of arms, vehicles, and uniforms, while life in the trenches provided a fertile ground for working-class propaganda.

Unemployment elsewhere in the world was not as visible. Japan and China had quite different stories. Japan devalued in December 1931 and recovered well using military expenditures, just as the Nazis did after 1933, to stimulate the economy. China was struggling to make its republic work when it was hit by the Depression in the West. It was making uneven progress when it was invaded by Japan in 1937. The Japanese conquered Beijing, Shanghai, and the capital, Nanjing—where the killing of 300,000 Chinese became known as the Rape of Nanking. Continuing occupation and warfare doomed the Chinese Republic, which emerged from the war too weak to defend itself against the communists. By contrast, Japan largely avoided the Great Depression by a quick devaluation followed by an aggressive military buildup.

Outside of Europe and North America, unemployment during the 1930s typically took the form of increased underemployment, for which no statistics are available. Several factors affected the rise in underemployment: the composition of output, the severity of the depression, and the economic policies followed by the government. In India, falling grain and rice prices resulted in widespread social unrest in the countryside during 1930–31, indicating that peasant conditions had deteriorated almost to the breaking point and, most likely, that underemployment was on the rise. The subsequent imposition of a tariff on wheat (but not on rice) imports provided only limited and temporary relief to the peasantry. China was peculiar in that the onset of the depression and increased underemployment was somehow delayed until 1933, probably due to an unintended but beneficial early devaluation of the silver-based currency. In 1930s Japan, unemployment was contained by the early devaluation of the currency, war, and the spree of military-related government spending. In Latin America, particularly in Argentina and Brazil, the fall in prices of the main export staples resulted in large increases in underemployment in the countryside.[42]

Contractionary policies in the United States were reversed only after Roosevelt took office in March 1933. He was forced to close banks to avoid their collapse, and he abandoned the gold standard and began the series of legislative changes known as the New Deal, signaling a new policy regime in the United States. Freed from the gold standard and the ideology dictating austerity as the cure for all economic evils, the US economy began to grow rapidly. Employment rose, but hardly enough to absorb all those who had lost their jobs in the long contraction, and unemployment remained high.[43]

At the same time as the gold standard was disintegrating, tariff warfare broke out once again, provoked by the deterioration in economic conditions and by the introduction of the Hawley-Smoot tariff in the United States in 1930. Britain finally abandoned its longstanding commitment to free trade at the end of 1931, and numerous other countries increased their tariffs in a desperate attempt to protect themselves from the deepening depression and the collapse of any attempt at international cooperation. In the judgement of the League of Nations, "there was probably never any period when trade was subject to such widespread and frequent alterations of tariff barriers. . . . Currency instability has led into a maze of new protectionist regulations and private trading initiative generally has given way to administrative controls."[44]

Chancellor Brüning was replaced by Franz von Papen in late May 1932. The Lausanne Conference in June 1932 effectively ended reparations and cleared the major political hurdle from Germany's path. Brüning's deflation was replaced by Papen's first steps toward economic expansion. Brüning had initiated a small employment program that had little effect in the context of his deflationary policy regime. This program was expanded by Papen and complemented by some off-budget government expenditures. In addition Papen introduced tax credits and subsidies for new employment. These were steps in the right direction, but they did not alter the perception of the policy regime. They still appeared to be isolated actions, not regime shifts.

The new policy measures (like the US Federal Reserve's open market purchases earlier that year) nevertheless produced some economic effects, which seem to have had an immediate political impact as well. The Nazis had leapt to prominence in Germany's 1930 election and increased their seats in the Reichstag from 12 to 107. They then doubled their large representation in the Reichstag in the election of July 1932. But that was their high point in free elections. They lost ground in the second election of 1932, in November, garnering 33 percent instead of their previous high of 37 percent of the vote and reducing their representation in the Reichstag from 230 to 196 seats. Further economic improvement could well have reduced the Nazi vote even more. If the recovery begun under Papen could have continued, the political courage to hold out a little longer with the Papen or the Kurt von Schleicher governments might have spared Germany and the world the horrors of Nazism. Germany, and hence the world, was balanced on a knife edge at the start of 1933 between the continuation of normal life and the enormous costs of the Nazis.[45]

However, only a slim case can be made for believing that the recovery could have been sustained. The instability of politics mirrored the instability of the German economy. The policy regime was in the process of changing, but there was no clear signal of change like the American devaluation in April 1933. There was no assurance that Papen's tentative expansionary steps would be followed by others. The recovery of 1932 consequently was neither sharp nor universal. Even though a trough can be seen in some data, other series show renewed decline into 1933. The economy fell back to its low point in the brief Schleicher administration, and the Papen recovery was abortive.

For Nazism to have been a transitory aberration, the recovery would have had to resume in early 1933. It would have had to be strong enough to repair the damage to the political fabric caused by the social and political effects of extensive unemployment. The expansive policies already undertaken would have had to have further effects—which they probably did—and the American recovery would have had to spill over into Germany. Both factors are possible, but neither was very strong; in addition, the latter could not have come for several months. One can argue that the future course of the German economy under elected governments would have limited the Nazis to continued minority status, but it is harder to argue that it would have led to a rapid decline in Nazi support.

Hitler was appointed chancellor at the end of January 1933 by the aged Hindenburg, who had championed the stab-in-the-back theory of Germany's defeat in the world war, and sustained economic recovery began only then. The advent of the Nazi government heralded the presence, as in the United States, of a new policy regime. The Nazis set out immediately to consolidate their power and destroy democracy. They turned away from international commitments to the restoration of domestic prosperity. They obliterated democratic institutions. And they gave their highest priority to the reduction of Germany's massive unemployment. Hitler conducted a successful balancing act. He reassured businessmen that he was not a freespending radical at the same time as he expanded the job creation programs and tax breaks of his predecessors. The First Four Year Plan embodied many of the new measures and gave them prominence as a new policy direction.

Employment rose rapidly in 1933 as a result. The new expenditures must have taken time to have their full effects. The immediate start of recovery therefore was the result of changed expectations when the Nazis took power —the result of anticipated as well as actual government activities. Even though the specifics of the Nazi program did not become clear—in fact were not formulated—until later, the direction of policy was clear. As we now can see more clearly than contemporaries could, the Nazi expansion was based on rearming Germany from the start. Hitler had been criticizing the deflationary policies of his predecessors for years, and the commitment of the Nazis to full employment was well known. As in the United States, a change in policy regime was sufficient to turn the corner, although not to promote full recovery.[46]

Contemporaries had trouble distinguishing the new administrations in the United States and Germany. Both Roosevelt and Hitler looked like "new men" who were taking charge from the paralyzed old guard. But it soon became clear—if it was not at first—that the two leaders came from opposite ends of the spectrum. Roosevelt acted to preserve democracy in an economic crisis; Hitler, to destroy it. The evils of the Nazi regime must be accounted among the worst effects of the Great Depression.[47]

The Nazi aim of dominating Europe if not the world was a continuation of the policies that led to the First World War. Germany had not given up its dream of replacing Britain as the hegemonic power. As before, Germany first sought the domination of Europe, but initial military victories enlarged its ambitions. We have defined hegemonic power in the context of cooperative actions, whereas the Nazis relied largely on coercion. Hitler went beyond the Kaiser and sought autocratic rather than hegemonic power. But even though it is usual to distinguish the Nazis from Germany's other governments, the common elements are equally important. Germany had started its bid for hegemony in the early twentieth century. It pursued this objective in war and peace, leading to a second Thirty Years' War. Only after the Nazis' total defeat in 1945 did Germany abandon its efforts to follow Britain as the next hegemon. Only then, as recounted in Chapter 1, did the United States acknowledge to itself and to the world its hegemonic status. But now Germany, as we discuss in Chapter 5, is once again resurgent in EMU.[48]

The British, French, and American governments released the Tripartite Agreement in September 1936. A large fraction of the declarations was devoted to avowals of belief in peace, prosperity, increased living standards, and truth, beauty, and goodness that the French favored. US Treasury Secretary Henry Morgenthau believed that the declaration would be significant in restoring peaceful conditions to the world. The declaration included references to relaxing quotas and exchange controls that the British wanted, although France was not specifically mentioned, and the French did very little to lower trade barriers after the release of the agreement. The British agreed not to retaliate against the coming French devaluation, but there were no promises about interest rates, because the British refused to constrain their domestic policy. The agreement also included announcements calling for increased cooperation among the central banks and the equalization funds of the Tripartite Powers. It avoided a round of competitive devaluation, and currency movements generally were mild in the few remaining years of peace. But it would have been far better for all of Europe if an agreement for a coordinated devaluation could have been concluded five years earlier, when Britain abandoned the gold standard.

The Tripartite Agreement marked the total failure of the gold standard to stabilize the international economy. The tangled negotiations needed to produce even this minimal agreement showed the tattered remains of international organization. Minimal and partial cooperation was possible with great strain, but more was unattainable. Germany and Italy were not interested and not welcome in international forums. The French and British were too weak to provide effective leadership. And the United States under Roosevelt had turned inward, providing more of an obstacle than an opportunity for cooperation.

The Netherlands and Switzerland followed France off the gold standard in September 1936, officially ending the gold bloc, three years after its inception. Recovery was quick in these two nations, as it had been in Belgium. Export markets recovered, and expansionary policies were implemented. The Italian government used the occasion of the French devaluation as an excuse to devalue the lira and reduce exchange controls, and Czechoslovakia devalued the crown a second time. The Tripartite Agreement was received negatively in France, where it was commonly believed that the Léon Blum government had reneged on its promises not to devalue, and the international accord was seen as a sham hiding the French devaluation.

Policymakers in the United States decided at this time that the rapid economic growth after 1933 meant that depression was over, even though unemployment remained stubbornly in double digits. The Federal Reserve decided that the growth of excess reserves in commercial banks threatened its control over inflation and doubled reserve requirements. The Roosevelt administration sharply reduced the federal deficit at the same time by not replacing the veterans' bonus that had been passed over presidential veto and by starting new taxes. More important than either of these changes was a new program of sterilizing the gold inflows that had increased the money stock and promoted the economic expansion. The monetary expansion stopped cold, and the result was a sharp contraction in economic activity known as the recession of 1937. The recession was short because it was an American phenomenon, not duplicated around the world, and the sterilization program was abandoned a year after it began.[49]

War was already raging in China, and preparations for war dominated the German economy. Other countries were making some war preparations, albeit nowhere near the German expenditures. The French, with the First World War in mind, constructed the Maginot Line on the border with Germany near where the trenches of the earlier conflict had lasted so long. However, the Germans repeated their earlier sweep around the Maginot Line and attacked through Belgium and Holland. They succeeded in stranding the British Expeditionary Force at Dunkirk, rescued in a heroic effort by the seafaring British and symbolizing the lack of preparation by Germany's foes.

Germany reprised the First World War not simply in its tactics. It also continued the strategy of using military force to bid for a hegemonic position. The continuity of policy ran from the military opposition to the Versailles Treaty, as embodied in the stab-in-the-back theory that was a critical stimulus to the growth of extremist parties like the Nazis in the 1920s. The aged General Hindenburg acted on this theory in appointing Hitler chancellor at the start of 1933. The brutality of Nazi policies and their virulent anti-Semitism serve to set them apart from the course of German history, but the constancy of Germany's efforts in the early twentieth century to fight its way to hegemonic status binds Nazi policies to the broad stream of German aims.

The Germans, however, could not achieve their aim. Initially they were more effective than in the First World War and avoided getting bogged down in static trench warfare. But they could not amass enough power to force the British or the Russians to surrender. The United States joined the war at the end of 1941 as a result of the Japanese attack on Pearl Harbor. As in the First World War, the American entry tipped the balance, and the United States emerged as the world hegemon, as we discuss in Chapter 4. The defeat of Germany took far longer than in the First World War for many reasons, but the end was even more devastating. No German was insulated from the Nazi war effort, and the Allies disdained negotiation with Hitler. Germany emerged from the war in a state of physical chaos and without a functioning government. It was hardly a hegemonic power.

Could any of this tangled history have been forecast at the end of the First World War? Recall the contrasting views of Cunliffe and Keynes as the war ended. Cunliffe faced backward and argued that a return to traditional ways would bring stability. Keynes faced the future under the Versailles Treaty and forecast disaster. He proved to be the better guide to the coming chaos.

THREE Keynes from the Macmillan Committee to Bretton Woods

BY 1930, KEYNES WAS A HUGE FIGURE on the world stage. He had created an enormous stir in 1919 when he published his *Economic Consequences of the Peace*. It was unimaginable that a senior Treasury official
should resign from the peace negotiations in Versailles and then publish a
devastating critique of what had happened. It was even worse that this book
should foretell the European tragedy of the 1920s and 1930s that we described
in Chapter 2. Keynes' actions turned him into a worldwide public intellectual, a status that he never lost. Some years later Lionel Robbins wrote:

> I often found myself thinking that Keynes must be one of the most remark-
> able men that ever lived.... Certainly, in our own age, only the Prime Minister
> [Churchill] is of comparable stature. He of course surpasses [Keynes]. But the
> greatness of the Prime Minister is much easier to understand than the genius
> of Keynes.[1]

By publishing such a fiercely critical book as *The Economic Consequences of
the Peace* in 1920, Keynes had cast himself out from the center of imperial
power in London. He had also thrown away the opportunity of rising to the
very top of the British civil service, something that was clearly within his
grasp, as he was obviously one of the cleverest people in the country, had a
mesmerizing personality, and was also a ruthless operator. Twenty years later,
at the beginning of the Second World War, he found himself back in the Treasury, where he became its widely respected leader; in 1942 he was appointed to
the House of Lords, thereby becoming the ultimate insider. And in 1944 he led
an international conference of seven hundred people at Bretton Woods, which

created a new international monetary system. But that was all later. In 1930, where we pick up our narrative, Keynes was still very much an outsider. And yet, extraordinarily, Keynes contrived to remain at the center of things. He obviously did so intellectually. But more than this, he had already acquired vast influence on economic policymaking, even if from the outside.

This chapter about Keynes might seem out of place in the present book, which is about practical policy choices facing the world. But Keynes himself once famously remarked that "practical men, who believe themselves to be quite exempt from any intellectual influence, are usually the slaves of some defunct economist."[2] In this chapter we show how Keynes invented the model of internal and external balances sketched out in Chapter 1, and we show that he did this to free himself from ideas about the gold standard that he had come to regard as defunct. This sets the stage for the integrated view of external and internal balances in the world today presented in the rest of this book.

We have already used Keynes' model to interpret the history presented in Chapter 2. We show in this chapter how Keynes' knowledge of this model led him directly to Bretton Woods. And we use his model even more extensively in Chapters 5 and 6 to illuminate the policy choices now faced by Europe and by the world. That is why a chapter about Keynes and his ideas belongs at the center of this book, demonstrating how hard it was and how long it took to understand this model for the first time.

Keynes was forty-seven years old in 1930. He taught economics at Cambridge and was a Fellow of King's College, after Trinity perhaps the most distinguished of the Cambridge colleges. In 1912, at the age of only 28, he had become the editor of the *Economic Journal,* the leading professional journal for economics at that time, a position he retained for the rest of his life. Ever since then he had been known worldwide as the standard-bearer of the Cambridge tradition of monetary economics—a school of thought that had been pioneered by Alfred Marshall, who held the chair in political economy at Cambridge from 1885 to 1908.

In international economic policymaking, Keynes worked in the early 1920s to rectify the economic effects of the Versailles peace agreement. He published *A Revision of the Treaty* and played a key part in reparation diplomacy. In 1923 he worked, partly in secret, with Carl Melchior, a German banker whom he had befriended during the Versailles peace negotiations. They tried, unsuccessfully, to bring about an Anglo-German financial agreement.[3]

Domestically, Keynes became a vocal critic of the British economic policy of deflation. In 1923, he became the owner and manager of the weekly news magazine *The Nation,* later to merge with *The New States-man,* in which he published his own attacks on government policy. That year he also published *A Tract on Monetary Reform,* which led to significant controversy. Then in 1925, he published the devastatingly critical *Economic Consequences of Mr Churchill,* which slammed the decision taken by the Chancellor of the Exchequer to return Britain to the gold standard. Quite remarkably, Keynes spent much of 1927 and 1928 helping entrepreneurs and working-class trade unionists in Lancashire to deal with the uncompetitive position into which the British cotton industry had slid, as a result of Britain's return to gold. He also became influential in the Liberal Party, and in the run-up to the general election in May 1929, he published the pamphlet *Can Lloyd George Do It?* in support of the Liberal Party leader. That pamphlet excited such extensive anti-government comment that Winston Churchill—who was still Chancellor of the Exchequer—took the extraordinary step of issuing a government White Paper to rebut Keynes' proposals. The resulting controversy was a major reason why, at the end of 1929, Prime Minister Ramsay MacDonald asked Keynes to join the Macmillan Committee, a Committee of Enquiry set up to investigate the state of the British economy. Keynes' presentations to that Committee laid the basis for his thinking about internal and external balances and for his later influence on actual policymaking.[4]

By 1930, Keynes also took part in an extraordinarily wide range of other activities beyond academic life and his concerns with economic policy. These date back to his time as an undergraduate at King's at the turn of the century, where he had become good friends with the famous philosophers Bertrand Russell and G. E. Moore. Keynes studied mathematics at King's, and his fellowship dissertation was not about economics at all but was an exercise in philosophy, exploring aspects of the theory of probability. He remained close friends with a number of Cambridge philosophers, including Frank Ramsey. It was Keynes and Ramsey who brought Ludwig Wittgenstein back to Cambridge from Vienna in 1929. And it was Keynes who encouraged Ramsey to work out his famous models of economic growth and of optimal pricing that are still at the heart of modern technical work in macro- and microeconomics. By 1930, Keynes was the chairman of the National Mutual Life Insurance Company.

His undergraduate friendships at Cambridge made him part of the Bloomsbury group of artists, writers, and intellectuals, which included Lytton Strachey and Virginia Woolf. In 1924, he married a Russian ballerina, Lydia Lopokova, which shocked the Bloomsbury intellectuals. Keynes' many artistic connections led him later in life to set up the Arts Council of Great Britain and to become the chairman of the Covent Garden Opera Company. Many of these activities of Keynes are fascinating—but they are well beyond the scope of our book. They are described in three rewarding biographies of Keynes, by Roy Harrod, Donald Moggridge, and Robert Skidelsky. Harrod's judgments about Keynes were particularly acute, because he knew Keynes well and was one of the best English economists of his generation.[5]

This chapter adds something significant to those biographies. We believe that Keynes' famous book *The General Theory of Employment, Interest and Money* was a way station toward his global achievement in creating the a new international monetary system at Bretton Woods. That much is common ground. But more than this, we believe that the macroeconomic model that Keynes developed in the *General Theory*—what has become known as the IS/LM model popularized in thousands of undergraduate textbooks using a diagram described in the Appendix—was also only a step toward his much more significant international economic model—the model of internal and external balance, which we deploy in this book. We demonstrate how this model underpinned Keynes' achievement at Bretton Woods. That is, we show that Keynes' intellectual progress made possible his practical achievement. And in our later chapters, we show that Keynes' model is still essential for thinking about current global policy problems. Our picture of Keynes' intellectual achievement is not something that is presented by his biographers. For example, Skidelsky believes that Keynes' central intellectual triumph was his *General Theory*. We hope to persuade our readers that Keynes' intellectual accomplishment was much larger than this.[6]

Britain's economic position at the end of the 1920s was particularly dire, as we have seen in Chapter 2. The country had returned to the gold standard at an uncompetitive exchange rate in 1925. And at a deeper level, the British economy had been radically weakened by the First World War. Its holdings of overseas assets, in its empire and elsewhere, had been significantly run down to pay for the war, thus curtailing Britain's income from abroad. Much of the country's productive capital had not been replaced or modernized since before the war, and its capacity to export had contracted significantly during the hostilities, never to be rebuilt. In these circumstances, Britain needed lower costs to make the country once again internationally competitive. Only then could it regain its position as a country with good growth prospects in which firms would invest and people had jobs and felt confident enough to spend their incomes. But the required improvement in competitiveness failed to materialize.

At the same time, Britain remained the only possible leader of the world. The persistence of the British Empire coupled with the alliance of Canada, Australia, and New Zealand, which all belonged to the new British Commonwealth, meant that the sun never set on this commonwealth. And London was still the center of the financial universe. By contrast, Germany was preoccupied with internal conflicts and was much more interested in maintaining its opposition to the former allies than in cooperating with them. The Americans had retreated into isolation, and in any case policymakers in America were not interested in any alternative to the orthodoxy of the gold standard. There was as yet no other power that could fulfil a leadership role.

Furthermore, everyone of substance in Britain—politicians, businessmen, financiers, civil servants, academics—knew what it was like to run the world. Many of them had done just that in the years leading up to the First World War. Such people still thought beyond the needs of their own country to the wider requirements of the world economy. But their country no longer had the means for them to exercise the leadership that they knew to be necessary.

The combination of two elements—a difficult economic position coupled with a sense of global responsibility—created particular difficulties for British politics. A new Labour government had come to power in the election held in May 1929. By October, policymaking was overwhelmed by the Wall Street Crash. Soon afterward, after much maneuvering, the Labour Prime Minister MacDonald did what British governments often do at a time of difficulty: he created a Committee of Enquiry. The terms of reference of the committee were

> To enquire into banking, finance and credit, paying regarding to the factors both internal and international which govern their operation, and to make recommendations calculated to enable these agencies to promote the development of trade and commerce and the employment of labour.[7]

This committee became known as the Macmillan Committee, after its chairman, a Scottish judge. It was not required to advise on any particular economic policy question but was, instead, meant to carry out a wide-ranging investigation of the options facing both Britain and the world.

Keynes was by far the most eminent member of the committee, but it also contained several other notable figures. Reginald McKenna was a Liberal politician who had been Chancellor of the Exchequer during the First World War and was now Chairman of the Midland Bank, and Lord Robert Brand was another distinguished banker and public servant. Ernest Bevin, the powerful General Secretary of the Transport and General Workers' Union, who was later to become the Foreign Secretary in the post–Second World War Labour government, provided a voice for a different constituency. The Treasury was represented by former Joint Permanent Secretary Lord John Bradbury and the Bank of England by Director Cecil Lubbock. The committee also included Professor Theodore Emmanuel Gregory, who held a chair in banking and currency at the London School of Economics, and who said much that was thoughtful in the course of its meetings. Other seats were filled by a Labour MP, who was a former communist, another banker, and two additional businessmen. This was a formidable group of people.

The committee sat from February until December 1930. Over 100 meetings were held, and evidence was taken on 49 days. The *Report of the Committee* was published in June 1931. Keynes was central to what happened, both in examining witnesses and in shaping the report. Remarkably, the committee gave Keynes a platform on which he could develop his ideas: he was asked to lead the members' thinking by presenting his ideas for five full days in February and March, in the early stages of the committee's work, and again for a further three full days in November and December, when the committee was beginning to draft its report. Thus Keynes was granted an extraordinary opportunity not just to shape its work, but also to present his own views, and through the minutes (which were published) and the report, to shape the discussion of these ideas in the wider world.[8]

To understand his influence, it is helpful first to get a sense of what Keynes was like in action. The Nobel Prize–winning economist Friedrich Hayek— who strongly disagreed with Keynes about economic theory—wrote that

[Keynes] owed his success largely to a rare combination of brilliance and quickness of mind with a mastery of the English language in which few contemporaries could rival him—and [something that] . . . seemed almost one of his strongest assets—a voice of bewitching persuasiveness.[9]

FIGURE 3.1   Keynes by Low

Source: British Cartoon Archive.

Note: Originally published in *New Statesman,* October 28, 1933, by David Low (1891–1963). Published courtesy of Associated Newspapers Ltd. / Solo Syndication.

The philosopher Bertrand Russell said of Keynes that "his intellect was the sharpest and clearest that I have ever known." He also added that "[when] I argued with Keynes I felt I took my life in my hands and I seldom emerged without feeling something of a fool." The famous Low cartoon reproduced here as Figure 3.1 gives some visual sense of Keynes at work: his penetrating eyes staring out with sustained concentration; his hands poised, ready to make some expressive gesture; his angular body completely relaxed.[10]

Keynes' presentations completely captivated the committee. The minutes of the relevant meetings are reprinted in Keynes' *Collected Works,* where they occupy nearly 300 pages. The text reveals a masterpiece of sustained logical thinking, even though it is a verbatim report of a set of oral presentations. Keynes held together the structure of his argument over a full five-day set of presentations. At the same time, he was extraordinarily careful in presenting each detail of his argument and made extended detours to answer specific questions from the members of the committee who formed his audience. At each stage he skillfully moved between general principles and particular examples, always showing a subtle command of language and a sense of the mood of the meeting—a sense of which ideas needed to be restated to ensure that those present fully understood what he said. Even now the reader can sense what extraordinary sessions these were. The chairman, Lord Macmillan, who was ignorant about finance but was an open-minded and sympathetic listener, summarized the feelings of the committee. At the close of the long fourth day of Keynes' presentations in February, Macmillan said that committee members "hardly notice the lapse of time when you are speaking."[11]

Keynes' preparation for the committee went back ten years to *The Economic Consequences of the Peace.* In Chapter 2 we described how, in that book published in 1919, Keynes foresaw the tragedy of Europe that was to emerge in the 1920s. But he was, by temperament, a practical visionary rather than a complainer. In the remarkable Chapter 2 of this book, called "Europe before the War," Keynes set out with extraordinary clarity a vision of how it was that the European economy, and the global economy, had functioned so well during the British century—that remarkable period of economic expansion described at the beginning of our previous chapter. Keynes' one short chapter —12 pages in all—mapped out the challenge that Keynes faced then and for the rest of his intellectual life: how could he help make such a miracle of growth happen again? The great Harvard economist, in his obituary for Keynes, uses a memorable phrase to describe the remainder of Keynes' intellectual career as a struggle to "make that vision of our age analytically operative." This was the task Keynes set himself in the Macmillan Committee.[12]

When writing *The Economic Consequences* in 1919, Keynes had argued that the magic of the late-nineteenth-century expansion depended on four things: a rapidly growing population; security of property and person; an unequal society in which wages were low, profits were high, and profits were invested; and an orderly international economic system in which Europe could obtain its necessary food and raw materials from the New World cheaply, and could export manufactures back to the New World in exchange. That is, Keynes described, even then, the system of export-led expansion that we described in our previous chapter. But, said Keynes, the war "had so shaken this system as to endanger the life of Europe altogether." He was pessimistic. "The Treaty," he said, "contains no provisions for the economic rehabilitation of Europe." The central task, as he described it in the final chapter of his book, was the renegotiation of the reparations that had been imposed on Germany. And he was already thinking beyond this to the need for a settlement of inter-Allied indebtedness, to the need for a large loan from the United States to Europe.[13]

But now in 1930, ten years later, Europe's tragedy had unfolded, as described in our Chapter 2. The economic rehabilitation of Europe would now depend on a much wider set of policy choices—about monetary policy and the constraints imposed by the gold standard—than those he had discussed in 1919. It was widely known that, for the past five years, Keynes had been working on a restatement of monetary theory, bringing Marshall's Cambridge tradition up to date, and that the resulting *Treatise on Money* was in the process of publication as the Macmillan Committee convened for its meetings. This is why Keynes was asked to guide the committee.

The trouble was that Keynes' presentations to the committee did not add up to a coherent view. He failed in his task. This is why the committee is of such interest to us: it shows the process of Keynes' growing understanding. It was obvious that Keynes' testimony did not add up—and this was also clearly obvious to Keynes himself at the time. As we aim to show, this great failure set the stage for the work that Keynes was to carry out for the next fifteen years. In an important sense it is Keynes' failure in the Macmillan Committee that provides the foundation on which he built the two astonishing achievements that we describe later in this chapter. His failure in that committee led him to focus on two specific questions in the final fifteen years of his life and to provide answers to these two great questions. It was his resounding answers to these questions that would enable him to turn his vision of his age, a vision he had expounded in the *Economic Consequences of the Peace,* into a system for managing the world economy.

Keynes began his presentations as follows:

I have decided that probably the best way will be to begin rather in the middle and then work forwards and backwards, starting from the things that are probably relatively familiar and keeping till the last some of the things which I hold of great importance, but which are likely to be less familiar. I think it will be useful if, first of all, we go through the more or less orthodox theory of how Bank rate works, the classical theory of Bank rate as it has existed in this country for the past fifty years.

So long as we are on the gold standard, the fundamental principle of our currency management has to be that the differences between our international receipts and payments which we have to meet or receive in gold shall never be very large. We cannot afford to use lose large quantities of gold, or at any rate to lose them continuously. So . . . the primary task of currency management is to keep an approximate equality between our international receipts and payments. This balance is made up of two parts.[14]

The first, short-term, component of the gold-standard mechanism, Keynes explained, worked as follows. If a country was exporting less than it imported, then it would be the task of its monetary authority (in Britain's case, the Bank of England) to raise the interest rate (or "Bank rate," in Britain's case) to attract funds from abroad, and thereby to cover the cost of imports. This action could cushion the deficit that a country was experiencing, ensuring that it attracted enough gold for it to use to pay for its imports. The Bank of England was at the center of this international financial system, and it had much experience in adjusting Bank rate in this way. Keynes describes how well the Bank of England was able to operate this short-term cushioning.

But such short-term cushioning could not, Keynes claimed, solve the underlying external difficulty facing an economy like that of Britain. He went on to describe a second, longer-term, component of the gold-standard mechanism. This required the interest rate to be held at a higher level for sufficiently long to cause a fall in investment and so induce a decline in the overall demand for domestic goods, which would lead to in an increase in unemployment. Such unemployment would cause wages to fall. What was required for the economy to become competitive again was that unemployment remain high for a sufficiently long period and wages fall by a sufficiently large amount. As a result, the economy would once again be able to gain export markets and so would export enough to match the need for funds to pay for its imports. It would not then need high interest rates to attract funds from abroad. There is, said Keynes, no other way by which Bank rate brings down prices, except by increasing unemployment. That, he concluded "is the beginning and end of traditional sound finance in this country."[15]

It is worth noting that the longer-term component of the adjustment mechanism was originally proposed by Hume in the mid-eighteenth century, in the price-specie-flow mechanism that we described in Chapter 1. But the short-term component, about the use of Bank rate, was missing in Hume's account, because Hume subscribed to what is now called the Quantity Theory of Money. In that Quantity Theory approach, expenditures are determined by the quantity of money. If gold flows out of country because the country is not exporting enough, then residents will have less money and will spend less, setting in motion the second, longer-term, component of Keynes' mechanism and causing prices to fall. By inserting an intermediate step that depends on the interest rate, Keynes was rejecting the Quantity Theory of Money.

To a modern audience, this may not sound like a radical innovation, but it was. In the famous Cambridge tradition of monetary economics, Marshall had used the Quantity Theory of Money to show how the level of prices in the economy is determined by the quantity of money in existence. This idea had become a central idea in economics teaching, for it was, as people then thought, a necessary part of any attempt to connect monetary phenomena (about prices) with real phenomena (about how many actual goods and services are bought and sold in an economy). Ever since Keynes began lecturing in Cambridge in 1909, the year in which Marshall retired, he had been the person who passed on this tradition to generations of Cambridge students. By the 1920s, he had become the leading authority on Hume, Marshall, the Quantity Theory, and the gold standard, not just in Cambridge but also worldwide. Yet now he separated the workings of the gold-standard mechanism into two components: a short-term effect on capital inflows, operating as a result of a rise in Bank rate, and a longer-term effect operating through an improvement in competitiveness stemming from the rise in unemployment, which was, in turn, caused by the increase in Bank rate. This argument seems rather trite to us today; it is something we all now understand. But it was a dramatic change of view for an audience in 1930.

The minutes of the Macmillan Committee show that its members came to agree with Keynes about this two-stage nature of the gold-standard adjustment process—a short-run component and a longer-run component. Toward the end of his first day's evidence, Keynes sought to bring together these two components. He asked, How long would it take for adjustment to happen? It all depends, he argued, on how resistant wages are to falling.[16]

We will see below that Keynes did not yet properly understand an important part of his own argument, and that this difficulty led to the first of two major problems for him. But the famed Governor of the Bank of England, Montagu Norman, understood almost *nothing* of what Keynes had said. This became evident later in the proceedings of the committee, when Governor Norman was called to give evidence. When asked to describe his own view of the workings of the gold standard, Norman categorically refused to accept Keynes' analysis. He thought the Bank of England's responsibilities extended only to the first, short-term, component of the gold-standard mechanism, that of ensuring sufficient capital inflow at times of inadequate exports to avoid the country losing gold. The idea that, as part of the workings of the gold standard, the Bank of England actually caused the unemployment problems described by Keynes was beyond his ken. Wage adjustment was, he said, a matter for industry and its workers: "I have never been able to see myself why for the last few years it should have been impossible for industry, starting from within, to have readjusted its own position."[17]

When faced with questioning by the committee, the minutes show both that Keynes made Norman look remarkably foolish and that the Committee agreed with Keynes' view that Norman's answers were hopelessly inadequate. Indeed, Norman's evidence was so threadbare and deliberately negative that, according to Norman's biographer Andrew Boyle, the deputy governor of the Bank of England was given the unenviable task of doctoring the evidence for the printed record.[18]

Toward the end of the first day of the committee's proceedings, Keynes expressed an important doubt about whether the longer-term component of the adjustment process could be made to work adequately, except when wages were growing and adjustment required only that wages grow less rapidly. Keynes maintained that is what had happened in the late nineteenth century and was why the gold standard had worked satisfactorily at that time. By contrast, Keynes denied that money wages had ever been downwardly flexible in the way that was now required:

> My reading of history is that for centuries there has existed an intense social
> resistance to any matters of reduction in the level of money incomes. I believe
> that, apart from the adjustments due to cyclical fluctuations, there has never

been in modern or ancient history any community that has been prepared to accept without immense struggle a reduction in the general level of money income. . . . The . . . deflation which followed the Napoleonic Wars, . . . very much like the one we are going through now, was one which brought the country to the verge of revolution.[19]

These problems of wage adjustment explained why problems had emerged since Britain rejoined the gold standard in 1925. That policy decision had, Keynes thought, led to the miners' strike and then to the general strike of 1926; the collapse of the Lancashire cotton industry in the years that followed; and high unemployment, which was widespread in Britain by 1930.

Such an allegation brought a sharp response from Lord Bradbury, who had chaired the committee that had recommended the return to the gold standard in 1925. There followed a lively debate between Bradbury and Keynes, joined by other members of the committee, a controversy that carried over to the beginning of the second day. Unlike Norman, these other members of the committee, including Brand, agreed with Keynes on how the adjustment process was meant to work. But unlike Keynes, they believed that it could, in fact, be made to work in the way required. This controversy seems eerily like that taking place at present in the European Monetary Union. The EMU countries on its periphery (Greece, Ireland, Italy, Spain, and Portugal) are now very uncompetitive in relation to Germany. But in the monetary union, these countries are unable to devalue their exchange rate relative to Germany, just as countries were unable to do so in the gold-standard system. There is now intense debate as to whether it will be possible to reduce wages in these countries to the extent necessary to enable economic growth to resume.

As the second day of evidence continued, Keynes ran into his first big difficulty. When describing the longer-term component of the adjustment process mentioned above, he said very simply that a higher Bank rate would cause an increase in unemployment, and he added that this was something "which we all now understand." But how, he asked, does this rise in unemployment actually happen? Keynes set about explaining this and got into a complete mess. His confusion—and how he later escaped from it—is invaluable to analyze, because it is very like the confusion that is bedeviling current discussions about policy, which we describe in Chapters 5 and 6.

If the interest rate rises, what would happen next? Keynes said that firms would tend to invest less in factories and productive capital. If the cost of borrowing went up, then fewer people would be prepared to borrow, and borrowing would fall. We might also say that if the interest rate went up, then people would tend to save more, but Keynes was not concerned with this. He was content simply to consider the effect of a higher interest rate on investment. Such a rise in the interest rate would make investment fall relative to savings. What would happen then?

Keynes proceeded by setting out a parable to reduce the problem to its simplest terms. This *banana parable* subsequently became famous and is worth quoting at some length. We provide a verbatim account of what Keynes actually said. This makes it all the more astonishing—even if, in the end, it is an intellectual morass.

> Let us suppose a community which owns nothing but banana plantations which they labour to cultivate. They collect bananas and they consume bananas and nothing else, and we will suppose that there has been equilibrium between saving and investment in the sense that the money income of the community not spent on the consumption of bananas, but saved, is exactly equal to the cost of production and new investment in the further development of banana plantations. You see that that part of their incomes which the community do not spend on bananas is exactly equal to the cost of new investment. Let us suppose that the selling price of bananas is equal to the cost of production, and that ripe bananas will not keep for more than a week or two.

Keynes was here being an economic theorist, assuming a simple world in which we can disentangle cause and effect more easily than in the messy real world. He then continued as follows:

> Into this Eden there enters the campaign urging the members of the public to abate their improvident practice of spending nearly all their current incomes on buying bananas for food. "You have no provision for your old age; save more money." But at the same time there is no corresponding increase in the development of new plantations—which may be the case for one or other of many reasons.

Keynes here found it easier to suppose that a gap between savings and investment comes about because of an increase in savings, even though his earlier discussion and his discussion of the short-term component of gold standard had involved a reduction in investment resulting from a rise in the rate of interest. This difference is in no way crucial to the relevance of Keynes' parable. The point in both versions is that savings exceeds desired investment.

Keynes made another innovation at this point, asserting that savings and investment decisions are made by different people. Consumers save, but businessmen invest. The lack of coordination between these two groups causes economic trouble. This idea is central to what has been taught as Keynesian macroeconomics to generations of students, and as a result it is very familiar to us. By contrast, in the Cambridge Quantity-Theory approach, what people spend depends on the quantity of money, and there can be no such gap between savings and investment. This innovation by Keynes is familiar to all economists, but it is typically attributed to Keynes' later publications, in particular to his *General Theory of Employment, Interest and Money*, published in 1936 and discussed below. However, this piece of the puzzle—the separation of decisions to save from decisions to invest—is clearly visible in Keynes' *Treatise on Money* of 1930, and it was clear in his presentations to the Macmillan Committee.

But Keynes had not yet worked out how businessmen decide how much to invest, and he went on to suggest any number of reasons why they might not invest in his banana economy.

> It may be that counsels of prudence are influencing the entrepreneurs, also, that they feel no confidence in the future price of bananas, they fear overproduction of bananas and are not disposed to enter on new development; or it may be there are technical reasons which prevent banana plantations from maturing until long after the laying of the plans, or it may be that the labour required for the making of new plantations is a highly specialised form of labour, which cannot be trained except after a generation, so that you cannot divert men from the harvesting of bananas to the preparation of banana plantations.

After this detour, Keynes returned to the main thread of his parable, asking what happens when savings rise and investment does not.

> What in that case will happen? The same quantity of bananas as before will continue to be marketed; they will not keep, so that they must be sold. But the amount of current income devoted to the purchase of bananas will be reduced

in proportion to the success of the thrift campaign. Since bananas will not keep and people are spending less on them than before, their price must fall, and it will fall exactly in proportion to the amount by which the savings have increased. The consequence will be that as before, the public will consume the whole stock of bananas, but at a reduced price level.

What follows in the parable at this point is absolutely crucial to Keynes' difficulty. Notice that he set out his story with employment staying constant and prices changing, rather than having employment fall while prices stayed constant. This reflected his thinking in his *Treatise on Money,* which was in the process of publication as he addressed the committee. But Keynes' task was to explain to the committee how an increase in the rate of interest might cause investment to fall short of savings, lead to a rise in unemployment, and in turn cause wages and prices to fall. That argument will not work if one has a model in which employment is assumed to remain constant. In short, Keynes made the separation of savings and investment in his analysis, but he could not incorporate any resulting changes in employment into it. All the effects of imbalances between savings and investment came out in prices in the banana parable.

> Well, that is splendid, or seems so. The thrift campaign will not only have increased saving, it will have reduced the cost of living. The public will have saved money without denying themselves anything, because owing to the reduction in the price of bananas they will be consuming exactly the same quantity of bananas that they were consuming but for the thrift campaign; and however much they saved, since the price of bananas will fall correspondingly because all the bananas must be marketed, there will never be any change whatever in the amount of bananas they consume.
>
> But unfortunately that is not the end of the story; because, since wages are still unchanged—and I assume for the moment that the selling price of bananas will have fallen, but not their cost of production—the entrepreneurs who run the banana plantations will suffer an enormous loss. What will happen is that you have just as many bananas consumed as before, but the entrepreneurs will lose an amount equal to the new savings of those people who have saved.

At this point the chairman, Lord Macmillan, interjected, "The savings will be in the hands of the banks, and the unhappy entrepreneur will have financed the bananas through the banks." Keynes replied as follows:

Yes; the public will provide the deposit and the whole of the deposit will be lent out [to] the businessmen to make up their losses. So that the aggregate savings have not increased the wealth of the community. The only way to increase the wealth of the community would be to have more banana planta-tions. The only effect has been to transfer the wealth of the entrepreneurs out of their pockets into the pockets of the public.

Lord Macmillan responded: "So all this financial jugglery does not increase the actual wealth of the world." At last, Keynes sees where he needs to go next.

The only thing that increases the actual wealth of the world is actual invest-ment. But that is not the end of the story. The continuance of this will cause entrepreneurs to try and reduce wages, and if they cannot reduce wages they will try to protect themselves, by putting their employees out of work.

Now I come to disclose the full horror of the situation. However much they do that it will not help them at all because as they reduce wages and throw men out of work, the buying power to purchase bananas will be reduced by that amount; and so long as the community goes on saving, the businessmen will always get back from the sale less than the cost of produc-tion, and however many men they threw out of work they will still be mak-ing a loss.

At last unemployment has arrived in the story. The minutes of the meeting show that Keynes was then prodded by other members of the committee to explain what would happen next. That is, they asked him to show how this cumulative process of throwing people out of work would end and how many more people would actually end up unemployed. But he did not know how to develop his model to the case where unemployment emerges, and his attempts, although intriguing, are totally unsatisfactory. He could not actu-ally say how an increase in Bank rate would cause unemployment. He did not understand how the longer-term component of his gold-standard mech-anism actually worked.

Keynes' contribution on this second day had been extraordinarily radical. He was not sure how well his presentation had gone. Two days later he wrote to Lydia, his wife:

On Friday they found my speech much more perplexing, as I thought they would. I think I did it all right. But it was unfamiliar and paradoxical, and

whilst they couldn't confute me they did not know whether or not to believe. . . .
I got back to Cambridge, very tired.[20]

It is not surprising that the members of the committee found his speech perplexing; Keynes' argument was incomplete. He knew the conclusion: higher interest rates will cause demand to fall, triggering a fall in output and thus an increase in unemployment. This is an argument we all now understand, but Keynes did not yet know how to develop it himself.

Keynes now had an argument in place—even if he did not understand part of it. In an uncompetitive country like Britain, which was on the gold standard, the monetary authority would need to raise the interest rate. This would cause unemployment—for reasons he did not properly understand—which was meant to reduce wages, so that the country would become competitive again. But Keynes did not believe that British wages would fall rapidly or far enough.

Thus the gold standard did not work. Some kind of remedy was needed. During the subsequent presentations of his evidence, Keynes outlined three remedies, just as he had discussed possible remedies of the parlous situation a decade earlier in the final chapter of *The Economic Consequences of the Peace.*

The first remedy proposed by Keynes was that of a devaluation of the pound; that is, a departure by Britain from the gold standard. Consequently, a British pound would buy less foreign currency and foreigners would be able to buy more British pounds with their foreign currency. This would cheapen the price of British goods in world markets when expressed in foreign currency; it would mean that the amount of British exports would rise. It would also raise the price of imports measured in pounds in Britain. As a result, the demand for British goods would also rise as people bought home-produced goods instead of the more expensive imports. This mechanism seemed to be what was needed.

Keynes, however, believed that such a route through devaluation of the currency was not a viable option for Britain, for the following reason. He had been a fervent opponent of the return to the gold standard at an overvalued exchange rate in 1925. But the outstanding point that must be noted about the Macmillan Committee's deliberations, including Keynes' presentations, is that members of the committee did not consider at any length the alternative of abandoning the gold standard, so great was the respect in which that standard was held. Yet only three months after the publication of the *Report of the Committee,* the gold standard was in fact abandoned. Keynes would have pushed for a devaluation if there had been the remotest chance of it being accepted; he did not lack the necessary courage, and he had previously devoted several years to strenuous opposition to Britain's return to gold. But once Britain had returned to the gold standard, Keynes believed that the country needed to stay the course. Anything else would reduce confidence in the City of London as a global financial center. And preserving that confidence was essential to ensuring global recovery.

Finding himself in this quandary, Keynes then produced a second possible remedy. This proposal was really remarkable for him. He suggested that some measure of protection for British goods by means of tariffs might be desirable as a temporary remedy for the current impasse. Up to this point, Keynes had been a determined free trader. But he now argued that protection would raise the demand for British goods and thereby boost British employment. However, the problem with protection was that, although it would cause an inrease in the demand for import substitutes within Britain, it would not promote exports in the same way as would a devaluation of the currency or a cut in wages. As a consequence, protection would be inefficient.

Keynes clearly thought workers would have a better standard of living if either the currency were devalued or they were to consent to a reduction in money wage rates. These options would ensure that the resources of the country were employed to the best advantage among various industries, and between exports and production for the home market. But if there was no devaluation, and if money wage rates were not adjusted, then there would be unemployment. Protection would undoubtedly reduce real wages and result in a less satisfactory distribution of productive resources compared with a devaluation of the currency. But if devaluation was not available, protection would ensure a higher level of employment than that which would result from doing nothing, and increasing employment was—for the moment—the central objective.

Keynes understood the damage that would be done to other countries and to the global trading system by acting in a protectionist manner against the exports of those other countries. The risk of possible retaliation was also significant. But he appears to have thought that this risk might be offset by a beneficial effect on the global financial system as a result of an increase in confidence in the City of London, and that such a boost in confidence would be produced by a more buoyant level of macroeconomic activity and employment in Britain. He also thought that without such an improvement in employment, the country's ability to remain on the gold standard might come to be undermined by a wish to devalue the currency, and that the resulting uncertainty would damage other countries and the global system.

Nevertheless, this conversion of Keynes to a protectionist position was remarkable, and it led to considerable controversy. At the same time as he was serving on the Macmillan Committee, Keynes was also asked by the government to chair the Committee on the Economic Outlook, whose task was to advise more precisely on policy than was the case with the Macmillan Committee. This other committee consisted of Keynes and just four other people: Arthur Pigou, the person who in 1908 had succeeded Marshall as Professor of Economics in Cambridge; Hubert Henderson, another Cambridge economist; the businessman Josiah Charles Stamp; and Lionel Robbins, then a young and ambitious Professor of Economics at the London School of Economics. This smaller group covered much the same ground as the Macmillan Committee, and Keynes also drafted its report. Robbins violently objected to Keynes' protectionist proposals, so much so that he refused to sign the report. After an acrimonious dispute, Robbins was allowed to issue his own minority report. He insisted on doing this to disown the protectionist suggestions, even though he agreed with Keynes on many other things.

Having made his protectionist point, Keynes then moved on. In the last part of his five days of evidence for the Macmillan Committee, Keynes returned to his quandary—that Britain's position was condemning it to an unacceptably high level of unemployment—and provided a third, and equally remarkable, remedy. He proposed a large increase in government expenditure on public works, what we now call a Keynesian expansion. This suggestion was not unexpected, because in *Can Lloyd George Do It?* Keynes had made such a proposal in support of Lloyd George, in the run-up to the general election of 1929.

This third and most important remedy proposed by Keynes got him into more trouble, creating his second big difficulty. This second difficulty had two aspects, both of which were important. The first aspect was that Keynes failed to convince the committee that an increase in expenditure on public works would not crowd out an equal amount of private expenditure. In other words, his fellow committee members were not convinced that an increase in public expenditure would not cause to an equal reduction in private investment. The argument against which Keynes was pitted was the following. Public expenditure needed to be financed by the issue of government bonds. These bonds would compete with other financial assets in the market for what we might call loanable funds, a term made famous by Keynes' Cambridge contemporary, Dennis Robertson. This competition for loanable funds would ultimately displace the bonds that private firms wished to issue to fund their own private investment. Private investment would thus be crowded out.

A good way of showing Keynes' failure to win this argument is to describe his interaction with Sir Richard Hopkins, the senior Treasury official who was called by the committee to give evidence on this point. Hopkins' appearance led to a resumption of the debate between Keynes and the Treasury, which had begun with the publication of *Can Lloyd George Do It?*

Hopkins dwelled on the point about crowding out. He repeatedly made it clear that he could not understand how crowding out could be avoided. Yet it is impossible to read Hopkins's testimony many years later without becoming immensely frustrated and feeling immense sympathy with Keynes. Hopkins' testimony steered very warily between two alternatives. As a loyal civil servant, he could not let down the Winston Churchill who had commissioned the white paper criticizing Keynes' *Can Lloyd George Do It?* And yet he also could not undermine the new Chancellor of the Exchequer, who was already undertaking a strictly limited scheme of public works.

When Keynes pressed him, Hopkins retreated, in a careful, measured, but entirely unsatisfactory way. A reference was made to the white paper issued in response to *Can Lloyd George Do It?* This paper had criticized the increase in public works that Keynes was advocating. Hopkins assured the committee that the Treasury had never adopted a hard and fast dogma on this subject, although it clearly was opposed to the kind of large scheme that Keynes was advocating.[21]

Keynes then asked if it was the Treasury position that "schemes of capital development are of no use for reducing unemployment." That, said Hopkins, was "going much too far." Keynes tried again, asking whether the Treasury really did believe that any capital that could be found for their schemes would be diverted from other uses. That, said Hopkins, was a "much too rigid expression of any views that may have come from us." It was the "atmosphere in which schemes may be undertaken" that conditions their consequences. He went on to say that the Treasury view is not a "rigid dogma." It is the "result of the view that we take as to the practical reactions of the scheme." Keynes finally, in exasperation, said that this view "bends so much that I find difficulty in getting hold of it." But Hopkins, not to be beaten, replied "yes; I do not think these views are capable of being put in the rigid form of a theoretical doctrine."[22]

Hopkins' replies in these exchanges were profoundly unsatisfactory, but Keynes was unable to convince the committee that Hopkins was wrong. The trouble was that Keynes' theory did not help him justify what he wanted to say. We have seen that Keynes wanted to say—and had said to the Macmillan Committee using the banana parable—that an increase in Bank rate would reduce investment, which would make expenditure fall, *and that this would create unemployment.* But we have seen that his argument did not work. He also wanted to say that an increase in government spending would not crowd out the investment of private sector entrepreneurs. It would instead create more jobs, *and reduce the unemployment that had been created by the higher Bank rate.* But his economic theory in the banana parable did not work that way, because the supply of output in the economy is assumed to be fixed. So the increase in government spending would, even if it did not crowd out private sector investment, merely cause a rise in the prices of bananas. Keynes thought that money wages would not keep up with prices, so that workers would be able to buy fewer bananas with their wages. He wanted to say, and did say before the Macmillan Committee, that higher prices, but no wage increases, would mean that production would become more profitable and that *this* would induce capitalists to produce more and reduce unemployment. But his theory did not allow him to say this. All his theory enabled him to say was that the increased government expenditure would increase the price of bananas and depress the real income of workers, because wages would rise less than prices and would depress the living standards of workers.

It is no wonder that Keynes had trouble on this issue with Hopkins. Their discussions were taking place in 1930 at a time of high and rising unemployment. A macroeconomic model that assumed that output is fixed at full-employment capacity was not particularly helpful. And the use of such a model to defeat Hopkins, by arguing that public expenditure need not crowd out private investment expenditure, because instead it would reduce workers' consumption, was hardly helpful to Keynes. This trouble with Hopkins exactly parallels Keynes' trouble showing that an increase in Bank rate would increase unemployment. If one assumes that output is always at full employment, then an increase in government expenditure cannot cause an increase in employment—for exactly the same reasons that an increase in Bank rate cannot cause a decrease in employment.

At the end of these exchanges, Lord Macmillan gave his judicial summary as follows: "I think we may characterise it as a drawn battle." Harrod remarked:

> It is always rash to indulge in a negative generalisation, but I do not recall another occasion on which Keynes, in the plenitude of his power, arguing on his own chosen subject, was not deemed by a good judge to have had somewhat better of the argument. If this is so, Hopkins has a unique distinction in his generation.[23]

And Keynes wrote to Lydia:

> Sir R. Hopkins is very clever; but did not understand the technique of what we were discussing,—so the combination made a good hunt. But it proved that the Treasury don't know any more than the Bank of England what it is all about—enough to make tears roll down the eyes of a patriot.[24]

Keynes might well have believed that, because of his failure, policymaking "remained driven by the ideas of "defunct economists" at the Treasury and the Bank of England.

There also was a fundamental incoherence in Keynes' advocacy of an increase in public works, when, in fact, his discussion of the gold standard had suggested that what the country faced was an external problem. He wanted to say that higher public expenditure would lead to an increase in employment and so to an increase in domestic incomes and expenditures. But that would cause an increase in imports, which would certainly make the external problem worse.

Keynes consequently had two problems on his hands. First, he had failed to provide an understanding of why an increase in Bank rate would cause unemployment and how an increase in public works could help reduce that unemployment. Second, he had failed to provide any alternative to the unsatisfactory workings of the gold standard.

We can understand the relationship between his problems by employing the simple model described in Chapter 1. This model was only properly formulated in the 1950s, but we need to be clear to describe Keynes' confusion and to understand his subsequent research program. We distinguished in Chapter 1 between internal and external balances. Without going into details again here, we need the conclusion that an outcome is only satisfactory when both types of balance have been achieved.

In 1930, Keynes did not understand how to achieve balance in either dimension. He opened his presentation to the Macmillan Committee with a description of how to maintain external balance under the gold standard. To make the argument—and to deal with the urgent demands on the committee—Keynes had to confront the issue of domestic balance, that is, unemployment. Today, we can distinguish these two interrelated issues because of contributions by Keynes after 1930 and subsequently by many others. However, we cannot be sure that Keynes saw them as two separate questions. Today we can understand how working with one imbalance could exacerbate the other, but in 1930, Keynes lacked the tools to do this.

We suspect that Keynes made the first step toward understanding by distinguishing the two issues. In his actions and in his extensive popular publications and public comment, he attacked the two problems one at a time. But given the urgency of unemployment, Keynes chose to tackle the domestic issue first. Dealing with the domestic issue led Keynes to the publication of his *General Theory of Employment, Interest and Money* in 1936. Tackling the second led to his important work on the creation of the International Monetary Fund (IMF) at Bretton Woods in 1944. In the rest of this chapter we survey these two developments one at a time, as did Keynes.

The process of discovery started from Keynes' *Treatise on Money*. Keynes clearly was troubled by his inability to convince the Macmillan Committee and saw the *Treatise* in that light. Looking back, that is what we see as well. The *Treatise* had been published in October 1930. By January 1931, as the Macmillan Committee was drafting its report, a group of Keynes' young followers was meeting in Cambridge to discuss the *Treatise*'s strengths and weaknesses. This group included Joan Robinson and Austin Robinson, Piero Sraffa, James Meade, and Richard Kahn, Keynes' young colleague at King's College. The gatherings of this group became known as the Circus. In the *Oxford English Dictionary*, one of the meanings of that word is "a disturbance or uproar; a lively or noisy display." This accurately captures what seems to have gone on.

Initially these gatherings were informal meetings held in Kahn's rooms in King's College, in the elegant, neoclassical Gibbs Building designed by Nicholas Hawksmoor, built in the 1720s and located next to King's College Chapel. The meetings subsequently were expanded into what would now be called a seminar held at Trinity College, next door to King's in a wonderful old-fashioned room called the Old Combination Room. Participation was strictly by invitation. Some of the very ablest of the undergraduates of that generation were invited, but only after they had satisfied an interviewing board. One or two research students were present, and one two other members of the teaching faculty sometimes attended. Keynes himself took no part in these activities. Nor did Arthur Pigou, who had succeeded Marshall as Professor of Political Economy; he regarded such adolescent frivolities with Olympian detachment.

Meade later enjoyed describing the workshop style of the Circus meetings. Although Keynes was not present, after each meeting, Kahn would go to see Keynes and recount to him the subject matter of the discussions and the lines of argument:

> From the point of view of a humble mortal like myself Keynes seemed to play the role of God in a morality play; he dominated the play but rarely appeared on the stage. Kahn was the Messenger Angel who brought messages and problems from Keynes to the 'Circus' and went back to Heaven with the result of our deliberations.[25]

The casting of Keynes in this role was first suggested by Meade's wife, Margaret, in 1934 when they were staying for the weekend with the Robinsons in Cambridge. During that weekend messages from on high appeared at regular intervals. God dominated the scene without making an actual appearance.[26]

The central problem with Keynes' *Treatise* was made clear in the banana parable that Keynes presented to the Macmillan Committee. When savings rise, they are bought back into line with investment by a fall in the price of bananas; however much more individuals save, the profits of firms fall by the same amount, so that overall the total amount of savings does not increase. This problem was similarly evident in Keynes' engagement with Hopkins at the committee session discussed above. When government expenditure increases, investment (including government expenditure) is brought back into line with savings by a rise in prices. Thus profits and overall savings rise to match the increase in government expenditure, because workers' wages remain unchanged. But output and employment do not increase. As in the banana parable, Keynes' story depends on a fixed national output (in the banana parable, a fixed output of bananas), and all adjustment, when investment changes relative to savings, takes place through the price of bananas. This story was clearly inadequate.

There is a lot of folklore about how this problem was solved. The most famous story is about a simple remark made by Austin Robinson. He put problems of the *Treatise* as follows: "If an entrepreneur, loaded with profits, decided on his way home to have a shoe-shine, was the effect solely to raise the price of shoe-shines? Was it impossible to increase the number of shoes shone?"[27]

Economists in the early 1930s were used to dealing in prices, not quantities. They could deal with the quantity of any single good or service, because Marshall had taught them how to do so. But when they came to think of the price level, that is, what we now call macroeconomics, they fixed the quantity of goods and services produced. That led to the Cambridge equation for the price level, that is, to the Quantity Theory of Money. To free the analysis from the assumption of full employment, Keynes also had to free himself from the Cambridge equation.

Kahn, Keynes' young colleague at King's College, had already drafted his famous article on the *multiplier* by January 1931. In this piece, Kahn showed that, if output is able to move in response to an increase in government expenditure, as in the discussions with Hopkins, an increase investment (or an increase in government expenditure) is brought back into line with savings by a rise in output, not by an increase in prices. Such a rise in output will bring about an increase in profits, because more people are brought into work; more goods are produced; and more goods are sold, on each of which there is some extra profit. Output, said Kahn, will rise by just enough to make savings out of profits rise to match the increase in government expenditure. It is output that rises to bring savings back into line with investment again, rather than prices rising enough to bring this about, as happens in the banana-parable economy. This extra increase in output means that output will increase by more than the initial increase in government expenditure—hence the famous name by which this response is still known, the multiplier.[28]

Meade, then a young graduate student from Oxford visiting Cambridge for a year, showed how Kahn's multiplier analysis could be connected with Keynes' previous argument in the *Treatise*. Meade described what happened:

I said the following to the other members of the Circus. "Haven't any of you read Marshall's *Principles of Economics?* In that book, in the short run, the economy lies on a short-run, upward-sloping, supply curve. But that curve adds an extra equation to the model. This means that—in comparison with the model in the *Treatise*—we can make *both* prices *and* output endogenous [that is, able to move] at the same time."[29]

Kahn acknowledged his debt to Meade in his article of 1931 and in his later account of the period. Once these ideas were understood, it led the Circus to the view that it is primarily variations in the level of *output* that bring savings into line with investment and so reestablish the conditions of macroeconomic equilibrium, rather than variations only in the level of *prices,* as had been supposed, in the banana-parable economy and in the *Treatise.*[30]

This crucial move established the second of the three fundamental breakthroughs Keynes needed to make if he was to escape from Marshall's Quantity Theory of Money. The first breakthrough was the one we have already described—the idea that savings and investment are separately determined. Savings are decided by households deciding what fraction of their incomes to consume and how much to put aside for the future. Investment is decided by firms when they decide how much capital equipment they need for production and so what they need to invest to acquire this capital equipment. That first breakthrough meant that to understand how much money was spent in the economy, one needed to know more than simply the amount of money in existence.

Taken together, these two breakthroughs meant that if one could understand the determinants of savings and investment decisions over time, one could understand how expenditure, output, and employment in the economy were likely to move over time. This advance involved a huge change in thinking about the way the economy worked. It would enable someone to explain properly the workings of the gold-standard mechanism—to explain how a higher interest rate could cause output to fall and thus unemployment to rise and so cause wages to fall, thereby making the economy more competitive. And it would enable one to establish a convincing counterargument to Hopkins's narrative by explaining how an increase in government expenditure would cause output to rise.

Keynes needed to make a third and equally fundamental move for him to dispense with the objections that had been raised by Hopkins. If the amount of total spending in the economy was determined by the balance between savings and investment, then what was the effect of the quantity of money? If an increase in the quantity of money did not increase total spending in the economy, what did it do?

The answer seems obvious to us now, but it was not clear then. An increase in the quantity of money would cause the interest rate to fall. This was because the interest rate was determined, not by the need to make savings equal to investment, but instead by the need to make the demand for money equal to its supply. The story turned out to be remarkably simple. The demand for money depended on the rate of interest as well as on the number of transactions for which people needed money and the price of these transactions, because some people might wish to hold their wealth in the form of liquid money if they were unsure whether the price of bonds or shares was going to move up or down. We all know this from our experience at the end of 2008, after the bankruptcy of Lehman Brothers, and followers of Alfred Marshall knew this too. In times of crisis, the risk of failure makes the value of bonds decline and leads bondholders to sell bonds to get cash. It is the rush to sell bonds that causes a panic.

But this idea had not been brought into the existing framework of analysis about how the economy works as a whole. This idea of Keynes became known, famously, as his theory of *liquidity preference,* a theory that resulted from the idea that one reason people might want to hold money was their wish to have liquid assets in addition to long-term bonds, or shares, which might happen to have a low price at just the time they needed to be sold to finance an expenditure. If that is how some of the demand for money is determined, then the interest rate will be that which makes the supply of money (controlled by the central bank) equal to the overall demand for money, including both the demand for money for transactions purposes and also this additional demand, which depends on people's preference for liquidity.

Armed with these three breakthroughs, Keynes' new theory added up to the following set of beliefs. Keynes believed that the amount of investment in the economy depends on the opportunities for investment and on the rate of interest. As in his discussion of the short-run component of the gold-standard mechanism, if the interest rate rises, then the level of investment will fall. So we have to ask how the rate of interest is determined. Keynes answer was: primarily by the quantity of money. If the supply of money is reduced, then this will cause the interest rate to rise. The Bank of England is able to increase Bank rate by reducing the quantity of money available.

What determines the overall level of expenditure and output in the economy? This depends on finding the level of output that will be big enough to make savings out of incomes just sufficient to equal investment. If, say, investment falls, then it will cause a reduction in the incomes of those working to make goods that are sold for investment purposes, and so the amount that people can spend will decline. As a result, income and output will fall in the economy. They will decline until the level of savings has fallen so that it is again equal to investment. Finally, what determines the level of employment in the economy? It is not determined by wage levels at all. It is determined by the level of output, because that determines how many people entrepreneurs will want to employ to make the output that they are able to sell. This paragraph sets out in a nutshell the view put forward by Keynes in his *General Theory*.

The interpretation of the *General Theory* made famous in the IS/LM diagram produced by John Hicks in 1937 adds one further, important, tale to the above story. If, says Hicks, the Bank of England holds the quantity of money fixed, then the level of output in the economy will influence the demand for this money. That will exert an influence on the rate of interest. So the argument put forward in the last paragraph becomes just one part of a more general, simultaneous argument. The rate of interest influences the level of output, and the level of output influences the rate of interest. That sentence comes from a discussion between Keynes and Harrod in August 1935, when the *General Theory* was at the proofs stage. Harrod put Keynes' theory as clearly as anybody had done up to that time, and Keynes categorically agreed with Harrod's interpretation. That sentence clearly summarizes what generations of undergraduates have been taught, using the IS/LM diagram, about Keynes' *General Theory*. John Hicks showed the genius necessary to express this theory in one simple diagram. We set out this diagram briefly in our Appendix.[31]

This is not to say that Keynes was unaware of the many limitations of this theory. It is also not to say that he was blind to the many ways in which it could be extended. We discuss one such extension, the generalization of the analysis to an economy that has international trade, later in this chapter. That extension is central to the discussion in this book and leads to the Swan diagram. A way of understanding what Keynes had achieved is to ask what happens if there is unemployment and wages are cut. According to Marshall, this would make firms demand more labor and would reduce unemployment, an effect on unemployment that would be magnified if some people decide to work less if wages fall. But according to Keynes, the reduction in wages will not cause a reduction in unemployment unless it leads to a drop in the interest rate (which would stimulate more investment) or to a reduction in the amount of their incomes that people are prepared to save. Only then will investment rise above savings; only then will the level of expenditure and output in the economy rise; and only then will unemployment fall. If this does not happen, then the fall in wages would just cause firms to lower their prices, rather than encouraging them to take on any new labor. Firms will only take on new labor if they can see an increased demand for their products.

If firms do not see this increased demand, then they will simply cut their prices commensurate with the fall in their costs. In an economy that is open to international trade and has a monetary system based on the gold standard (or is a member of a monetary union, like EMU at present), a cut in wages is certain to stimulate employment in a way rather different from that described above. In such an open economy, unemployment will fall, because a cut in wages will cause a reduction in domestic costs and prices, and so will encourage an increase in exports. It will also encourage consumers and firms to prefer purchases of domestic output over imports. Both the increase in exports and the reduction in imports will simulate demand for domestic output, which will in turn cause a reduction in unemployment. These ideas become important in the next section of this chapter.

The path Keynes took to reach his *General Theory* illuminates two important things for us. In developing both of these things, the Circus—the gathering established by Keynes' young colleague in Cambridge in 1931—was crucial to Keynes' progress.

First, the participants in the Circus learned a new macroeconomic method of analysis. This method gives a sense of how macroeconomic outcomes are determined in more than one market at a time as part of a "general equilibrium" for the economy as a whole. Keynes' young co-workers in the Circus—John Hicks, Roy Harrod, Richard Kahn, James Meade, and Joan Robinson—all came to understand this method. An understanding of this method is important for our understanding of the world's problems today.

Marshall did not understand the method. For Marshall, prices are determined by money, the interest rate is determined by what is needed to make people invest what they have saved, and wages are determined to make the demand for labor equal to its supply. The microeconomic method used by Marshall is the following. First figure out which market you are talking about, then figure out how prices are determined in that market to make demand equal to supply. If you are considering the labor market, then wages are determined to make the demand for labor equal to its supply. Unemployment can arise only because wages are too high, and it can be removed simply by cutting wages. If you are thinking about the goods market, then the interest rate is determined to make savings equal to investment. If there is a reduction in investment, then the interest rate will simply fall enough to make investment rise again, and/or make savings fall so that, again, savings and investment come to be equal, and there will never be a shortage of demand for goods. And if you are thinking about the money market, the price level is determined to make the demand for money equal to its supply. If the quantity of money is increased, then that will cause the level of prices to rise—because that is what an increase in the quantity of money does. Similarly if the quantity of money is reduced, then prices will fall. A fall in the quantity of money does not cause an increase in unemployment.

The *General Theory* enabled Keynes to escape from such a confined way of thinking. For Keynes, by contrast, the amount of employment is determined by the demand for goods, which is in turn determined by the level of income in the economy. The level of income is the one at which the level of savings will equal that of investment. It is not the case that wages are determined to make the demand for labor equal to its supply. Similarly, the rate of interest does not make savings equal to investment. And the price level is determined by the level of wages, not by the quantity of money. As we say to our students: macroeconomics is the study of a subject in which everything depends on everything else. But good macroeconomics requires understanding which bit of everything influences which other bits of everything else in the most important way. That is why macroeconomics is such a challenging subject. Keynes led the way in showing economists, and the wider public, how to think in a macroeconomic manner.

In a later generation, Paul Samuelson understood that the way to think about Keynes' *General Theory* was in terms of what economists call general equilibrium theory and the way to understand the connection between markets is the one we have just described. The IS/LM model, taught to generations of undergraduates from Samuelson's *Principles of Economics,* is an example of this method. The Swan diagram, which is explained in the Appendix and underlies much of the analysis in our book, is also an example of this general equilibrium method used for an economy open to international trade. Macroeconomics in this general equilibrium view consists of integrating two or more markets. In any single country, Keynes distinguished the markets for goods and for money. Hence the IS/LM model. For an open economy that has international trade, Keynes later would replicate this process and distinguish between the market for goods produced at home and the market for goods traded internationally. This was conceptualized in the less-well-known Swan diagram.

Sometimes Keynes himself failed to understand how to do such systems thinking, although he saw that it was necessary. It fell to Meade, Hicks, and Harrod, the younger members of Keynes' Circus, to understand this and to show Keynes how to use his own method. Such a failure by Keynes is clearly revealed in letters between Keynes and Harrod written at the time that the *General Theory* was in proofs. Harrod provided exactly the kind of comparison between Keynes and Marshall that we have provided above. Keynes tried to reject this comparison and in his *General Theory* goes on and on about Marshall's incoherence, in a way that annoyed Harrod and many others. It is not that Marshall was incoherent. It is just that Marshall did not understand the kind of general equilibrium thinking described above that Keynes himself had made necessary. It is ironic that Keynes so vigorously attacked his great teacher, when he was not able to fully slough off the analytical methods he had learned at his teacher's feet.[32]

As we will see in later chapters of this book, the necessity to think in a macroeconomic manner is fundamentally important when thinking about the world's problems. Many of the difficulties described in Chapters 5 and 6 come from an inability of economists—and more importantly, an inability of policymakers and politicians—to think in this manner.

The second great and important thing learned by members of the Circus, and something that we can learn from them, is that they developed a form of group working. Keynes is someone who had many bright, intuitive ideas about the kind of analysis we have been describing. But he lived much too busy a life to work out much of the relevant theory for himself. It is possible that he had the wrong sort of mind for doing this. Nevertheless, he gathered a group of clever, technical young people around him to carry out the formal analysis.

Keynes did something very similar ten years later when preparing for the Bretton Woods negotiations, which led to the creation of the IMF. He brought together an extraordinary group of young economists to work with him in the Treasury. And a generation later, Meade did something similar in his work in macroeconomics, which he did during the 1970s and 1980s:

> Meade's young colleagues came to experience his skill at running a group of researchers—which I have begun to think he partly inherited from his experience in the Cambridge Circus so many years previously. As he passed eighty years of age, Meade presided over a weekly programme of meetings. . . . The day after each meeting, Meade would sit at home, in his village outside Cambridge, and write down an algebraic formulation of what we had all discussed. He would then walk to his local post office and send us a letter containing a photocopy of these handwritten notes. We would all then analyse his algebra and diagrams, in preparation for the next week's meeting.[33]

The remarkable aspect of this management of work by junior colleagues seems to have involved giving the young people their head, a strategy that we think Meade learned from Keynes. Keynes never came to the Circus, and Meade left his group to work alone each week. But both Keynes and Meade took pains to listen carefully to what their young colleagues said, and to articulate what they said back to them in conversation and in writing. In seeing this similarity with Meade, we see an important part of the way in which Keynes worked.

The writing of his *General Theory* provided Keynes with the tools he needed to answer the skepticism of Sir Richard Hopkins on whether an increase in public expenditure would crowd out private investment in an economy at less than full employment. The *General Theory* provided the equipment to enable one to say that it need not do so. The analysis in the *General Theory* makes it clear that, providing monetary policy is sufficiently loose to prevent crowding out happening through a rise in the interest rate, an increase in public expenditure will cause output and employment to increase in the economy. That will cause savings to rise and also, in an economy with a public sector, will cause taxes to rise. Income will rise to just that point at which the rise in private sector savings, coupled with the rise in taxes, is just as large as the initial increase in public expenditure. There need be no crowding out.

But the *General Theory* did not deal with the second problem identified above about the international setting of policymaking. How should an economy like Britain's in 1930 deal with rising unemployment, when the economy is insufficiently competitive internationally? Any increase in public expenditure of the kind that Keynes was advocating to Hopkins would only make the international position worse. Something else must be necessary if that problem is to be addressed, along with ensuring that unemployment is dealt with. To use the language we introduced in Chapter 1, policymakers need to ensure both internal balance and external balance. It is to this problem that we now turn.

Keynes could not immediately commence writing down his bigger set of ideas about the international economy. He had a heart attack that nearly killed him after finishing the *General Theory,* and then came preparations for war. From 1937 on, Keynes focused on the problems that emerged as Britain neared full employment and started its war preparations. Of particular concern was the need to create room for rearmament without running into inflationary or balance-of-payments pressures. Policies were needed to reduce domestic demand to what was available after the needs of the war effort and trade had been met. This set of issues was about ensuring both internal and external balance.

But what framework did Keynes have available with which to carry out this analysis? Early on Keynes saw that to achieve two kinds of objectives— internal and external balance—two kinds of policies were needed, which we state in modern terminology. He needed expenditure-changing policies to reduce domestic demand to what was available after meeting the needs for the war effort and trade to achieve internal balance. But he also needed expenditure-switching policies to ensure a balance of external account consistent with the war effort. He knew that the first of these needs could be analyzed using the tools that he had developed in the *General Theory.* The second required that he return to the difficulties of an economy open to international trade that he had discussed in the Macmillan Committee, and the tools of analysis that he had been developing in the *Treatise on Money.*[34]

The setting in the *Treatise* is not that of a closed economy (as in the *General Theory*) but instead the international system, a system of the kind he described and analyzed for the Macmillan Committee. Quite remarkably, the *Treatise* contains a discussion of the need for both separate national monetary autonomy in the face of difficulties facing individual countries, and also an analysis of the need for a uniform, unaccommodating international monetary standard to stabilize global price levels and the global economy. The culminating chapter of the *Treatise* includes a discussion of the possibility of fulfilling these needs.

Keynes did not understand how to use this framework when he was talking to the Macmillan Committee. As we have seen, the *General Theory* dealt with Hopkins' criticism about crowding out. It provided Keynes with the tools for thinking about internal balance. But the open economy problems raised by Hopkins—all the issues about external balance—remained to be dealt with.

Keynes' objective in the discussions from 1937 to 1940, as war loomed and then began, was to make internal balance possible—to ensure that inflation would not be the means of paying for the war as it had been in the First World War. He also did not want the war to be fought with tight money, which would benefit the rentier class. Some other way to reduce internal demand and so release the resources required for the war effort was needed. Thus was born *How to Pay for the War*. This marvelous piece of applied economics explained Keynes' plan for compulsory savings, along the lines of what we now know as the Singapore model. But Keynes' plan was adopted only to a small degree.[35]

The discussions of Keynes' plan, however, rapidly led to the ideas of Keynesian macroeconomic management becoming entrenched in Whitehall beginning in 1941. This aspect of history is well known. It starts with the Treasury dominated by a pre-Keynesian, Hopkins-like, view of what makes for responsible policy. This view holds that if the government's nonwar deficit is balanced, then private savings would be forthcoming to finance the war effort. It is hard now to understand how anyone could have thought this. Keynes' alternative view quickly came to dominate. According to his view, one must instead compute the likely level of economywide demand for goods— that is, "aggregate demand"—and ensure that there is no inflationary gap between this amount and the residual of overall supply in the economy, after the devotion of resources to the war effort. These discussions about domestic macroeconomic policy, and the need to ensure internal balance, led to Keynes' role at Treasury as an advisor. Although he never held a paid job there, he quickly became the Treasury's effective leader. He used this position as a platform on which he carried out his role in all the international economic discussions that we are about to discuss.

At the beginning of the war, the need for wartime external balance in Britain imposed two requirements, which differed according to their time frames. For discussion of these requirements, Keynes used the international framework of his *Treatise,* amended by incorporating the ideas from his *General Theory.* Given the achievement of internal balance by the use of domestic macroeconomic policy in the ways laid down in the *General Theory,* external problems can be analyzed simply by inspecting the balance between exports and imports. This is what Keynes did, using both a short- and a long-run perspective.

In the short run, just as under the gold standard, there was a financing need. The level of imports (both military and nonmilitary) required for survival needed somehow to be paid for, and yet the conversion of a large proportion of Britain's export trades to the production of armaments made payment impossible. As a result, the country became dangerously dependent on the United States for its short-run survival, a problem exacerbated by Britain's commitment in the summer of 1940 to "victory however long and hard the road may be." The process of engaging the United States in this need led to Churchill's famous letter to Roosevelt of December 8, 1940, "one of the most important that I ever wrote," and to Roosevelt's generous response in the form of Lend-Lease. This program was announced on December 17, 1940 "in the homely image of lending a neighbour a hose to put out a fire." As a result of Lend-Lease, Britain was able to fight the war without the kind of daily threat of financial crisis that had characterized its economy during the First World War.[36]

But the need for long-run external balance imposed the need for the economy to become competitive again after the war ended, in a way that had never happened after the First World War. Keynes' long-run strategy was to save enough external and financial strength for Britain to preserve its freedom of maneuver to regain—in time—a satisfactory external position.

Keynes aimed to establish a policy framework in which individual countries like Britain would be able to promote high levels of employment and output by means of demand-management policies, mainly in the form of fiscal policy. This would, it was hoped, avert slumps in growth and would prevent the reemergence of the kind of global depression that had occurred in the 1930s.[37] Each country would pursue internal balance.

But Keynes saw that such policies would need global support, because they would have to be reconciled with the need for each country to be sufficiently competitive. That is, each country would need to be able to export enough to pay for the imports that would be purchased at full employment.

Keynes' first step was the plan he put forward for a new postwar international monetary system in late 1941 that was designed to make such global full employment possible, which he called a Clearing Union. His plan drew on the theoretical arguments in his *General Theory* and also on the harsh practical example provided by Britain's return to the gold standard in 1925. In his Clearing Union draft, he was concerned that a shortage of global lending to countries in balance-of-payments difficulty might trigger global malfunction in the form of a worldwide recession. He feared what had happened in 1931, which we discussed in the last chapter—a fear displayed in 2012 in the face of the borrowing difficulties experienced by many European countries. Keynes thus wanted a global monetary system in which international money would be sufficiently accommodating. His global Clearing Union was thus to be something like the clearing system in a national banking process— something that would enable global liquidity needs to be met without any international risk, hindrance, or restraint. Such a union would act for the world like a national central bank acts in a country; it would lend to countries that have balance-of-payments difficulties and so act as a lender of last resort to those countries. Balance-of-payments difficulties might continue for a considerable period of time, and Keynes' proposal was designed to provide finance during the (possibly prolonged) adjustment period. And he wanted this to happen at a low level of global interest rates. This final requirement was to prove a massive stumbling block in the negotiations between Keynes and Harry Dexter White of the US Treasury from 1942 to 1944, in the run-up to the Bretton Woods conference, negotiations that are discussed below.[38]

Our use of economic theory in this book can help us make further sense of Keynes' position, one that is easily misinterpreted in the manner of White. Keynes was not just being naively expansionary. As well as worrying about the risks of postwar recession, Keynes, like many others, was alive to the opposite risk that postwar recovery might be so vigorous that global restraint would be required. He wanted a postwar world in which countries could achieve both internal and external balance. But he did not want the equivalent of a gold-standard mechanism for achieving external balance, because it would put internal balance at risk.

Keynes actually believed that a gold-standard kind of mechanism could be both too expansionary and too contractionary. His reasons appear to be very modern. As we show in Chapter 5, the European Monetary Union, in which separate countries have fixed exchange rates among them in the manner of the gold standard, has features like those that concerned Keynes. Not only has this system forced countries in the European periphery to have excessively contractionary policies since the onset of the European crisis in 2010. It has also meant that policies in these countries were excessively expansionary in the period before that crisis, in the way Keynes had feared would happen after the Second Word War.

The need for something different from the gold standard was discussed in much detail over the next two years with White and others from the United States, including during a visit that Keynes made to Washington in 1943. In these discussions, which elaborated on the views he had presented to the Macmillan Committee, Keynes had argued that since the 1920s the gold standard had been broken, and he now understood more clearly why this was so. He had claimed in the *General Theory* that the wage and price adjustment does not work well; in the Macmillan Committee he had argued that it does not work fast enough or well enough to accomplish the expenditure-switching component of the balance-of-payments adjustment process. Keynes reiterated that such wage-and-price adjustments could not be brought about in this way; the attempt to use them had resulted in conflict and chaos in the interwar period. (We are watching a similar difficulty in Europe at present, which will be discussed in the next chapter.)

This first failing of the gold-standard system created a second one. At the same time as recession was spreading from the export trades, the gold-standard rules of the game required that monetary policy should raise the interest rate and lower spending and so required that policy deliberately augment the Great Depression. This was, Keynes thought, no longer practical politics for the postwar world. Keynes had already argued before the Macmillan Committee that it was not practical politics for prewar Britain. The gold-standard mechanism, said Keynes, should be prevented from working in this way. This perverse policy is what his Clearing Union proposals were designed to avoid.[39] Today many are arguing that adjustment in Southern Europe will only come when this problem is solved for those Southern European countries now experiencing difficulty in EMU.

Furthermore, in these circumstances, said Keynes, the short-run component of the gold-standard mechanism is likely to be destabilizing. Countries suffering external shocks and experiencing a spreading recession would be likely to come under political pressure to suspend membership in the gold standard. Capital holders would take fright at this possibility, and capital would thus tend to flee those countries experiencing negative external shocks rather than to cushion the adjustment of such countries to these shocks. Here Keynes was already beginning to produce ideas about self-fulfilling speculative attacks and financial crises.[40] Here too there are parallels with what is happening in Europe today.

How could external adjustment be achieved? What were the policies that countries could pursue to achieve external balance, alongside their policies to promote internal balance? In terms of the language we have introduced above, what expenditure-switching polices were available to ensure that countries could become sufficiently competitive and sell sufficient exports to pay for their imports at full employment?

Here Keynes, and Britain, ran up against a sting in the tail of Lend-Lease—the "fire hose" that Roosevelt had provided for Britain. At the end of 1940, Article VII of Lend-Lease, which became known as the "Consideration," had stipulated that in return for donating resources through Lend-Lease, the United States would have the right to determine the institutional structure of the postwar world. In effect, it was proposed that Lend-Lease would give the United States complete control over the form of Britain's long-run rehabilitation. In particular, the United States would be able to determine the conditions under which Britain could recover the export markets that, during the war, it had abandoned. And, using their new-found power to control their old imperial masters, the United States firefighters were determined to impose tough conditions. Roosevelt himself was passionately determined to dismember the British Empire, as was Cordell Hull, the US Secretary of State. There can be no doubt that the destruction of empire was an American objective, consistently pursued. Reasons abounded for this wish; it was not just a moral argument. There was a push for markets (for example, Argentina), a belief that Britain was the past (and Russia the future, a view held by White), a hope by New York bankers to exert ascendancy over London, and an ideological belief in free trade (as held by Hull). It became a war aim of the US State Department that imperial preference should be dismantled. But, catastrophically, it also became a war aim of the US Treasury that Britain would be denied the use of an imperial payments system (or indeed of any serious balance-of-payments restrictions) that the competition for its imperial markets might make necessary. A fundamental contradiction lurked in these requirements.[41]

The effect of the United States' acting on this objection to imperialism was to be the eventual destruction, as collateral damage, of the entire British economic system. The crucial casualty was to be Britain's free trade area with the Old Commonwealth countries—Canada, Australia, New Zealand, and South Africa. For a hundred years, these primarily agricultural countries had supplied the mother country with raw materials in exchange for British manufactured goods, and since the 1930s explicit trade preferences had supported this arrangement.

Although the United States was insisting during the Second World War that this would have to stop, the contrast with the American position of the past ten years is striking. Britain's defense of its free trade area is consistent with the "new regionalism" promoted by the United States since 2000, which has been designed to create trade between its members at the expense of outsiders who remain excluded by tariffs and other barriers. The United States, voluntarily excluded two hundred years earlier from the British Empire, now wished to make good its loss and to expropriate the empire's gain. The war and Lend-Lease gave the Americans their chance.[42]

Keynes came to see that, because it was essential that the United States provide Britain with support, there was no way to escape from the sting contained in Lend-Lease. Nevertheless, he saw, at first dimly and then in the end with great clarity, that perhaps there was a way out of the impossible contradiction into which the United States was pushing his country. This escape route required him to remake the whole world. Suppose that free trade (including the absence of general balance-of-trade restrictions against the United States and the unwinding of more specific imperial preference) were to be imposed on Britain along with open international finance. Then the position of Britain could only be maintained if trade were freer and international finance were managed on a *global* basis. Could a multilateral world of global free trade and open international finance really be made to work, to replace the imperial system of the late nineteenth century? Could Britain earn an important and prosperous place in such a brave new world?

Keynes' activities in Whitehall from 1942 to 1944 required him to confront this issue. His resulting negotiations with White in the run-up to the Bretton Woods conference were perhaps the most conceptually difficult international negotiations ever conducted about anything—except possibly those about how to fix the Eurozone crisis at present.

Keynes' first thoughts deliberately did not presume the kind of multilateral response with which he has become associated. That is, he did not initially propose the use of the exchange rate as the expenditure switching policy. His initial thoughts were illiberal and protectionist and ran along the following lines. The financial system should differ from the gold standard by providing generous international liquidity, sufficient to allow time for the required adjustments to work. Capital controls should be used where necessary (perhaps all the time) to rub out the malfunctioning of international capital flows. In particular, he was worried about speculative attacks on countries in difficulty. But in the longer term, balance-of-balance restrictions (that is, tariffs and quotas) should be used as the necessary expenditure-switching mechanism to reequilibrate exports with imports, in exactly the way that he had proposed to the Macmillan Committee.[43]

At the core of these illiberal ideas was the view, which we have been stressing in this book, that balance-of-payments problems might stand in the way of full-employment policies—the difficulty that he had faced in the Macmillan Committee. But, in the face of insistence by the United States that the world move to a more open international trading system, why did Keynes not immediately move to the view that we have been putting forward and see exchange-rate depreciation as the way to deal with this difficulty? Partly the reason was what became known as "elasticity pessimism"—a sense that exports and imports might not be responsive enough to exchange-rate change. Partly it was a fear that the global economic system was likely to malfunction, as it did in the 1930s—and as it has again from 2008 to the present—and that, as a consequence, the risks of full exposure to it (which a country experiences when protectionism is dismantled) might be too extreme. Without protectionism, a country might need to resort to aggressive beggar-thy-neighbor depreciation of its currency to protect itself against such a global slump. Keynes thought this behavior was surely not desirable.[44]

But crucially, there was also an important fear that the United States would be protectionist. The change to protectionism by Britain in 1931 and the subsequent growth of imperial preference within the British Empire had added to the risk of global protectionism, and Keynes could certainly see a global interest in free trade; he could understand why the United States was promoting a move in this direction. But Britain faced the postwar prospect of having to deal with a United States that—although its rhetoric was pro–free trade—was actually likely to act in a protectionist manner to defend its own industries. The United States had the financial power to prevent Britain from being protectionist—something that would require Britain to abandon the protectionism it had embraced since 1931. And the "Consideration" clause in the Lend-Lease agreement gave it the ability to exercise such power. This was a grim economic prospect for Britain. It is no wonder—in the face of this threat—that Keynes sent James Meade away one weekend in 1942 to produce a draft document on how to set up a body devoted to the liberalization of international trade. These proposals for an International Trading Organisation led to the establishment of the General Agreement on Tariffs and Trade (or GATT) in 1948, which ultimately became the World Trade Organization in 2003. The British negotiating position was built on the hard-nosed idea that Britain needed a form of global institutional protection, to ensure that the global Prisoner's Dilemma game of protectionism would not end up being played in the worst possible way—one in which the United States would remain protectionist but Britain would be forced by the United States to dismantle imperial free trade and so to pursue trade liberalization.[45]

Thinking about this issue makes one realize why Keynes took so long to be persuaded that the expenditure-switching balance-of-payments adjustment mechanism in the Bretton Woods system should be through exchange-rate change rather than through fine-tuned changes in the level of protectionism. If the rest of the world were to remain protectionist, then exchange-rate devaluation by Britain would not be much use for Britain in remedying any balance-of-trade deficit that it might have. But one day in 1944, in a particularly tedious meeting at the Board of Trade, Keynes sketched something like Table 3.1 on the back of an envelope. He passed the envelope to Meade and said, as he did so, "At last, I am convinced."[46]

How did Keynes reach this conclusion? In the decade or so since he had written *The General Theory,* he had incorporated macroeconomic thinking into his framework. No longer would he struggle against Marshall; instead he was firmly asserting that several markets needed to be in equilibrium for

TABLE 3.1   The international policy system according to Keynes

Objective	Instrument(s)	Responsible authority
Full employment	Demand management (mainly fiscal)	National governments
Balance-of-payments adjustment	Pegged but adjustable exchange rates	International Monetary Fund
Promotion of international trade	Tariff reductions etc.	International Trading Organisation
Economic development	Official international lending	World Bank

the economy to be in equilibrium. Building on Hicks's IS/LM system, but well before Samuelson's neoclassical synthesis, Keynes had become comfortable with the new field of economics he had created. His objectives were multidimensional. Having understood what he was doing, Keynes came to see that to achieve a well-managed national economy, one needed to consider not just the market for domestic goods and the need to achieve full employment—that is, internal balance. One also needed to include the market for goods traded internationally and the need to achieve external balance (that is, a satisfactory balance-of-payments position). The first two lines of Table 3.1 make the necessity of joint dependency clear—and this has been the central message of our book. It would take economists many years to figure out how to model this analytically, but Keynes leapt to this next step without effort. In developing his new model, Keynes continued his procedures from the early 1930s, sending messages to his colleagues and students, as he had done with the Circus, and letting them work out the details. The big difference was that he now understood more thoroughly what he was doing and could send more complete messages.

This model of international macroeconomics was not written down until 1952, when it was published by Meade in *The Balance of Payments,* for which he was awarded the Nobel Prize. As Howson and Moggridge show, Meade was a key player in Keynes' invention of the model. Meade described his work as one that "does not claim to make any significant contribution of original work in the fundamentals of pure economic analysis" and one that has an "indebtedness to the ideas of Lord Keynes [which] is too obvious to need any emphasis." This model became easy to grasp as a result of the Swan diagram, but it only came into popular use in the mid-1980s. Since then it has become a core part of international macroeconomics.[47] It will be central to our discussions in this book. This model is explained in the Appendix. It shows the way in which the exchange rate necessary to ensure external balance and the domestic macroeconomic policy necessary to ensure internal balance are jointly determined. Keynes saw that domestic macroeconomic policy influences both the internal position of an economy and its external position; a more expansionary policy raises the level of demand and output and also increases the level of imports. The exchange rate similarly influences the level of domestic economic activity as well as influencing the external position of the country, and it can move a country toward or away from internal balance. Both need to be thought about together.

We can put this simply as follows. The aim of policy in a well-managed economy must be to ensure both external balance—which requires that exports are sufficient to pay for imports—and internal balance—which requires that resources be fully utilized. It is clear that to achieve both objectives at the same time requires a difficult balancing act. Adjustment in the face of an external deficit—the kind of problem that Britain would face after the war—requires that domestic expenditures be reduced so that imports will be reduced. But to preserve internal balance means that these domestic expenditures must be replaced both by an increase in exports and also by a move away from imports toward demand for domestically produced goods. Clearly the increase in exports and the reduction in imports require an improvement in the international competitiveness of the economy; that is to say, it requires a depreciation of the country's exchange rate. This is what is shown in the Appendix.

Without a gold-standard mechanism to enforce wage cuts as a means of bringing about the necessary improvement in competitiveness, it is clear that a devaluation of the currency will be necessary in these circumstances. If such a devaluation were not contemplated by policymakers, then we can see why Keynes initially believed that protectionism might remain necessary for countries in external difficulty. But once such protection was put to one side, he and others recognized that exchange-rate depreciation would be a required part of the policy to bring about adjustment.

It is clear that Keynes invented this model between 1942 and 1944, and that he used it in his discussions with White about the postwar relationships between Britain and the United States. Keynes then went on to increase the number of countries considered to more than one. He saw, for example, that with two countries, it is necessary to achieve internal balance in both countries and also achieve external balance between them (that is, a satisfactory balance-of-payments position between them). We use this model extensively in what follows, and we show how it can be used—as Keynes used it—to think not just about policies in one country, but also about how policy should govern the relationships among countries.[48]

Keynes understood the properties of this model even without writing it down. He argued that we needed as many policy instruments as we had objectives. This requirement would emerge gradually after the war as economists became familiar with Keynesian models, but Keynes stated it clearly in 1944. For one country, two goals could only be reached with two policy instruments; for two countries acting together, three objectives (internal balance in both countries and external balance between them) could only be accomplished by the use of three policy instruments. Remarkably, Jan Tinbergen was to win the Nobel Prize in 1969 for another more general and abstract version of the same idea.

In addition, long- and short-run goals had to be considered together. For the international economy to be stable, short-run expedients had to be consistent with long-run arrangements. Measures to deal with temporary crises should not destroy the long-run conditions. These short-run measures need to bring the world economy closer to its long-run equilibrium to be effective. This lesson has not yet been properly incorporated into formal models, and it is a valuable lesson for today.

Finally, Keynes had the audacity to envisage new institutions. If the policy levers did not exist, Keynes would create them. He had such intellectual dominance at this stage of his career that he could envisage remaking the international economy according to the model he had created. This was an astonishing amount of bravado, and it could have sent the world economy down some primrose path. It may be Keynes' greatest contribution and perhaps the one he would have been most proud of—that the IMF, the World Trade Organization, and the World Bank are still operative today. True, these agencies have been modified many times in the intervening seventy years, but they still fulfill the roles assigned to them in Table 3.1. The World Trade Organization has faced many difficulties recently in the failure to negotiate the Doha round of trade liberalization, and the World Bank often has been much maligned. But the work of these three institutions continues to be crucial—and the initial arrangement that the Europeans choose the head of the Fund and the Americans choose the head of the Bank endures.

Why didn't Keynes properly work out the model that underlies Table 3.1? We can only speculate, but it was Keynes' method to sketch out the main ideas in messages to junior colleagues and let them work out the math. He had used this framework in the Circus to produce the *General Theory*, and he clearly hoped to use it again here. Had he lived, perhaps he would have written another book that would have been as innovative and influential as his previous ones.

However, this would have required Keynes to live for many more years after 1944. He was far ahead of his students in thinking about the interconnections among different markets in different countries. It has required more than a generation of economists steeped in Keynesian thought to come close to the world model that was anticipated in his message to Meade. Perhaps it requires a different kind of intelligence to write down the analytic version of Keynes' summary. Perhaps it requires the calm of a Cambridge or Oxford to pull it together.

This last speculation gets to the real point. The actual Keynes, as opposed to the hypothetical one just conjured up, was actively involved in making economic policy. Keynes had been working and writing in this area since *The Economic Consequences of the Peace* in 1919. He had spent a quarter-century actively working in this area, with many successes and failures; he was unlikely to have retired from this public arena while he was still able to contribute to it. We must be grateful that his interests were so practical.

In July 1944, two years after the initial circulation of Keynes' Clearing Union proposals, 730 delegates from 44 nations met at Bretton Woods, in the White Mountains of New Hampshire. Their deliberations were led by two people—John Maynard Keynes from Britain and Harry Dexter White from the United States. Keynes and White shared a determination to avoid another Great Depression after the Second World War. More than this, they wished to ensure the return of worldwide growth—as there had been in the great Victorian era before the First World War—and that it would happen in a world with open international markets and growing international trade. They desired that this growth would take place in all countries. Discussions on these matters by delegates lasted three full weeks.

Those gathered at Bretton Woods saw that, if they were to achieve what they desired, the world economy would need a new form of leadership and global cooperation. Such leadership had been exercised by Britain in the late Victorian era of expansion. But there had been no such leadership in the interwar period, and the resulting lack of cooperation was part of the reason why the world had fallen into the Great Depression, with disastrous consequences. Global leadership now needed to pass from Britain to the United States. But Keynes wanted to ensure that the emerging global system was a truly multilateral and cooperative one, in which the United States was unable to impose unacceptable constraints on the second-tier countries, such as Britain, which faced such enormous balance-of-payments difficulties.[49]

In March 1946, nearly two years later, Keynes again met with a large number of delegates from around the world, this time in Savannah, Georgia. They were there to celebrate the baptism of the two new creations, the IMF and the World Bank, which had been brought to life at Bretton Woods. In his speech Keynes drew an analogy with the christening party in *The Sleeping Beauty,* a ballet that he had just seen at the reopening of the Covent Garden Opera House in London a few weeks earlier. Keynes hoped that the Bretton Woods twins, Master Fund and Miss Bank, would receive three gifts from their fairy godmothers: first, a many-colored coat "as a perpetual reminder that they belong to the whole world"; second, a box of vitamins to encourage "energy and a fearless spirit, which does not shelve and avoid difficult issues, but welcomes them and is determined to solve them"; third, "a spirit of wisdom . . . so that their approach to every problem is absolutely objective." Keynes warned the delegates that this was asking a great deal: "There is scarcely any enduringly successful experience yet of an international body which has fulfilled the hopes of its progenitors." So he hoped that the malicious fairy would not bring its curse on the twins: "You two brats shall grow up politicians; your every thought and act shall have an *arrière pensée;* everything you determine shall not be for its own sake or on its own merits but because of something else." And if the IMF were to become politicized, then, Keynes said, it would be best for the twins "to fall into an eternal slumber, never to waken or be heard of again in the courts and markets of Mankind."[50]

FOUR

The American Century and the
Global Financial Crisis

THE UNITED STATES HAD TAKEN OVER FROM Great Britain as the world's
leading economic power by the time of the Bretton Woods meetings in
1944. America was in position to play a key role in managing global economic developments, and it maintained its economic hegemony until the
end of the twentieth century. This chapter tells how the United States achieved
its leading position in the world economy, surveying the roles of both internal factors and external pressures on the nation's rapidly expanding wealth.
It assesses America's role in putting the world back together again after
the Second World War, especially through the Marshall Plan, and it traces
the subsequent fortunes of the American economy in relation to both internal factors and the external pressures it faced.

This discussion of the American economy and the role it played in the
larger global economic environment is followed by an analysis of Europe in
the years leading up to the euro crisis in Chapter 5. Together, these chapters
provide crucial insights for Chapter 6, where we return to global developments in the second half of the twentieth century, when America was the
key player in the global economy, and point the way forward.

The large shock of the Second World War was not followed by the same
economic strains as the interwar period. The First World War followed the
economically tranquil Victorian and Edwardian periods; there was no expectation of and no preparation for the forces unleashed by the war. By contrast,
the Second World War followed the Russian Revolution, the Great Depression, and the Nazi domination of Europe. Policymakers had ample warning
—if they cared to learn from history—that the world economy would not
heal itself from the injury of the war quickly or smoothly without help.

The United Nations, the IMF, and the World Bank were all planned while the war was still going on, but it became apparent by 1947 that these new institutions were not going to be sufficient to guarantee economic—and therefore political—stability in Europe. President Harry Truman, in one of the great actions of an international hegemon in the past century, extended aid to Europe in the form of the Marshall Plan.

The cooperation stimulated by American generosity was a hallmark of postwar European progress. The European Currency Union, the European Coal and Steel Community, and other such organizations cemented the practice of cooperation among the countries of Western Europe. They culminated in the Treaty of Rome of 1957 that founded what would become the European Union. This led in turn to EMU, which introduced the euro as a common currency for many members of the European Union.

The Truman administration had to work hard to extend this aid, because Congress feared that the cost of aid would be large, added to the already huge cost of the war itself. The congressional point of view is hard to recapture in light of the great postwar boom that followed, but we must remember that the boom was still in the future. History was not that hopeful; the Great Depression was scarcely over. A little thought might have enabled Congress to realize that the costs of aid to Europe would be small, but who could be expected to foresee the future when it was so different from the recent past and so dependent on current actions? Congress consequently delayed and discussed the proposed plan in detail. Truman later said he called it the Marshall Plan because Congress would not have approved a "Truman Plan."[1]

This brief legislative history raises an important question. If the expected cost of aid was large, why was the Truman administration so intent on overriding congressional caution? Was the administration's motive to promote the interests of the United States or was it simply altruism? Economic and political conditions in Europe were very unstable in the late 1940s. Communists were coming to power in Eastern Europe and seemed ready to take Western Europe as well. Having just vanquished Nazi domination of Western Europe, Truman did not relish repeating the experience with Soviet domination. Foreign aid was a way to tip the political balance in favor of democracy and ensure a measure of political tranquility. What was in it for the United States?

A bit of game theory known as the Prisoner's Dilemma helps us understand and prepares for the discussion of international cooperation in Chapter 6. In this game, a prisoner does not know what his confederate in a separate cell is saying. If he denies any wrongdoing while his confederate implicates him, he suffers for both his guilt and his false statement. However, if he admits his guilt, then he does better than the worst-case scenario when he denies it, but he gives up the possibility that both he and his confederate deny their guilt and go free. (See the Appendix for more on simple game theory.)

Extensive exploration of this abstract game has yielded two conclusions. First, people playing this game one time only are likely to choose the conservative strategy of admitting guilt. If both prisoners act this way, they both admit guilt and are punished. Second, if people play the game repeatedly, they can get to a better equilibrium, where they both deny guilt and go free. How do they get there? The most popular theory is called tit-for-tat. If you choose to admit guilt, in the next episode your partner does too. If you choose to deny guilt, in the next episode your partner does too. If you both take a chance and deny guilt in the first episode, you will reach the good equilibrium by the second.[2]

Think of the Marshall Plan as an offer by the United States to help Europe recover. If the Europeans reciprocate, maintain democratic societies, and cooperate with one another and the United States, everyone wins. By contrast, if the United States had declined to offer the Marshall Plan and several European countries had gone communist, the postwar world would have been far less pleasant.

This theory is a problem for the deliberations about the Marshall Plan. Postwar conditions were changing rapidly; there were not many opportunities to go back and replay the same choices. The United States had to choose between the policies implemented by the Allies after the First World War (and by the Soviets after the Second World War) of extracting reparations from the losers and the actual American policies taken after the Second World War of extending aid to friend and former foe alike. Congress had to decide on the Marshall Plan without knowing what Western European countries would do.

If the countries of Western Europe were rational (in the game-theoretic sense), they would go communist and enjoy the gains promised to them by the Soviet Union, whether or not United States gave them aid. But there was a probability that Western Europe would play tit-for-tat. In other words, it would respond to aid by staying democratic but go communist without that aid. In this case, even though Western Europeans did not envisage replaying this precise game over again, they thought of other kinds of cooperation that would be relevant in the years to come. They chose to signal the United States that cooperation would be the norm in whatever future games were to be played. This general expectation transformed a single game into a repeated game.

Similarly, the United States clearly thought of this decision as part of an ongoing relationship with Western Europe. The Marshall Plan was a discrete program, but it was also only part of the postwar relations between the United States and Europe. It was only one part of the aid given to Europe, which ranged from the immediate postwar aid before the Marshall Plan to the support of other measures like the European Payments Union thereafter. The Truman administration learned from the Great Depression that the aftermath of world wars stretches out over many years, as described in Chapter 2.

The probability that Western Europe was playing tit-for-tat must have been high enough to make the cost of having Western Europe be communist loom large even when discounted by the probability that Western Europe would not respond favorably to American actions. The Truman administration was asking Congress to take a gamble. It was not only that the anticipated cost of communism was larger than of the Marshall Plan and other aid. It was also that the Europeans would understand that the Marshall Plan was a signal of an economic policy regime to promote cooperation with Western Europe and among the Western European countries. It was this double estimation that makes the argument for the Marshall Plan so complex.

The Marshall Plan, however complexly justified, was a major step in the American assumption of hegemonic status. America had the economic and military power to dominate at least the noncommunist world, and it showed that it was willing and able to use this power in constructive ways. The result was several decades of spectacular economic growth whose benefits were shared by both American and Europeans. It confirmed American hegemony, the power to induce cooperative actions by other countries, and it has become the iconic example of postconflict generosity.

Contrast this gamble with prospects after the First World War. Keynes, after predicting the chaos that would follow the Versailles Treaty, asked whether anything could be done to alleviate the continuing contest. One possibility was an international loan from the United States. But, Keynes admitted,

> There is no guarantee that Europe will put financial assistance to proper use, or that she will not squander it and be in just as bad a case two or three years hence as she is in now. . . . If I had influence at the United States Treasury, I would not lend a penny to a single one of the present Governments of Europe. They are not to be trusted with resources which they would devote to the furtherance of policies in repugnance to . . . the United States.

America in 1947 took the gamble that a loan would not turn out this way after the Second World War. Without the acrimony of the Versailles Treaty, there was an opportunity for cooperation. A program of loans and grants given generously by the United States was the stimulus for reciprocal acts by the Europeans. A hegemonic power has to be able to take such major gambles and to have them come out well.[3]

As Keynes had hoped, the international monetary system built around the IMF and World Bank in Washington also played a significant part in ensuring that catch-up growth was possible in Europe. The system enabled countries, including those in Europe, to promote high levels of employment and output by means of domestic macroeconomic policies. Each country was able to aim for full employment of its resources and to use its own macroeconomic policy, at that time mainly fiscal, in the pursuit of this objective. Of course such policies would have been at risk if a country wished to import more at full employment than it was able to cover from its exports. Those meeting at Bretton Woods were not prepared to return to a gold standard system in which the adjustment in such countries would be brought about by means of deflation. Instead, the IMF oversaw a global system of pegged-but-adjustable exchange rates. A deficit country was declared to be in "fundamental disequilibrium" if it wished to import more at full employment than it was able to cover from its exports. Exchange-rate pegs were not to be adjusted (unless there was a fundamental disequilibrium) to prevent countries from stealing jobs from one another by beggar-thy-neighbor devaluations. But deficit countries in fundamental disequilibria were required to adjust their exchange rates. Lending from the IMF was available to cover liquidity problems during the adjustment period. Surplus countries in fundamental disequilibrium—that is to say, countries exporting more than the amount required to pay for what would be imported at full employment—were also required to adjust.

The resulting international monetary system followed the intentions of its founders only inexactly, because countries in fundamental disequilibrium turned out to be reluctant to alter their exchange rates, and the Bretton Woods system broke down by 1971, as described in more detail below and at the beginning of Chapter 5. Nevertheless, it provided an important element of stability for the international financial system; supplying three components that the American economist Fritz Machlup brought together in the memorable phrase "liquidity, confidence and adjustment." Liquidity was to be provided at times of difficulty by the IMF, adjustment was to happen in the way just described, and confidence was preserved in that, for some period, crises were avoided.[4]

The twin of the International Monetary Fund in the Bretton Woods system was the World Bank; within the Beltway in Washington these are often known as just the Fund and the Bank. The role of the World Bank was to lend money for longer periods than did the IMF, initially for reconstruction after the war and later to help provide finance for development. Keynes once helpfully remarked that to comprehend the Bretton Woods system, one has to understand that the Fund is a bank, and the Bank is a fund! That is to say, the purpose of the IMF was—and still is—to provide short-term finance. By contrast, World Bank lending was designed to enable countries to borrow abroad (in a world in which there was little international mobility of private capital). Borrowing from the World Bank enabled a country to import capital goods from abroad, even though this might otherwise cause them to run balance-of-trade deficits. Governments used these capital goods for investment purposes to grow more rapidly; the World Bank particularly financed infrastructure, such as roads, bridges, ports, schools, and hospitals. In other words, the IMF generally dealt with macroeconomic issues, whereas the Bank focused more on microeconomic ones.[5]

In addition, a conference in Geneva in 1947 established the General Agreement on Tariffs and Trade (or GATT) to supplement the Bretton Woods system by encouraging the growth of international trade. A series of GATT rounds brought about tariff reductions that helped create markets for exports as countries expanded. Even though trade was liberalized, financial systems and private capital movements typically remained restricted until the 1970s; even the United States resorted to forms of capital control in the 1960s. The globalization of finance with which we are all familiar only gathered pace in the 1980s.

There is still some disagreement as to how quantitatively important the IMF, the World Bank, and the GATT were in sustaining the golden age of growth. But there is no disagreement that the initial impetus provided by the Marshall Plan was significant and that the cumulative effect of the three institutions was deeply important.[6]

The United States was able to impose this world order because it clearly dominated the world after the war. But a little thought is needed to understand why the whole twentieth century, not just the last half, deserves the title of the American century. For that we need to return to the world wars of the early twentieth century and the American role in them. People often say war is the failure of politics, but war also is politics in the sense that wars need to end. The most common end is for both sides to agree to stop fighting; they draw up an armistice, which in most cases leads to a peace treaty. But even if these steps toward returning to some sort of antebellum status quo are not completed, stopping the fighting is the only way to end a war.

The First World War became a stalemate when neither side could convince the other to stop fighting. Lines were drawn, trenches were dug, and fighting continued. The war ended only when the United States entered the war after it had been going on for three years and tipped the balance. There was an armistice and a peace treaty, but many Germans thought that the treaty had been forced on them by the Allies. This failure of political will created chaos in the Weimar Republic and was influential in the political fallout of the Great Depression. The roots of the Second World War were laid in the faulty resolution of the First.

We described the turbulent period between the world wars in Chapter 2. We return to it here to contrast American loans then to the Marshall Plan. Recall Keynes' hypothetical advice about American loans to Europe after the Versailles Treaty. America extended the Dawes Loan to Germany five years later to help end the imbalances that produced the German hyperinflation, and it extended the Young Loan five years after that in an attempt to arrest the imbalances in Germany that led to the currency crisis of 1931. These loans were extended to fight fires rather than to promote cooperation; they were extended in the poisonous atmosphere of the Versailles Treaty. The unwillingness of the United States to promote cooperation and the reluctance of the Europeans to work together doomed these loans to be seen as too little, too late.

The use of tanks and planes in the Second World War restored to offensive operations the power they had lacked in the First World War. France's Maginot Line was a tribute to the fixed trenches of the previous war, and it had no impact on the course of the Second World War. The Nazi blitzkrieg utilized the new technologies in offensive actions and bypassed the Maginot Line. The Allied invasion of Europe, once it got off the beaches, similarly showed how modern armor could advance quickly and almost completely suppress successful opposition.

The point of this brief narrative is that America played a dominant role in the world wars of the early twentieth century. The United States made the difference in the stalemate of the First World War, and it rescued Britain in the second. It was the dominant nation in the first half of the twentieth century, just as it was in the last half. By the end of the Second World War, the Americans understood their world position, and they employed it first to rescue its allies from the devastation of the war. The United States was able to dominate militarily in this way because of its economic dominance. By 1950, it produced over one quarter of all goods and services produced in the world.[7]

The seeds of American dominance were sown in the nineteenth century as the United States grew from a coastal to a continental country. In contrast to the other possible hegemons, the United States was able to achieve both internal and external balance during this growth process. It did not adopt an export-led growth strategy; instead, it directed its attention primarily to settling the American continent and satisfying the consumption of a mobile and relatively egalitarian population. As described in Chapter 1, the United States took shape at the end of the eighteenth century with a constitution that provided for an executive branch of government and gave it resources by allowing the federal government to tax individuals in the component states. The country became in effect a currency union of the states that lasted for two centuries due to the mobility of the population, the national tax system, and the ability to divert resources to alleviate the effects of regional shocks.

The United States stayed in both internal and external balance throughout the nineteenth century except during various shocks. The first one, known as the Jacksonian inflation, was eerily like the current problems analyzed in Chapters 5 and 6. Anglo-American trade with China was disrupted in the 1830s in the run-up to the Opium Wars. Mexican silver that used to flow to China through this trade lodged in American banks. Bank reserves rose, prices rose, and the price of land rose most of all. The appreciation of the real exchange rate was financed by capital imports from England until the Bank of England called a halt in 1836. The result was a financial crisis in 1837 that led to a temporary American devaluation and then to default on the debts of several states in the following few years.[8]

The United States fought a bloody and extended Civil War a generation later to keep the growing nation together. As might be expected, this brutal conflict created both internal and external imbalances in the American economy. The inability of the government to acquire sufficient resources to fight the war from its tax revenues and its consequent need to borrow extensively led it to abandon the gold standard—as many countries would do in the First World War. This led to a depreciation of the dollar, expressed as the discount of "greenbacks" (paper dollars) against the nominal equivalent of gold. The war ended with greenbacks heavily discounted and with the government determined to return to the gold standard, as the British Cunliffe Commission would later echo. It took the United States almost two decades to reduce the discount enough to return to gold in 1879.

The domestic imbalance was widely recognized, but the external imbalance was not identified until quite recently because of the great size of America and the regional conflicts that emerged. The Civil War was a conflict between the North and the South. The postwar deflation became a contest between the East and the West. Western farmers, who typically were in debt and suffered from deflation, did not understand why prices needed to be forced lower. The deflation continued after the resumption of the gold standard due to gold scarcity in the late nineteenth century, and it was seen as a conflict between staying on gold and going to a silver standard—silver being mined in the West. The plea "You shall not crucify mankind upon a cross of gold" was made in 1896, long after the Civil War devaluation had been forgotten.[9]

The resolution of these conflicts was difficult, but it created favorable conditions for the American economy to flourish in what economic historians know as the Second Industrial Revolution of the late nineteenth century. The First Industrial Revolution consisted in large part of the substitution of mechanical, hydraulic, and fossil power for human power in productive processes. This English revolution allowed Britain to dominate the world in the nineteenth century, but it was based on small-scale industry. The growth of the railroads in the United States created large markets and made large-scale production profitable, just as a high ratio of wages to power costs had made the initial industrial discoveries profitable in late-eighteenth-century Britain. Large managerial business firms grew in the United States and became leaders in their respective industries. They grew most prominently in industries in which the vertical integration of different stages of production was profitable, whether from a need to have stable supplies of raw material, careful treatment of products on their way to market, or customer service after the products were sold.[10]

American manufacturing was known by the middle of the nineteenth century for its reliance on what is called the American System, consisting of machines making interchangeable parts. This approach had its start in making muskets and was in full flower for Singer sewing machines. It formed the basis for assembly lines as the volume of production increased, and it was used most famously by Henry Ford in 1914. His five-dollars-a-day pay scheme was a dramatic wage increase for workers who would stay on the job and enable the assembly line to continue at a steady pace. It was coupled with a reduction in hours to eight, also helping to maintain the pace of production. The growth of mass production often is known as Fordism.

The effect of these innovations was to put the United States' current account into surplus in the first years of the twentieth century. However, the surpluses were far smaller than those during and after the First World War, as the United States supported Britain and its allies in that struggle even before joining militarily. In general the gold system worked well for the United States as it moved from an agricultural to an industrial exporter. Tariff debates energized politicians, but industrialists produced largely for the domestic market.[11]

The results of these advances are shown in Table 4.1. The first two columns compare aggregate growth in Western Europe and the United States over the twentieth century. The higher growth rate for GDP in the United States comes in part from the massive immigration that increased an input to growth when combined with the plentiful American natural resources. The difference in aggregate growth rates decreases over time as immigration was restricted after the First World War. The last two columns show the

TABLE 4.1 Economic growth in Western Europe and the United States (percent per year)

Period	GDP		GDP per capita	
	Europe	United States	Europe	United States
1870–1913	2.1	3.9	1.3	1.8
1913–50	1.2	2.8	0.8	1.6
1950–73	4.8	3.9	4.0	2.5
1973–2003	2.2	2.9	1.9	1.9

Source: Maddison (2007), pp. 380, 382.

growth of per capita GDP and again show the United States to be leading Europe in most periods. The exceptional period is 1950–73, which was an unusual period that proves the rule; it only demonstrates American primacy at midcentury, as described earlier in this chapter.[12]

The unusual period in Table 4.1, known in Europe as the golden age of European growth, was the only period when Europe had faster growth of per capita income than did the United States. One might attribute this phenomenon to convergence, where the Europeans catch up to the economic leader, but that is not accurate. The rapidity of European growth was specific to this historical period; it was not a feature of Europe for the whole century and therefore was not a part of a long-run process. Instead, the growth of Europe was the result of catching up on economic development that had been impeded by the world wars, assisted by the spirit of cooperation fostered by the hegemonic United States.

Globalization ebbed and flowed in the course of the twentieth century. Before the First World War, international commerce and travel were free and open, more or less as they became again after the Second World War. But between these two endpoints, the flow of goods, finance, and people was interrupted by world wars and depression. Authors disagree among themselves about whether today's globalization actually existed a century ago, but there is no disagreement about the interruption during the world wars and Great Depression.[13]

International trade was interrupted by the First World War. The postwar settlement created many new boundaries that provided the opportunity to impose tariffs on trade. And the Great Depression led to restrictive trade policies that reversed whatever expansion had taken place in the 1920s. The volume of exports for the major Western European countries was lower in 1938 than it had been in 1913, in sharp contrast to its rapid growth both before and after this period.[14]

Trade promoted economic growth in the postwar world because the closed economies of the interwar years did not undertake the reallocation of resources needed to increase productivity. They did not exploit their comparative advantages, and they did not end their reliance on domestic agriculture. Before the First World War, participation in international trade promoted industrialization. One has only to recall the discussion of Britain's climacteric in the late nineteenth century to see the importance of international trade in economic growth (see Chapter 2). Britain was surpassed because the United States and Germany were better able to exploit world markets.[15]

It follows that the lack of international commerce during the world wars and Great Depression generated barriers to the continued industrialization of European countries. This slowdown in the process of industrialization created disequilibrium after the Second World War. As suggested by Table 4.1, the supply frontier continued to expand during what we may call the second Thirty Years' War. The United States, insulated from the wars if not from the Great Depression, was able to continue its transformation from an agricultural to an industrial economy. Its exports were primarily food and raw materials before this protracted conflict; they were manufactures afterward.[16]

European countries emerged from the Second World War with a developmental deficit. This disequilibrium is not the same as that caused by low income, which generates conditional convergence. In the standard story, low income is produced by low levels of physical and human capital relative to savings rates. The developmental deficit highlighted here is produced by a misallocation of resources. The first takes place in a single-sector economy; the second, in a disaggregated model of development.

The misallocation of resources caused by autarky in the first half of the twentieth century can be measured by the share of the labor force in agriculture. There are many ways to divide up the economy, but the division between agriculture and all other activities appears to be the most important. Denison analyzed the misallocation of resources in Europe during the golden age of European growth, showing that European countries were growing rapidly when they were transitioning away from agriculture.[17]

Therefore, growth was rapid in Western Europe during the golden age of growth due to disequilibrium. The normal catch-up that works in general was not important right after the war, but other kinds of disequilibrium were. The most important of these was the misallocation of resources that came from the lack of international trade during the preceding thirty years. In this state of arrested industrialization, too many resources still were employed inefficiently in agriculture. Reallocated labor rapidly enhanced the labor supply. Cooperation stimulated by the Marshall Plan and other European institutional arrangements helped create the needed demand.

Different countries grew at different rates during the golden age because of their initial positions. National policies had secondary effects relative to these initial positions. Labor relations were tumultuous in both Italy and Britain, but Italy grew rapidly, while Britain did not. Some of the bitterness of policy debates in slowly growing Britain may have been the result of slow growth instead of its cause. Germany grew at an intermediate rate; its "miracle" was more a result of delayed industrialization than of pro-market government policies. It was helped by the fast recovery from wartime destruction, continuation of Nazi economic policies, and a small German debt. The last of these was a gift of the Marshall Plan that was in addition to the support described earlier.[18]

A similar growth spurt took place in the United States, albeit for different reasons. Gordon called it one big wave of economic growth. It appears to have started before the war when productivity grew rapidly, even though the economy was depressed. In fact, total productivity grew more rapidly in the 1930s than in any other decade of the twentieth century. The fruits of these technological advantages became apparent once the depression and war ended. The United States had a golden age of its own.[19]

Four groups of innovations contributed to this wave of growth. The first was electricity, introduced before the First World War and gradually applied to more and more activities in the first half of the twentieth century. The internal combustion engine similarly gave rise to a variety of new activities, mainly centered on transportation. Although cars were increasingly common in the 1930s, the expansion of suburbia after the Second World War and the production of an integrated highway system led to increased reliance on automobiles. A third group derived from the increased use of oil, giving rise to petrochemicals, plastics, and pharmaceuticals. The spread of antibiotics after the Second World War was a major step in health care. Fourth and finally, the growth of consumer entertainment in the form of radios, movies, television, recorded music, newspapers, and magazines made life more fun in ways not always picked up by national income accounting.

All this postwar growth in America was accomplished with a stable distribution of income. The share of income captured by the very richest—the top 0.1 percent—declined during and sometimes just after the war for all countries for which we have data. Their share in total income then stayed more or less constant across the board until the 1980s. After then, top incomes in English-speaking countries rose as a share of the total, whereas those in other European countries did not. These patterns are replicated if the top 1 percent or even the top 10 percent is examined. However, the share of the top 1 percent rose as a share of the top 10 percent in English-speaking countries after 1980.[20]

Unions in Europe were brought into government efforts to promote economic growth to make sure that workers reaped benefits from higher productivity commensurate with their contribution to production. There was an implicit bargain between workers and capitalists. Workers committed to desist from claiming all the gains and disrupting production. Owners committed to invest their earnings for greater production and productivity. These promises were time inconsistent, as workers had to show forbearance before they knew what capitalists would do with their profits. Governments put unions on company boards and in other ways as well assured the unions that their implicit bargain would be kept.[21]

The story was more complex in the United States, which lacked a long history of unionization. The nonmarket mechanisms that shaped the postwar golden age had roots in the Great Depression and the New Deal. At first glance, it is surprising that norms and institutions—microeconomic policies—grew out of a macroeconomic crisis. But macroeconomic policy as we now understand it did not exist in the Great Depression—Keynes' *General Theory* was not published until 1936, as discussed in Chapter 3. In 1933, Roosevelt's first year in office, unemployment stood at nearly 25 percent, and microeconomic policies appeared to be the only tools at hand. Lacking a theory of aggregate demand, Roosevelt's New Deal policies focused on other goals—in particular, trying to stop what the administration saw as ruinous price deflation.[22]

This theory was implicit in the first major piece of New Deal legislation, the 1933 National Industrial Recovery Act (NIRA) that gave the government control over employer contracts and encouraged labor and industry to nego- tiate industry codes that shortened work hours, increased wages signifi- cantly, and raised prices. The NIRA also gave workers the right to organize and bargain collectively with their employers, and this was a bone of conten- tion. Roosevelt supported union organizing, but Hugh Johnson, charged with administering the NIRA, was eager to get industry codes with or with- out collective bargaining. Roosevelt formed the National Labor Board, led by Senator Robert Wagner, which mediated the resulting conflicts. The con- fusing implementation of the NIRA made both sides tense and combative.[23]

Congress passed the National Labor Relations Act (NLRA)—the Wagner Act—in 1935, endorsing the rights of labor, limiting the means employers could use to combat unions, and transforming the informal National Labor Board into the legislatively directed National Labor Relations Board. The Supreme Court outlawed the NIRA in 1935, citing it as an overreach of fed- eral power into state interests and probably easing passage of the Wagner Act. Unions grew dramatically under the NLRA as workers' reactions to the unemployment of the Depression complemented congressional actions.[24]

The minimum wage was introduced in 1938, and it was set to raise wages significantly in concert with other supports for unions and collective bar- gaining. In 1938, annual earnings at the first minimum wage represented 27 percent of the economy's average output per worker. Between 1947 and 2005, the value of the minimum wage exceeded that percentage in only four other years and today stands at less than half that percentage.

Given the widespread belief that the stock-market boom and the subse- quent collapse of the financial system was the major cause of the Depression, it is not surprising that the government also took control of the financial sector. The Federal Securities Act initiated government oversight of new securities, which was transferred to the new Securities and Exchange Com- mission in 1934. The Glass-Steagall Act of 1933 reformed the banking system in many ways. It separated deposit and investment banking on the argument that the combination had led to bank failures. It introduced federal deposit insurance to prevent bank failures from cumulating into panics. And—as extended by later revisions—it created a genuine central bank out of the Federal Reserve System.

When the United States entered the Second World War, mobilization and production became the focus of the economy. The military saw unions as detrimental to the war effort and took several initiatives to undercut union power. The civilian government countered with the National War Labor Board to settle labor disputes, which obtained no-strike and no-lockout pledges from unions and companies, effectively freezing wages for the duration of the war. The agreement created an uneasy peace, with continuing tension among unions, the government, and industry throughout the war.[25]

As the war drew to a close, many feared that the end of wartime strike controls would bring labor market disruption and the potential for a second Great Depression. At the war's end, organized labor erupted on cue with work stoppages involving over 3 percent of the workforce each year between 1947 and 1949. Business supported the Taft-Hartley Act of 1947, which defined restrictive administrative policies to constrain unions. Although the Taft-Hartley Act clearly rolled back some union gains from the Great Depression and the subsequent war, it fell far short of dismantling the Wagner Act and the National Labor Relations Board.

Walter Reuther assumed control over the United Auto Workers in this context. The relationship between the union and the "Big Three" automakers (Ford, General Motors, and Chrysler), previously plagued by turmoil, entered a new phase of negotiation. Reuther hoped to overhaul industrial relations in favor of labor interests, but the postwar setting created significant obstacles to his social vision. Workers faced price inflation while wages remained inert, and the government's division between the president and congress indicated the situation would not improve.

Charles Wilson, the head of General Motors, was aware that inflationary pressures generated by Cold War military spending promised to be a permanent feature of the economic scene. The company recently had begun a $3.5 billion expansion program that depended on production stability. Stress created by inflation could instigate the unions to interrupt production with a devastating strike, and Wilson thought a long-term wage concession would be a profitable exchange for guaranteed production stability.[26]

General Motors' two-year proposal to the United Auto Workers included an increase in wages and two concepts intended to keep wages up over time. The first, a cost-of-living adjustment, would allow wages to be influenced by changes in the Consumer Price Index, adjusting for rising inflation. Second, a 2 percent annual improvement factor was introduced, which would increase wages every year in an attempt to allow workers to benefit from productivity gains. The annual improvement factor resembled the European process of putting workers on company boards, but it was more rigid and contentious than the European arrangement.

The union would allow management control over production and investment decisions, surrendering job assignment seniority and the right to protest reassignments, in exchange for the cost-of-living adjustment and annual improvement factor. Reuther and his advisors initially opposed the plan, but workers needed assistance, and Reuther agreed to the plan and wage formulas, "only because most of those in control of government and industry show no signs of acting in the public interest. They are enforcing a system of private planning for private profit at public expense." The contract was signed in May 1948.[27]

Workers saw wage increases and gains from productivity for the next two years; General Motors enjoyed smooth, increasing production and established a net income record for an American corporation in 1949. When the time period for the contract ended, the union and the company readily agreed to a similar plan that included several changes. A pension plan was added, initially through Ford in 1949, which had an older workforce and progressive managers. The resulting plan was presented to General Motors as a precedent to create industrial conformity in a process known as pattern bargaining, and Chrysler, the last of the Big Three automakers to adopt it, agreed after an expensive strike. Agreements to the pension plan ultimately spread to other industries, including rubber, Bethlehem Steel, and then United States Steel. The final, five-year agreement was named the "Treaty of Detroit" by *Fortune* magazine: "GM may have paid a billion for peace but it got a bargain. General Motors has regained control over one of the crucial management functions . . . long range scheduling of production, model changes, and tool and plant investment." Wage adjustments and productivity gains became recognized as necessary and just, union membership increased, and industry reaped the profits from the Treaty of Detroit's stability.[28]

The Treaty of Detroit initiated a stable period of industrial relations. The use of collective bargaining spread throughout industry, and even nonunion firms approximated the conditions achieved by unions in an extension of pattern bargaining. Unions acknowledged the exclusive right of management to determine the direction of production in return for the right to negotiate the impact of managerial decisions. Unions crafted an elaborate

set of local rules that constrained management in its allocation of jobs and
bolstered the power of unions over jobs. Managers used the framework of
the Treaty of Detroit to tighten their grasp on production decisions. Labor
complaints had to go through paperwork, and the burden to oppose or
modify change was placed on the workers.[29]

The Treaty of Detroit was underwritten by the stability of American trade
during the golden age. Relative prices were stable, and large American firms
exploited their market power to earn generous profits. These profits then
were shared with their workers according to the Treaty of Detroit. We can
see in hindsight that this favorable condition was sustainable only for a limited time. As peace returned and economic growth resumed around the
world, new companies would grow and threaten the market power of American firms. Pressure on their sales would translate into pressure on wages
and perhaps hiring and in turn to labor conflict.

Growth slowed in the 1970s and 1980s, because the disequilibrium that
had generated unusually rapid growth no longer existed. The developmental
deficit of a generation was eliminated in a generation. The European Common Agricultural Policy kept some excess labor in agriculture, but the misallocation of resources had ceased to be a large macroeconomic issue by the
time of the oil crises in the 1970s. These crises muddied the historical waters,
confusing short- and long-run factors. It is only with the hindsight of
another thirty years that we can see that although the oil crises were disruptive, the slowdown of growth would have taken place even if they had not
occurred.

However, the transition was accelerated by the turbulent economic conditions of the 1970s. The United States embarked on the Vietnam War in ear-
nest in 1965. President Lyndon Johnson intensified the war at the same time
as he promoted many domestic reforms. He hesitated to raise taxes in the
midst of all these controversial activities, and he threw the United States into
a replay of the internal and external imbalances during the Civil War. In an
uncanny rerun of events of a century earlier, the US economy overheated
from the new demands made on its resources, and the current account went
into deficit. In terms of our simple model, the United States experienced
domestic inflation and had an international deficit, caused jointly by an
increase in domestic demand.

The US import surplus created strains on other Bretton Woods countries,
and pressure grew for the United States to devalue, but that was hard to do

in view of the dollar's use as a reserve currency. There was an alternative: the Allies' former enemies, Germany and Japan, could have appreciated their currencies. However, they did not see why they should help the richest and most powerful country in the world. Countries converted their gold holdings into gold, and the gold backing of the dollar decreased. This pressure threatened to turn into a run on the dollar, and President Richard Nixon acted to forestall that disruption. In the Nixon Shock of 1971, he "closed the gold window," imposed a 90-day wage and price freeze and a 10 percent tariff. Only the first of these measures lasted; several abortive events to settle on a new set of exchange rates were abandoned in favor of floating exchange rates.

The resulting devaluation corrected the external imbalance, but it made the internal balance worse by intensifying American inflation. Inflation turned into stagflation around the world as the scarcity of oil and wheat in 1973 sent prices skyrocketing and led to capital outflows from industrialized countries to the Middle East at the same time as unemployment rose. Economic theory had followed Keynes in focusing on demand shifts, and there was no theory of the supply side that related to economic policy. The high prices of raw materials were supply shocks, which cried for explanation. Macroeconomics was in disarray. Economic policy in the 1970s was a sequence of confused efforts to end inflation. Success finally came at the end of the decade, when President Jimmy Carter appointed Paul Volcker as Chairman of the Federal Reserve System. Volcker dramatically reduced domestic demand—absorption—by highly deflationary monetary policy. Interest rates skyrocketed, and the misery index, composed of the inflation and unemployment rates, went out of sight. President Carter failed in his bid for reelection, and his successor, President Ronald Reagan, got the credit for ending inflation.[30]

Inflation returned to its previous low levels, but the world economy did not return to the *status quo ante*. New policies ruled in developed countries, and Asian countries previously on the outskirts of the world industrial economy moved onto center stage. Reagan and Margaret Thatcher were elected leaders of the United States and Britain in 1979. They both rejected the policies that had prevailed during the golden age and began to refashion public policy. Deng Xiaoping became General Secretary of the Communist Party of China at almost the same time, and he too reversed previous economic policies. Deng similarly began to reduce the size of government in the Chinese economy and provided room for private enterprises to expand. Thatcher and Reagan emerged as leaders during the economic stagflation of the West; Deng emerged after Mao died. It is hard to find a causal connection between these events, but the coincidence of dates when economic policies changed is remarkable.

President Carter of the United States floundered in the absence of clear direction, arguing in 1978 that "The two most important measures the Congress can pass to prevent inflation . . . [are] the airline deregulation bill . . . [and] hospital cost containment legislation." He appointed the chairman of the Civil Aeronautics Board to head the administration's anti-inflation program. His field was government regulation, and his plans were to reduce regulations that supported monopoly pricing.[31]

Reagan made three decisions that proved central to the distribution of income in his first year in office. He gave the Federal Reserve's tight-money anti-inflation policy his full backing. He introduced a set of supply-side tax cuts lowering the top income tax on nonlabor income from 70 to 50 percent to align it with the top rate on labor income. And when the air traffic controllers' union, one of the few unions to support Reagan, went on strike, he gave them 48 hours to return to work or be fired. His stance ultimately led to the union's decertification.

Thatcher argued that the stop-and-go policies of postwar Britain had been the cause of its comparatively slow growth. This assertion confused cause and effect. Britain grew slowly because it was not subject to arrested development during the world wars and the Great Depression. British agriculture had declined to something like its long-run equilibrium by 1913, and it did not have any backlog of development to make up once the wars were over. But no one did any serious analysis, and the narrative of national frustration was persuasive. Thatcher set about deregulating business and opposing unions.

Japan had grown rapidly during the golden age by expanding its exports of mechanical equipment. Starting from exports that were unreliable, Japan learned how to maintain quality, and its exports began to gain a reputation for higher quality than that of American-made goods. Japanese manufacturers migrated from air conditioners to automobiles, and by the 1980s, they began to threaten the American industry, the birthplace of the Treaty of Detroit. Foreshadowing later Chinese practice, Japan loaned the United States the funds with which to buy Japanese products, and government deficits under Reagan were financed in part by the Japanese. In the words of our model, the United States was out of external equilibrium, enabled by an opposite imbalance in Japan.

Chinese policy under Deng increasingly favored private industry. The specific policies differed from those in the West, because the starting points were different. Town and village enterprises in China produced exports without having the clear definition of private property that Western economists have identified as a prerequisite for economic growth. Despite this ambiguity, China's economy expanded rapidly. As urbanization increased, private firms that looked more familiar to Westerners proliferated.

China adopted an export-led pattern of growth. Just as the United States, Germany, and Japan had shifted from agriculture to industry and from the countryside to cities, China also wanted to shift its economy from agriculture to industry. To speed this process, China adopted the policies used initially by Britain and then more recently by many smaller Asian countries, especially Japan. Instead of waiting for domestic demand for industrial goods to rise, the Asian countries tapped into the existing demand of richer countries that had already made the transition away from agriculture.

Japan and later China went from imitation to innovation as they implemented their export-led strategies of economic growth. Japan used this strategy to raise consumption levels of its citizens to levels previously seen only in Western Europe and the countries populated by their emigrants. China has started down this road, and its residents have seen their consumption rise substantially as a result. The difference between these two countries comes not only from the timing of their industrialization, but also from their size. China has an order of magnitude more residents than does Japan—1.3 billion rather than 130 million today—and its effects on the world economy have been proportionately larger.

An important result of this convergence was that the United States no longer enjoyed an absolute productivity advantage with its trading partners. Comparative advantage determined the composition of trade and put pressure on wages in the United States. The results are shown in Figure 4.1, where it is clear that the bottom four-fifths of the population lost as much share of total income as the top 1 percent gained since 1980. It is hard to know how much of the increase in income inequality was due to the growth of the Asian exporters and how much was due to domestic policies initiated by Reagan. Empirical research has not found clear evidence of the impact of the expan-

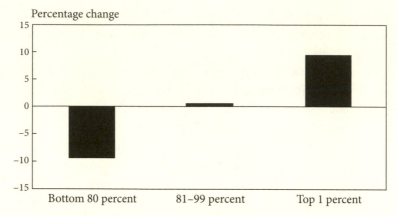

Percentage change

FIGURE 4.1   Changes in income shares, 1979–2007
Source: Krugman (2011a), using after-tax data from Congressional Budget Office, October 2011.

sion of trade on wages and unemployment in the United States, but recent theoretical and empirical work shows that the role of trade increased over time.[32]

International comparisons suggest that this was not simply a result of competition for less-skilled occupations. The policy reversals in Britain, the United States, and China were not duplicated in Western Europe. The results of this policy divergence can be seen in their contrasting patterns of income inequality. We discuss other differences between British and continental Europe's economic strategies in Chapter 5.

The rise of the financial sector and its accompanying high salaries in the United States represented a major part of the widening income gaps. We have to inquire into the composition of the economy to understand both the implications of economic policy for American lives and the roots of the current economic mess described in Chapter 1. The financial sector grew as the economy reacted to the new competition from Asia. The perceived need for change was promoted by the new policy direction that grew into a complex of deregulation and privatization policies and became known as the Washington Consensus.

Financial innovations had emerged in the 1970s, but the financial sector first attained its current prominence in the macroeconomic events of the 1980s. Volcker's policy of deflation raised nominal interest rates as inflation fell, raising real interest rates in the early 1980s. The high rates restricted profitable investment opportunities for mature firms in many industries, resulting in free cash flows that made these firms targets of takeovers. Lower rates after the 1981–82 recession led to a reallocation of capital across firms and industries. In earlier postwar years, investment came from mature corporations utilizing their own cash flows. Now, new corporations were financing investment through financial intermediaries. The result was increased demand for financial professionals—the financial sector—to create and sell the new debt involved in capital reallocation. The financial sector's importance was further increased by the rapidly growing US Treasuries market, a result of the Reagan budget deficits. Between 1975 and 1984, total credit market debt grew from $2.5 trillion to $7.2 trillion.[33]

Mortgage-backed bonds are a microcosm of these developments. As interest rates rose during the 1970s and early 1980s, savings and loan institutions were under pressure to sell low-interest mortgages in the hope of reinvesting the proceeds at higher returns. There was little investor interest in buying individual mortgages, but the introduction of mortgage-backed bonds created a market in which these mortgages could be sold. By the early 1980s, the mortgage-backed bond market had taken off and, as a by-product, helped to redefine income norms. The story of Howie Rubin, a graduate of Salomon Brothers' training program in his late 20s who was assigned to trade mortgage-backed bonds, illustrates the process. In 1983, Rubin's first year, he generated $25 million of revenue and was paid $90,000; he moved in his third year to Merrill Lynch for a three-year guarantee of over $1 million a year. Many of Salomon's other successful mortgage bond traders soon left the firm for similar offers.[34]

Similarly, junk bonds had been developed in the late 1970s to finance corporate takeovers, attempts to wrest control of the corporation's assets away from its current managers. Here, too, a by-product was very high salaries for both the junk bond salesmen and the investment bankers and lawyers who advised in the transactions. This history is summarized in Figure 4.2, which shows for selected industries the sum of compensation and corporate profits, a surrogate for economic rents, per full-time equivalent employee. From 1950 through the end of the 1970s, economic rent per full-time employee in the finance, insurance, and real estate industry grew at a rate similar to rates in other industries. Beginning in the mid-1980s, economic rent per full-time employee in this industry grew at an accelerating pace in line with the expanding bond market and a revived stock market.[35]

Compensation plus corporate profits (2005 dollars)

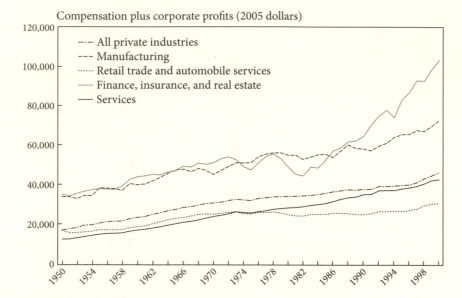

FIGURE 4.2   Compensation plus corporate profits per full-time equivalent
Source: US Department of Commerce, National Income and Product Accounts, 6.2, 6.8, and 6.16.

All these developments set the stage for a decline in the hegemonic power of the United States. But it would be misleading to think of this process as a downward spiral caused by shocks in the 1970s. The following decades were full of choices that could have produced different results. Because we are discussing the American century, we demonstrate the role of crucial decisions by focusing on the economic fortunes of the United States. However, we need to understand the implications of economic growth in other countries for the United States. The rise in exports from abroad reduced the rents available to American firms and consequently led to lower wages. Where wages were inflexible, the growth of international competition led to unemployment.

This shift in public policies brought the ideas of Adam Smith into prominence. Starting from the late twentieth century, this meant a return to ideas developed before the Industrial Revolution—and therefore before the Second Industrial Revolution—that gave rise to the world we now inhabit. The main idea taken from Smith was that collective action should be largely abandoned in favor of individual activity. This meant deregulation and privatization on one hand and low taxes on the other. The only permissible exception of this rule was military action in support of national goals.[36]

Just as the governing ideas of the golden age of economic growth were symbolized by the Treaty of Detroit, so the new ideas can be symbolized by the Washington Consensus. This set of ideas emanated from the hegemonic power in the 1980s and 1990s and was exported to the rest of the world. It started as intellectual advice being directed to developing countries, but it developed to be universally applied. The Washington Consensus argued that economic growth was promoted by open economies with minimal governments. Openness was achieved by stable exchange rates and low tariffs and barriers to the mobility of international finance. Minimal government meant privatization and deregulation in a mix that depended on a country's initial position. It followed that minimal government activity should be associated with low taxes. This American ideology was sharply at odds with the prevailing ideology in Western Europe. Chinese leaders did not refer to Adam Smith or the Washington Consensus, but they pursued parallel aims.[37]

The prominence of these Enlightenment ideas generated several cumulative processes that gained speed over time. The first one was a widening distribution of income. The rising wages of financial workers in the United States was balanced by the stagnation of wages in other sectors after 1980. Figure 4.1 showed that the income shares of the bottom 80 percent of the population fell in the two decades before 2007. They fell so much that there was virtually no rise in incomes for the vast majority of American families. The upper 20 percent minus the top 1 percent maintained their share of income, and the top 1 percent increased its share by as much as the bottom 80 percent lost. The top 1 percent of the population garnered most of the gain in national income in the two decades before the current contraction.

The drastic effect of the Washington Consensus can be seen dramatically in the Gini coefficient of household incomes in the United States. The Gini coefficient measures equality. It ranges from zero—indicating full income equality of all American households—to one—indicating that all income has been concentrated in a tiny group of rich households. The data since the Second World War are shown in Figure 4.3. The Gini ratio bounced around in a narrow range from 1950 to 1980; it then began a steady rise to a value that makes the United States one of the most unequal countries in the world today.

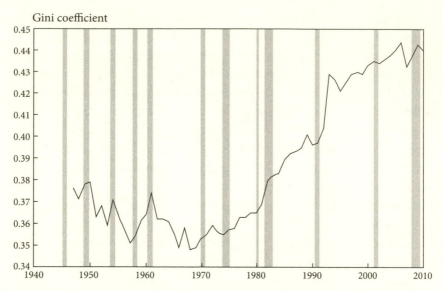

Gini coefficient

FIGURE 4.3   Gini coefficient for family income in the United States, 1947–2010

Source: US Department of Commerce, Census Bureau. Available at http://research.stlouisfed.org/fred2/.

Note: Shaded areas indicate US recessions.

The growth of large incomes led to government policies that encouraged even larger incomes that were balanced by policies to keep wages down. Unions had been encouraged by government policy in the postwar era, but they were discouraged and eventually attacked as this process continued. The opposition to unions was presented as an increase in worker choice, and similar arguments were used to promote deregulation in other markets as well.

American workers also suffered from the effects of Chinese imports. The first avenue was unemployment in manufacturing that had gone abroad. In addition, wages in other activities declined in areas affected by imports. The combination of increased unemployment and lower wages clearly decreased family incomes. Finally, areas more open to trade had more government transfer payments through disability, retirement, and medical services. The national gain from trade is decreased by these offsetting effects.[38]

Families tried to continue their previous annual increases in production by a variety of paths. Because wages were stagnant, both parents went to work to keep family income growing, as indicated by the rise in Figure 1.2 showing the employment-population ratio after 2000. More important for the source of the recent crisis was borrowing to consume more even as incomes were flat. The ability of people to borrow was encouraged by financial innovations that underlay the increase in financial incomes shown in Figure 4.2. Lenders were deregulated, and they devised complex ways to encourage ever more borrowing. Security for much of this borrowing was furnished by mortgaging households' largest asset, their house. This in turn gave rise to increasing incomes in finance and eventually to a giant housing boom. Economic theory, thrown into confusion by the events of the 1970s, also harked back to Adam Smith. As we discuss further in succeeding chapters, Smith replaced Keynes as the patron saint of macroeconomics. Theory thus justified the practice of deregulation already noted. It also made modern macroeconomics unsuitable to deal with the world of our current crisis.[39]

The limits of these theories were masked for two decades as the "Great Moderation" seemed to confirm all the assumptions of the new macro theories. The United States had steady growth, although there were small crises that we now know foreshadowed our current problems, and economists talked as if financial crises and even economic fluctuations were things of the past. This period came between two bouts of American borrowing, and the government, particularly under President Clinton, appeared to be bringing its external relations into balance. The success of Europe and the emergence of exports from Asia forced the United States to be more aware of its external balance.

The United States had two periods of extensive government borrowing in the 1980s and the 2000s, both of which were associated with wars. The exception that proves the rules of the Washington Consensus is the military. Smaller government did not mean a smaller military budget, rather it meant that fighting wars became the only legitimate function of government. This view reprised the role of the eighteenth-century British state. It also echoed the role of government in the Roman Empire. Both these models of course preceded industrialization.[40]

Reagan built up the military for the Cold War against the Soviet Union, whereas George W. Bush initiated wars in Afghanistan and Iraq. In conjunction with the earlier lowering of taxes, these expansions were financed by borrowing. Government deficits are shown in Figure 4.4. The first, beginning in Reagan's terms, set of deficits looks small in comparison with the later set. It would be even smaller had not a recession at the end of George

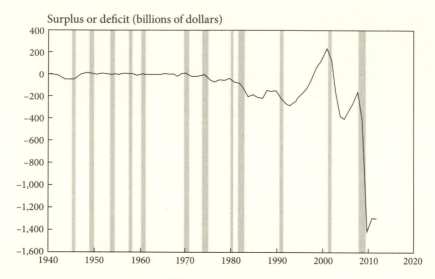

FIGURE 4.4   US federal surplus or deficit, 1940–2011

Source: White House, Office of Management and Budget. Available at http://research.stlouisfed
.org/fred2/.

Note: Shaded areas indicate US recessions.

H. W. Bush's term made the deficit balloon. The effort by Clinton to correct this imbalance in the 1990s brought the government budget into balance briefly at the end of the century, but the effort was short lived. The effect of these deficits can be seen in the growth of US government debt. This dissaving by the government had to be offset by a decline in domestic investment, a rise in private savings, or a rise in capital imports—that is, foreign savings. As will be seen from the progress of the American balance on current account, the last one of these was the result.

The first expansion was characterized by several small financial crises. The second contained one very large crisis, what we have been calling an end-of-regime crisis. The first crisis began in the 1970s. Savings and loan associations (S&Ls) were created during the Great Depression to extend mortgages to people; like banks, these institutions had illiquid assets financed by short-term liabilities. In the monetary contraction that ended the inflation of the 1970s, S&Ls found it impossible to finance their lending when nominal interest rates rose rapidly, and they sustained losses that continued when real interest rates were high during the deflation. The policy taken to deal with this crisis was to deregulate S&Ls. The thinking was that perhaps they could function better in a freer environment and return to solvency. In the event, having lost their equity, they became "zombie banks" willing to take any risk. If they won their gambles, they reaped some of the gain; if not, they simply walked away. As interest rates declined, banks regained solvency and invested heavily in booming Texas real estate. The boom collapsed, taking down many of the deregulated and adventurous S&Ls.

The resulting insurance claims on the government were honored, but the insurance agencies needed more funds. No one wanted to admit how big the government's obligation was, and only a decade later, in the administration of George H. W. Bush, was the obligation paid off by spending $50 billion from general revenues to clear the government's obligations. These costs were labeled horrendous by contemporaries, but they seem small by the standards of the 2008 crash. The S&L crisis provided a preview of the recent crash, replete with low interest rates, a real estate boom, and loose regulation of financial intermediaries. The costs were small enough, however, for most people to ignore them, although taking responsibility for the debts may have cost the first President Bush a second term.[41]

Fannie Mae, like the S&Ls, dated from the Depression. It was joined by Freddie Mac in 1970, and the two government-sponsored agencies bought mortgages and resold them to investors. The two mortgage giants were having trouble reselling the mortgages that were neither very safe (AAA in current parlance) or very lucrative and risky (junk bond level). Freddie Mac figured out in 1983 how to get around this problem by selling mortgages in tranches. The top tranches had the most senior claim on revenues from the mortgages, and lower tranches had progressively less senior claims. The bottom tranche, known as "toxic waste," clearly would take the first hit from any failures of the underlying mortgages. These tranches were called collateralized mortgage obligations, and they and their descendants played large roles in the expansion of financial activity at the end of the century.

The Black-Scholes formula to value options had been derived a decade earlier, and it provided a way to evaluate the risks of the various tranches in collateralized mortgage obligations. Using models derived from this formula, rating agencies gave the top tranches AAA ratings, which allowed all sorts of fiduciary institutions to buy them. The toxic waste yielded more, and there are suspicions that the apparently risk-loving investors who bought them did not understand the extent of the risk they were taking. In particular, the Black-Scholes valuation formula used data from recent history. Data from rising house prices in a housing boom provided little information about risks once the boom ended.

The problem of maturity mismatch—borrowing short to invest long—was illustrated vividly in failures of Thailand, South Korea, Indonesia, and Malaysia—the Asian tigers—in 1997. These small, open countries had industrialized and increased their exports rapidly in the preceding years. Their governments and banks financed this expansion by borrowing internationally and rolling over short-term loans. When the investors declined to renew their funding, the countries did not have liquid assets to replace the loans, and a crisis enveloped in East Asia. The IMF came to their rescue and pressured the Asian countries to adhere more closely to the Washington Consensus.

Russia seemed far away from Asia, and an American hedge fund decided that the low price of its bonds was an unwarranted extension of the Asian risk to another market. Long Term Capital Management (LTCM) went heavily into Russian bonds, and when Russia defaulted on its bonds in 1998, LTCM was insolvent. Hedge funds were lightly regulated, like the S&Ls of the 1980s before them. They typically invested for short-term gains and made their money by increasing their leverage. They could multiply small earnings on arbitrage by the extent of their leverage. A return on assets of 0.2 percent from a trade would give a return on equity of 2 percent if leverage was 1:10 and a return on equity of 20 percent if leverage was 1:100. LTCM was somewhere near the upper end of this leverage range.

Hedge funds were not banks subject to the scrutiny of the Federal Deposit Insurance Corporation; nor were they S&Ls with their own regulator. Nevertheless, the New York Federal Reserve Bank orchestrated a rescue of LTCM, so that it would not fail. Twenty investment banks agreed to contribute almost $4 billion to pay LTCM's debts. They in effect gave back some of their earnings in LTCM before the fatal misjudgment. LTCM investors lost 90 percent of their investment, but they were not poor.[42]

Why did the Fed rescue LTCM? They said it was to prevent a market breakdown. Of course, this is what central bankers always say, and no one knows if the failure of one highly leveraged hedge fund would have shut down international finance markets. If this dire prediction has merit, then this mini-crisis foreshadowed the 2008 world financial meltdown. The S&L crisis showed how excessive leverage encourages taking risks and failing when bad outcomes turn up. The LTCM crisis suggested that even one rogue firm could imperil the interconnected world system, but this conclusion was overdrawn. Barings failed in 1995 without bringing down the house. The Fed's actions need another explanation.

A more plausible view is that the Fed was unwilling to admit that it had let LTCM get as highly leveraged as it was. This tiny crisis was smaller than the S&L crisis, but it also foreshadows the problems of 2008. Lots of risk and high leverage make a volatile mixture, as Fisher explained during the Great Depression.[43] Central bankers have to choose their actions when risk taking results in losses. Even though Fed Chairman Alan Greenspan favored deregulation, he supported the bail-out of LTCM.

Greenspan's intellectual inconsistency may serve as an indication of the complex trends converging at the end of the twentieth century. The inequality of income shown in Figure 4.3 was progressing in the 1990s, and politics increasingly were subject to the influence of the very rich. It is hardly surprising that they championed their own interests, although some of their myopia may be surprising. Their influence was felt throughout the process of governmental decisionmaking, from elections to the underlying rules of administration. The nouveaux riches of the late twentieth century made their weight count through their ownership of communication media, political contributions, and lobbying. Given US election rules, it was hard to resist their pressure.

There was still room for decisions to affect American finances, as shown by the path of the government savings in Figure 4.4. Recall that the government saves when it takes in more in taxes than it spends and dis-saves when it spends more than it taxes, that is, when it runs deficits, shown in the figure as negative savings. The Reagan expansion of debt looks paltry relative to the deficits after 2000, but they were seen as dramatic at the time, because they had a major impact on the US exchange rate.

The fiscal balance changed dramatically under Clinton. Government savings rose in every year of his two terms of office, leaving the budget in surplus as the twentieth century ended. Although both parties are subject to the influence of the nouveaux riches, Clinton's budget revision was passed on a straight party vote, with no Republican votes. This upward path to surplus was reversed sharply in the administration of George W. Bush, and the United States ran deficits far larger than those of the 1980s. The largest deficit, however, reflected the effect of falling taxes during the Global Financial Crisis.

The cumulative effect of these government reversals is shown in the graph of government debt in Figure 4.5. It began to grow as a result of the Reagan deficits, and it continued to grow even as Clinton reduced the deficits, albeit at a slower speed. Only at the end of Clinton's term did the government actually run surpluses, and they were not large enough in these few years to repay much of the existing debt—even though informed discussion at the time wondered how monetary policy would operate in the absence of government debt. As Figure 4.5 makes obvious, these discussions were far off the mark. There is a noticeable inflection point in the growth of federal debt after 2000, as Clinton's surpluses were replaced by George W. Bush's large deficits. If Clinton's budgetary policies had remained in place, the ratio of debt to GDP—if not the size of the debt itself—would have been reduced over time.

Because the government dis-saved as it did after 2000, something else must have changed as well. Domestic investment and private savings did not change much, but foreign savings rose to offset the United States' dis-saving. The transfer was accompanied by changes in the US balance of payments on current account, shown in Figure 4.6. The balance on current account fluctuated in the 1980s and 1990s, exciting great interest in the waves of capital imports. These movements were dwarfed by the massive deficits in the last decade, as foreign investment transferred foreign savings to the United States to offset the government's dis-saving.

This foreign investment came from Asia. Japan had pursued an export-led strategy in the 1980s with the aid of an undervalued yen. The policy innovations in China under Deng generated rapid economic growth in a similar export-led strategy. Wages were held down through this expansion both by the massive flight from the countryside typical of industrializing countries and by government policy that otherwise repressed consumption. Chinese growth was based on expanding exports, as Japan's growth in the 1960s and 1970s had been. As noted already, the difference is that China is a much larger country.

It is hard to disentangle the causation in this apparent collusion between the United States and Asia. On the American side, President George W. Bush ramped up domestic demand by lowering taxes and raising government—military—expenditures. The Asian countries, as we describe more fully in Chapter 6, kept down domestic demand while expanding their exports. The result could only be American deficits in its balance of payments. Was this a

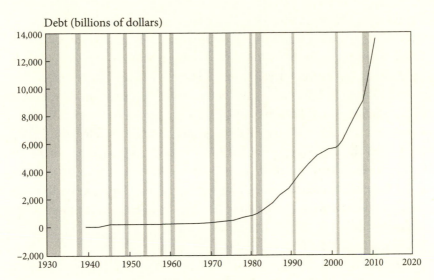

FIGURE 4.5 US Federal government debt, 1940–2011

Source: White House, Council of Economic Advisors. Available at http://research.stlouisfed.org/fred2/.

Note: Shaded areas indicate US recessions.

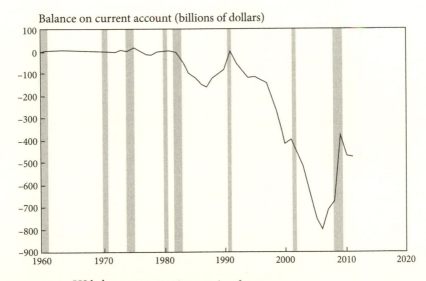

FIGURE 4.6 US balance on current account, 1960–2011

Source: US Department of Commerce, Bureau of Economic Analysis. Available at http://research.stlouisfed.org/fred2/.

Note: Shaded areas indicate US recessions.

fortunate coincidence? Was the United States accommodating itself to Asia? Or were the Asian countries taking advantage of American profligacy?

China pegged its exchange rate to the dollar to promote exports, producing a surplus on current account instead of the currency appreciation that followed Reagan's deficit spending. The Chinese development policy led to an accumulation of dollar assets as America ran an import deficit. This trend was upset after the 2008 financial crisis, because imports to the United States declined in the following recession. As with total US government debt, the foreign holdings of this debt did not reverse anywhere nearly as dramatically as did the annual trade balance. China was not accumulating more dollars as rapidly as before, but it continued to increase its dollar holdings during the recession.

The effect of these financial transactions is shown in Figure 4.6. Chinese imports to the United States grew by leaps and bounds. As with the earlier use of export-led growth by Japan, this influx of Chinese goods was greeted with cries of American obsolescence. That is part of the story, and the rapid transformation of the Chinese economy from agriculture to industry is another.

The decline of American education also is part of this story. Not only did the United States have a large labor force at midcentury, but it also educated them more than anyone else. For example, the GI Bill of Rights established in 1944 in the United States paid for *college* education of veterans, whereas the British Education Act of the same year only funded *high school* education for its youth. The high school movement in New England spread across the country in the early twentieth century, so that graduation rates in most states were over 50 percent by the start of the Second World War. No other country came close to this level of education at midcentury; the United States dominated the world economy at midcentury through both the quantity and quality of its labor force.[44]

American education prospered after the Second World War and was extended to African-American students through civil rights legislation in the 1960s. Educational gaps between whites and blacks decreased in the following decade, as improved methods of education were extended widely across the United States. This trend was reversed in the 1980s, when federal policy under President Reagan promoted inequality in education as in income. Innovative educational initiatives were replaced by standardized tests, and educational funds were diverted from increasingly segregated urban schools. The United States today scores low in international educational tests because of the resulting inequality. White schools in America fare well in comparison with schools elsewhere, but the national average is depressed by the poor performance of black schools.[45]

These factors cannot be the whole story, because part of the reason for the expansion of Chinese exports was the Chinese policy of keeping the exchange rate between the renminbi and the dollar stable. We further discuss the complex issue of causation in succeeding chapters.

Our discussion of finance and of fiscal and monetary responses in the United States summarizes the outcomes for the country in the past decade. It is time now to review the choices that have been made. As the fiscal policies reflected in Figure 4.4 show, there were alternative paths that could have been taken.

The first choice was the repeal of the Glass-Steagall Act in 1999. Undertaken during the Clinton administration, this repeal also revealed the influence of the nouveaux riches. Congress was responsive to the new wealth, and the enthusiasm for deregulation ran high. Financial actors were eager to combine commercial and investment banking in ways precluded by Glass-Steagall. This decision was made just prior to the reversal of fortune started by the 2000 election. Policymakers and economists may have supported this deregulation as part of the Washington Consensus, in the expectation that the government's fiscal house was being put in order with resultant balance in international accounts following suit. As it turned out, this repeal became part of the consumption boom that followed.

A second choice was made by George W. Bush in his first year. He proposed a massive tax cut to the richest taxpayers, which passed in 2001. Like Clinton's efforts to balance the budget in 1993, this tax cut was passed in a largely partisan vote. Some Democratic legislators could not resist the allure of tax cuts, and the vote was not as stark as under Clinton. To get all the Republicans in line, the administration engaged in trickery that came back to haunt the government later. The tax was made temporary—to last only a decade—to keep the anticipated budget deficit generated by the tax small enough for some recalcitrant senators to go along with it.

This tax cut, followed in 2003 by another tax cut and the invasion of Iraq, set the US government on the path shown in Figures 4.4–4.6 after the turn of the century. All these choices followed the same trend toward more freedom of individuals to run their businesses as they wished and a corresponding freedom of the government to spend without reference to tax revenues.

The combination of these choices shows the effect of the growing inequality of income, as the influence of the financial community and other rich persons was evident in them all.

The tax cuts were accompanied by the beginning of a new war in Iraq. This is another example of American military activity without a corresponding rise in taxes to divert spending to the government. As in the Civil War and the Vietnam War, the expansion of domestic demand—absorption—led to both internal and external imbalances. The policy choice made by President Bush was pernicious because it coupled tax cuts and military spending. Previous presidents had not raised taxes (or not raised them enough) to offset the rise in demand from the military. Never before, however, had they cut taxes while increasing spending. Of course, Reagan had built up the military while cutting taxes, but he was not actively engaged in war. The combination of the Bush tax cuts and military expansion helped set off a consumption boom just in the same way Reagan's policy had done twenty years earlier.

The third choice was that made by Fed Chairman Greenspan to respond to the stock market correction of 2000 when the dot-com boom crashed. His policy became known as "the Greenspan put," that is, creating enough cheap money to keep asset prices up and enabling firms to sell even depreciated assets at good prices. The Fed lowered the discount rate from 6.5 to 3.5 percent in 2001 and lowered it to 1 percent by 2003. The rate stayed this low until mid-2004, making the real discount rate negative. Investors had free money to invest.

An obvious alternative adjustment path, in which growth could have been maintained, would have been one in which the dollar fell along with a reduction in US interest rates. If this path had been taken, the fall in American interest rates need not have been so large, because some of the recovery from the dot-com crash would have happened by means of an improving current account position. The American current account deficit was, at the time, around 4 percent of GDP, a level that was historically unprecedented. A reduction of a large proportion of this external deficit, brought about by means of a depreciation of the dollar, would have compensated for the fall in investment.

But the dollar did not depreciate sufficiently at this time. The pursuit of undervalued exchange rates in East Asia—to ensure a rapid growth of exports —meant that American interest rates had to fall by a great deal and be maintained at extremely low levels for three years, so that the growth of demand in the United States would be rapid enough to ensure full utilization of resources. This policy resulted in global current account imbalances, with surpluses, principally in East Asia but also among other fast-growing emerging market economies and commodity exporters, counterbalanced by large and growing current account deficits in the United States, Britain, Australia, Spain, and Ireland. Taking on the obligations of "spender of last resort"— which caused American interest rates to remain low for longer than otherwise might have been the case—had very significant consequences for the United States and for the global economy, which we discuss in Chapter 6.[46]

The world seemed awash in savings, according to contemporary observers. The Chinese pursued their export-led strategy by buying US government bonds to keep their exchange rate low. The results were the United States needing to have a fiscal deficit and low interest rates to achieve internal balance and ending up with a balance-of-payments deficit. Financial intermediaries took advantage of this profit opportunity to expand their mortgage investments. The innovation of combining loans into tranches with varying risks allowed firms to offer securities of any apparent risk to their customers. Collateralized mortgage obligations were joined by more general CDOs (collateralized debt obligations) and other exotic combinations of assets in tranches designed to remove the risk from them. It was, in retrospect, a kind of financial alchemy. The CDO boom began in 2003, but most of the CDOs that crashed in 2008 were based on mortgages initiated in 2005–6.

All this funding flowed into the housing market with predictable effects. Capital inflows raise the demand for consumption in the importing country. The price of tradable goods is constrained by the abundant supply of goods to import, but the demand for nontraded goods results in higher prices. Housing is the ultimate nontradable good, as location is the most important characteristic of houses. The inflow of capital from China was compounded by the growth of structured finance, increasing the pressure on house sales. Housing prices rose and reached boom proportions by the middle of the decade.[47]

Banks and other financial intermediaries who used to hold mortgages began to repackage and sell them, changing from principals to agents. Their incentives changed as a result. The decomposition of the mortgage industry created many agents with little or no regulation in these increasingly complex markets. As the lure of easy profits attracted all sorts of investors, all sorts of shady activities were introduced. Put simply, agents were paid for the initial mortgage loan and for each modification. They had no interest in its eventual fate.

The rating agencies colluded in this credit expansion. They rated all securities coming from the tranches as they rated industrial bonds. They assumed that each mortgage was an idiosyncratic loan, which would fail only if someone moved or lost her job or suffered some other purely personal loss. Then the relevant risks could be modeled as a series of independent draws from some underlying probability distribution derived from historical records of mortgage defaults. The rating agencies made their criteria for AAA ratings public, so that financial intermediaries could tailor their submissions to get the higher ratings.[48]

This calculation ignored the conditions under which new mortgages were being made. The first problem was the changing incentives just described. The agencies' procedures assumed that new mortgages were of the same quality as old ones. Given the incentives to agents granting mortgages, this assumption was unwise. A second problem was that the procedures ignored the boom in housing prices that was generated by the increasing flood of new mortgages. The new financing, coupled with low mortgage rates, increased the demand for housing. Where houses were built on the plains, more houses could be built. But in older cities and coastal cities where space was not available, house prices rose. The result was a giant housing boom that rose in the middle of the decade and crested in 2006, reminiscent of the land boom of the 1830s.

As house prices stagnated and even began to decline, mortgage defaults increased. Also gone, but largely unnoticed in the early stages of the crisis, was the independence of mortgage defaults. As prices fell, many mortgages failed, and the previous calculations of relative risk gave no indication of which derivative assets were safe and which were risky. Investors became leery of all these assets. The risks were spread around the financial system by another, related financial instrument called a credit default swap, a form of financial insurance structured as a sale to avoid being classified as insurance with its requirements for reserves. In the spirit of the boom, credit default swaps were assembled into tranches called synthetic CDOs, joining other exotic derivative assets.

The first sign of trouble came from BNP Paribas, a large French bank that terminated two hedge funds engaged in buying and selling these assets in August 2007. The London Interbank Offered Rate (LIBOR), which is the

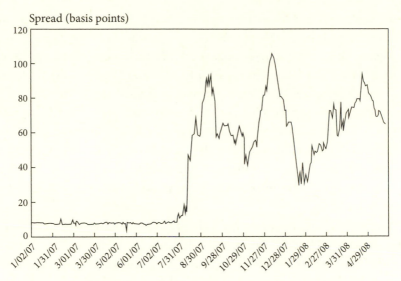

FIGURE 4.7   LIBOR–Federal Funds rate spread, 2007–8
Source: Cecchetti (2009).

basic interest rate of the London financial market, jumped dramatically and stayed high, as shown in Figure 4.7. Because the US federal funds rate did not change, the rise was an increase in the risk premium in LIBOR relative to the safe federal funds rate. This rise signified an increase in the price of risk as investors started to avoid assets that were beginning to seem more risky than advertised. The US Fed reduced its interest rates and began to accept questionable assets to get reserves into troubled banks. Outside the Fed, the six months after LIBOR rose were like the Phony War in 1939: Investors tried to convince themselves that nothing was wrong, but the clock was ticking.

Bear Stearns, an investment house not regulated by the Fed, was close to bankruptcy in March 2008. It could not borrow. It was experiencing the modern form of a nineteenth-century bank run. Instead of having depositors rushing the bank to get their deposits out before the bank's reserves were exhausted, the bank's creditors rushed to get their assets out before the bank's assets were exhausted. The Fed lent Bear Stearns money and then brokered its sale to JP Morgan Chase. As with LTCM, the Fed papered over the wider implication of one firm's demise. A Monday morning quarterback argued that the Fed should have let Bear Stearns fail. The example would have led other banks and investment houses to restrain themselves to avoid a similar fate, averting the panic of September. It is an intriguing suggestion.[49]

Again, there were a few months of financial calm. Then the quasi-governmental mortgage lenders Fannie Mae and Freddie Mac foundered and had to be rescued by the government in August 2008. They started life as government agencies and then had been sold. They acted like private financial intermediaries, but used their political clout to preserve the advantages of being public. In particular, they preserved the idea that the government would bail them out if they got into trouble. This claim enabled them to borrow more cheaply during the boom, and it turned out to be accurate as the boom ended.

The pace quickened in September. Lehman Brothers was in the same kind of trouble as Bear Stearns had been, but the Fed and the Treasury decided not to lend it money. Without the sweetener of government support, Lehman was not salable, and it was allowed to go bankrupt on September 15, 2008. This appeared to be a signal that the government was stepping out of the financial collapse; firms that had taken excess risks in the boom were vulnerable in the collapse.

But hard on the heels of Lehman Brothers' failure came trouble at American International Group (AIG). Although AIG was not an investment bank but a multinational insurance company, it had taken too many bets on what were now toxic assets and was about to collapse. The financial epidemic had escaped the mortgage market and infected the whole financial system.

Henry Paulson, Ben Bernanke, and Timothy Geithner—the Secretary of the Treasury and the governors of the Federal Reserve Board and New York Bank, respectively—threw in the towel and nationalized AIG on September 17. Their commitment to the free market had lasted one day; Congressman Barney Frank suggested we call it "Free Market Day." The nationalization of AIG, coming on the heels of Lehman's failure, only confused the market. Investors could not predict what would come next. Financial markets froze. All tranches of structured finance looked alike despite their disparate credit ratings. The risks were dependent on housing prices and were highly correlated. The end of the housing boom rendered the ratings irrelevant, because the assumption of independent risks underlying the ratings clearly was inaccurate. Fire sales of assets wrecked balance sheets; the United States went into recession.

As the initial warning from BNP Paribas indicated, the crisis was European as well as American. International companies like AIG and banks from many countries had tried to ride the bubble and had gotten caught at the end. Many governments in Britain and Western Europe followed the American lead and rescued their banks to avoid an even bigger financial collapse. The result was to socialize the bad debts of the private financial intermediaries. Governments always run deficits in recessions as tax revenues fall, and the assumptions of bank debt exaggerated this movement.

The Great Moderation swiftly was replaced by the Global Financial Crisis and the world economic mess described in Chapter 1. We argue in this book that the world economy collapses in this spectacular way when there is no hegemonic power to encourage harmony in economic policy. The argument applies as well in the United States for its part in the boom and bust of the past decade. In keeping with the dialogue in the United States since the crash, we discuss the various threads of causation in the language of blame. Without a hegemon, everyone and everything is to blame; the outcome is bad for all sorts of reasons.

There are many groups that appear appropriate to take the rap. First and most obvious are the consumers who bought all those mortgages they could not afford when house prices went down. However, they probably are the group least at fault. As noted above, wages have been stagnant for the past thirty years, and consumers borrowed to maintain their consumption. They were neglected by a government in thrall to the Washington Consensus, and they took the only actions they could to maintain growth in their consumption. In addition, the availability of cheap money allowed mortgage brokers to offer mortgages that looked like free money. Mortgages *were* free money as long as housing prices continued to rise. It is hard to fault ordinary working stiffs for not identifying a housing boom when many sophisticated observers were denying its existence. This absolution does not ignore those consumers who knowingly entered into bad bargains without intending to uphold their obligations; it says instead that these examples beloved of newspapers and TV were a symptom of the boom and bust, not a cause.

Financial intermediaries also were at fault. They diverted effort and resources into zero-sum bets instead of investing in real investments. They created investment vehicles so complex that even experts could not evaluate their risks. They too were taking advantage of cheap money. Turning a profit is their nature, not their problem. However, they are supposed to earn profits subject to the constraints of law. Evidence is accumulating that many financial intermediaries cut too many corners in their rush to get into the honey pot. The use of robo-signers (signature machines) to transfer ownership of loans so they could be combined into tranches may have violated laws of ownership. Foreclosures may not be possible because lenders cannot show they own a note from the mortgagee. This is only one example of fraudulent actions undertaken by financial intermediaries during the boom. The consolidation of financial firms in the crisis has transferred the liability from these questionable practices to the largest financial firms.[50]

Fannie Mae and Freddie Mac, the quasi-governmental lenders, stand apart from the other financial intermediaries. Started by the government and then cast loose, they belonged neither to the government nor to the private sector. They are a sort of quasi-government. As such, they had the advantages needed to grow larger. Did they also have the obligation to be cautious? They seemed to have been aggressively supporting the sale of questionable loans. Was this a misuse of their quasi-governmental position? This is a murky area of thought, but these entities appear to have shared the faults of the private intermediaries and overstepped reasonable bounds.[51]

The US government shares in the blame for constructing the framework in which the boom and bust took place. The rush to deregulate and to ignore regulations in place let private firms loose to do as they wished. Conditions in the 2000s were the culmination of the Washington Consensus. Firms supposedly did not need regulation, because good firms would chase bad ones out of the market. That may be true in the long run, although even that is debatable; it clearly does not work in the short run.

But there is circularity in choosing this villain. The government is elected by consumers in elections where firms also have influence. If firms can be absolved because the government gave them permission to increase their leverage, cannot the government be absolved as the instrument through which firms determined their fate? This objection is opposed by the implications of the rising Gini coefficient shown in Figure 4.3. The rise in inequality meant a rise in the influence of the newly wealthy members of the electorate. Government policies may reflect their interests rather than the interests of the population as a whole.

The Federal Reserve can be blamed for keeping interest rates low in the early years of the decade and not being quick enough to recognize the crisis later. The Fed clearly is subject to political winds, but it maintains enough independence to think of it as being causal. However, this critique seems to assign preternatural skills to the Fed, imputing to it the ability to have seen the financial crisis well in advance. It appears that the Fed was no better than anyone else at predicting the future, which may be cause enough to blame it.

Finally, one can assign blame to the Chinese for holding on to their export-led development strategy. The government of China bought un-limited amounts of US debt to keep its exchange rate low and its exports high. This action raised the price of American bonds and lowered the rate of return. That in turn lowered the interest rates throughout the world financial system. The Fed may even have been a victim of the Chinese policy. This line of argument introduces questions we deal with in Chapter 6; here we only suggest that there is enough blame to go around for the crisis that signaled the end of the American century.

How do we know that this is the end? We know because of the lack of leadership from the United States to resolve the crisis. The United States turned belligerent after the suicide attacks on September 11, 2001, echoing the frustrated policies of Germany between the world wars and leaving the world economy leaderless. The United States set the example for bank bail-outs during the crisis itself, but then it vanished as a world economic leader. After a hotly contested stimulus act sponsored by the incoming Barack Obama administration, American politics joined the rush to seize the con-fusion of the postcrisis world to shrink its government. It is as if the IMF were treating all the major industrialized countries as developing ones and insisting on the Washington Consensus. Alas, it is internal pressure that is leading the United States toward this policy, and the result is that the coun-try has become part of the problem rather than a leader orchestrating the search for a solution to it.

This can be seen in the defeat of President Obama's effort to pass a second stimulus bill in late 2011 to restore some of the lost employment in the US economy. Republican senators blocked this effort. They had voted against President Clinton's bill to raise taxes to restore balance to the government budget in 1993, and they continued the policy of opposing measures to bring the economy into balance over the intervening two decades. Democrats had enough power to pass a tax increase in 1993 by a slim margin; they lacked the votes to pass the expenditures in 2011. The paralysis of the American government is clear. Like Britain roughly a century earlier, America has become part of the problem, not the solution. American states, which are not allowed to run continuing deficits, have been contracting since the crash as their tax revenues have fallen. Total government spending continued to fall as the Global Financial Crisis spread.[52]

In short, the choices the United States made in the face of its declining international strength were crucial. The tax cuts, financial deregulation, and choice of a low level of interest rates—instead of ensuring that the dollar devalued—are fundamental to our story. They left the United States in internal balance but with an external imbalance. The United States encouraged expenditure through financial deregulation and a low level of interest rates. This unhappy combination caused the financial bubble, which led in turn to the crash.

Our thesis is that US policy is made in a global context, even though most US policy discussions concern only internal balance. If American macroeconomic policy had promoted a tighter fiscal policy and a devalued exchange rate, internal balance could have been ensured in a way that did not expose the economy to external vulnerability and a financial crash. The next two chapters show how this story played out in Europe and in the rest of the world. Chapter 7 studies the options available to us all from now on.

FIVE   Restoring International Balance in Europe

THE AMERICAN STORY IN CHAPTER 4 reveals how the Global Financial Crisis started. The data in Chapter 1 showed imbalances endemic in Europe as well as in the United States. To understand how structured finance in the United States destabilized both continents, we need to expand the account of European cooperation stimulated by the Marshall Plan to reveal how vulnerable Europe has become. This exploration looks back to the discussion of the gold standard in Chapter 3 and forward to the analysis of world disequilibria in Chapter 6. We look back because the European Monetary System has fixed exchange rates like the gold standard. We look forward because the adjustment process with a fixed exchange rate between the United States and China has broken down along the lines described by Keynes to the Macmillan Committee in 1930. This approach reveals that the three exchange systems in our story—the gold standard, the euro, and the dollar-renminbi rate—share the same adjustment malfunction.

The end of the Second World War was totally different from the end of the first, as narrated in Chapter 4. There was no recession at the conclusion of hostilities and no punitive treaty. The United States joined and helped to lead the United Nations. This was a very different outcome from what had happened after the First World War with the League of Nations. The Bretton Woods Institutions—the IMF and the World Bank—had been created, and they were joined by the GATT (which eventually became the World Trade Organization); the Marshall Plan followed in 1948. The United States used its hegemonic position to reach out to former friends and foes to rebuild the world economy and preserve peace. This resulting international system helped to underpin a golden age of economic growth, a period that lasted from 1945 until 1971.

We describe in this chapter how the golden age flourished in Europe and discuss why Europe was propelled toward the creation of a common currency, the euro, after the golden age had ended. We then turn to the current crisis in the Eurozone, arguing that this crisis has happened for two related reasons. We argue that the common currency was established on the basis of a faulty analysis of how a monetary union is meant to work, focusing on the failure to understand ideas about internal and external balance that are central to the argument of this book. We show also that the common currency was established without an adequate level of political support, directly as a result of a political deal between France and Germany struck at the time of German reunification. We expose the way in which the failure of analysis and inadequate political support came to feed upon each other in a particularly insidious manner.

The golden age from 1945 to 1971 was the most remarkable period of economic expansion that the world had ever known, a time in which growth was even more rapid than that experienced in the late Victorian era, when the world was presided over by the British Empire. During this postwar period, the motor of global growth was a process of rapid economic growth in Europe as it erased the developmental deficit from the second Thirty Years' War, accompanied by economic catch-up in Japan. The same process of catch-up is happening today in emerging markets.

The supportive global environment described in Chapter 4 set in train a series of cooperative actions in Europe itself. European citizens were determined that they would never again engage in the kind of conflict that they had endured twice in the previous thirty years, and they were led by statesmen with this cooperative vision. As we look back now, we need to understand the choices that these statesmen made. That will help us understand the difficulties in which Europe now finds itself. Crucial errors were made, and these errors have had long-lasting significance.

Leaders in France and Germany after the war believed that there would be no prolonged peace in Europe if the states of Europe simply were reconstituted on the basis of national sovereignty. These leaders thought that European countries were too small to guarantee their citizens the necessary prosperity and social development if they stood alone. They were led by Jean Monnet, a French economist and diplomat who believed that European states must ultimately constitute themselves into a federation, but who was also determined to do this in an incremental, nonthreatening manner.

An opportunity to initiate European integration came quickly. There was significant postwar tension about access to coal in the Ruhr Valley—just as there had been after the First World War. Monnet determined to solve this problem through high-level cooperation. In May 1950, French Minister of Foreign Affairs Robert Schuman launched the European Coal and Steel Community, declaring at its founding:

> Through the consolidation of basic production and the institution of a new High Authority, whose decisions will bind France, Germany and the other countries that join, this proposal represents the first concrete step towards a European federation, imperative for the preservation of peace.[1]

Shortly thereafter, France and Germany were joined in the Coal and Steel Community by Belgium, Italy, Luxembourg, and the Netherlands.

Monnet's ambition was shared by a number of statesmen in West Germany, of whom Konrad Adenauer was the most outstanding. He was Chancellor of West Germany from 1949 to 1963 and led his country from the ruins of the Second World War to the point where it became a powerful and prosperous nation once more. Adenauer did this by forging close relations with old enemies: both France and the United States. It was the time of the Cold War, and Adenauer was deeply committed to restoring the position of West Germany on the world stage with a Western-oriented foreign policy. He played a central part in enabling West Germany to come to terms with France, which helped make possible the further integration of Western Europe. He opposed his country's rival in East Germany, and he made his nation a member of NATO and a firm ally of the United States.

The outcomes could not have been more different in Britain, which declined to join the European Coal and Steel Community. From the beginning of the postwar period, Britain faced a fundamental choice that it has never fully resolved. Did its future lie with the Anglo-Saxon world, with those countries that were once members of the British Empire and with whom it had been so closely allied during the war? Or did its future lie with continental Europe, and in particular with Germany, with whom it had been in fierce conflict so recently? Europe was near at hand and had a highly educated labor force, and it obviously offered enormous potential. But it was with the Anglo-Saxon world that Britain shared a history, a culture, and a language. And Britain was still strongly integrated economically with its former colonies—not only Canada, Australia, and New Zealand, but also India and many countries in Africa. These countries together provided much of Britain's food and other raw materials; they produced a vast array of animal and vegetable products of every type, grown in every kind of climate, and they contributed an enormous range of mineral supplies. Furthermore, the citizens of these countries were still deeply connected to Britain, although their countries were no longer colonies. For a hundred years they had supplied the mother country with raw materials in exchange for British manufactured goods, and since the early 1930s protectionism had supported this arrangement through the system of imperial preference. What is more, their educational systems and legal frameworks were still basically British. This difference in view about the advantages of European integration, between Britain on one hand and mainland European countries on the other, has continued to be profoundly significant.

On the European mainland, the nations of Western Europe swiftly moved toward further economic and political integration, which soon went beyond iron and steel. The European Economic Community (EEC), commonly known as the Common Market, was established by the Treaty of Rome of 1957, with the purpose of freeing up trade among European countries.

The Common Market had at its core a shared approach to agricultural policy. The founding members of the EEC had just emerged from over a decade of severe food shortages both during and after the Second World War. As part of the project of trade liberalization, tariffs on trade in agricultural products among these countries would need to be removed. But this would be difficult; policies toward agriculture remained highly interventionist in each country, and the rules of intervention differed radically from state to state. Freedom of trade would interfere with these interventionist policies. Some Member States, in particular France, wanted to maintain a regime of strong state control, a view that was shared by the professional farming organizations throughout the EEC. But this objective could only be achieved if the interventionist policies were harmonized and managed at the EEC level rather than at the national level. The resulting Common Agricultural Policy (CAP) had the desired interventionist features. But it did so by being highly protectionist with respect to the outside world: the CAP introduced a system of subsidies, price supports, and protection from import competition. Besides being highly damaging internationally, the CAP was and still is extraordinarily costly to run. Expenditure on the CAP in 2006 was €50 billion, which represented nearly 50 percent of the EU's budget.

This level is due to fall, but only gradually, because of the continuing political clout of farmers. Reform has been immensely slow.

It was within the framework provided by the Common Market that rapid economic growth spread to Europe in the 1950s and 1960s. Early on, economists such as Jacob Viner in Chicago and James Meade in London came to understand the trade creation that a common market could induce as countries increasingly substituted imports from other common-market countries for goods produced less efficiently at home. This understanding went hand-in-hand with a fundamental transition that took place within Europe, turning the region from an agricultural to an urbanized, industrial economy, a transition that took place much earlier in the United States and Britain and to which we have given so much attention Chapters 2 and 4.[2]

As described in Chapter 4, the Bretton Woods system broke down in August 1971. The golden age of economic growth in Europe and Japan had weakened the US dollar's role at the center of the Bretton Woods system. Balance-of-payments difficulties began to emerge in the early 1960s, and by the latter part of that decade, the United States ran a large balance-of-payments deficit as it fought the Vietnam War. As a result, a belief gradually emerged that the dollar price of gold might rise. Central banks ceased their efforts to control the dollar price of gold in private markets in 1968, which meant that the prevailing fixed price of gold applied only to central bank dealings. The market price of gold rose, and in August 1971, following a massive speculative attack on the dollar, the US government ended the gold convertibility of dollars held by central banks. As a result, the entire gold exchange standard—the one brokered at Bretton Woods—fell to pieces. This outcome resulted from several features outlined below. They remain relevant to the economic situation that developed in East Asia in the past fifteen years—the "Bretton Woods II system"—which we discuss in Chapter 6.[3]

The Keynesian macroeconomic policy framework established after the Second World War had no clear method of preventing inflation. Although there were periods of (generally unsuccessful) price controls or incomes policy, in Europe as well as in the United States, the roots of incipient inflation were created by this omission. Such inflation took place at different rates in different countries, creating unsustainable differences in competitiveness, which eventually required exchange-rate changes.

Many countries were unwilling to adjust the exchange rates for their currencies in the face of fundamental disequilibria, as was required by the Bretton Woods system. This was especially true of Germany, which acquired an increasingly massive surplus, and it was also true of Japan, which was also in surplus. It was particularly problematic that the core country, the United States, was in deficit and was unable to adjust its exchange rate, because its value was tied to that of gold. Because the American rate of productivity growth lagged behind that in the countries that were catching up with it, and especially Germany and Japan, the trade position of the United States was at risk by the late 1960s. In addition, the United States fought the Vietnam War and launched its Great Society programs at the same time without adequately raising taxes.

The result was a large balance-of-payments deficit for the United States, which we have already identified as an external imbalance. The correction of this imbalance required both a depreciation of the United States' real exchange rate and a restraint on domestic expenditure within the country. Neither of these actions was forthcoming. When a crisis eventually came in 1971, there inevitably were large moves in exchange rates and domestic spending.

Finally, the growth of international capital flows—which was in part a result of the international stability associated with the golden age—helped to undermine the Bretton Woods system by rendering it liable to speculative attack. The 1967 sterling crisis demonstrated that it was no longer possible for the IMF and national governments to set exchange rates without reference to the forward-looking perceptions of private markets about sustainable exchange rates. With increasingly mobile capital, once a suspicion arose that devaluation of a country's currency might be needed to preserve external balance, speculation could make it difficult or impossible for central banks to defend an existing rate.

By 1971, the balance-of-payments deficit of the United States had caused a large buildup of mobile dollar holdings in offshore or Euro-dollar accounts. This movement was encouraged by Regulation Q in US banking regulations, which prevented banks from paying interest on demand deposits, and encouraged depositors to hold their money abroad. These funds were used to finance the massive speculative attack on the dollar in 1971 that brought down the whole system.

The collapse of the Bretton Woods system led to a decade of macroeconomic chaos, in both the United States and Europe. The decade began with the great inflation of 1973–74 provoked by the Arab-Israeli war, which caused a fivefold rise in the price of oil—from $2 per barrel to $10 per barrel. That inflation caused significant movements in the real exchange rates among countries, which destroyed nearly all of the (many) attempts being made at the time to reconstruct an international monetary system with pegged exchange rates. There was only one lasting, but partial, attempt to reconfigure such a system. This attempt took place in Europe, and it eventually led to a process of monetary unification within Europe. Discussion of what happened occupies much of this chapter.[4]

As a result of the move to floating exchange rates, the IMF's Articles of Agreement were revised in 1976; the changes came into effect in 1978. The Bretton Woods system was one in which the IMF managed a pegged-but-adjustable exchange-rate system. The IMF's revised articles ratified a new form of monetary system in which a country did not have to establish a par value for its exchange rate, but could instead have exchange rate arrangements of its own choice.

The great inflation of the 1970s led to more than the collapse of the Bretton Woods fixed-exchange-rate system. The entire structure of Keynesian, interventionist, high-employment policies, which had been at the center of the postwar policy architecture, came tumbling down, both in the United States and in Europe. For the ten years after 1971, macroeconomic policy was in a state of worldwide disarray. It even appeared that the Keynesian approach to macroeconomic policy might be replaced by noninterventionist policies of a monetarist kind in which all that the monetary authorities needed to do was "fix the money supply."

Subsequent decisions in the United States and Britain reasserted the value of an active macroeconomic policy, although this active policy was now conducted within what became known as an inflation-targeting regime and was combined with moves toward fiscal discipline. The inflation target was to be pursued by the central bank by interest rate changes rather than by manipulations of the money supply or the changes in fiscal policy that Keynes had pioneered. The basic idea was very simple—when inflation rises, the interest rate needs to be increased to discourage demand in the economy and create unemployment of resources to discipline the rate of inflation. The central bank might even follow something like the famous Taylor Rule. That rule is named after the eminent macroeconomist from Stanford University, John Taylor, who was Undersecretary for International Affairs in the Treasury Department during part of the presidency of George W. Bush. A Taylor Rule suggests the extent to which the interest rate should be raised in response to an increase in inflation. If, for example, inflation rises by 1 present, then nominal interest rates, according to this rule, should be increased soon afterward by 1.5 percent, that is, by 150 basis points. If such a rule is in place, financial markets know what to expect for interest rates when inflation rises. And because the number is more than one-for-one, they know that higher inflation will lead to a higher real interest rate and tighter monetary conditions. They know that tighter monetary conditions will follow simply by looking at the inflation numbers, because the rule is in place. We encounter this idea again later in this chapter when discussing the behavior of the European Central Bank (ECB) and in Chapter 6 when describing how macroeconomic policy is now run in a number of countries.

Although an approach to policy of this kind focuses on the control of inflation, it also enables the central bank to influence the level of spending in the economy to keep the economy close to full employment. In normal times, if inflation is under control, then it will be the job of the central bank to cut interest rates and thus stimulate spending to counter unemployment, and to raise interest rates if demand appears to be too high. A successful central bank will only allow the economy to move away from the full employment of resources if this is necessary to control inflation. Thus, if inflation is rising too fast, interest rates will be raised to cause unemployment and bring down inflation, and when inflation has come down, interest rates can be reduced again to their normal level; the opposite is true if inflation is too low. But otherwise, monetary policy can influence spending to manage demand for goods and services in the economy and promote the conditions in which producers ensure that resources are fully employed. This is what the ECB strove to ensure for the Eurozone as a whole

Such policy is very different from that pursued when the Bretton Woods system was set up; it diverges drastically from what a follower of John Maynard Keynes might have done. Keynesian policymakers put an emphasis on fiscal policy in control of the economy, but by the beginning of the present century, the use of fiscal policy to control the economy had become regarded as old fashioned. Monetary policy could—it was thought—control the economy, and it should be allowed rein to do so on its own. By contrast, fiscal policy is subject to considerable lags, because tax arrangements can be changed only slowly. And those who are able to borrow can do so to defend themselves from a tax increase; when taxes are cut, they will know that in the future taxes will again need to be raised. It also is difficult to avoid fiscal policy being subject to significant political interference, for example, by being expansionary in the run-up to an election.

Paradoxically, the new framework became known as a "New Keynesian policy," even though it concentrates on the use of monetary policy rather than on the use of fiscal policy. This moniker came about because it is an activist, interventionist policy. The monetary policy committees of central banks meet roughly once a month and decide at these meetings whether to change the interest rate up or down, or leave it unaltered. This activity is Keynesian in that, as we have seen from Chapter 3, Keynes himself was always highly interventionist, rather than cautious, when it came to the making of policy. Such interventionism is in contrast to the stance of the Governor of the Bank of England, Montagu Norman, whom Keynes confronted at the Macmillan Committee in 1930 and who did not believe that it is the task of a central bank to influence the overall workings of the economy. It is also in contrast to the position of the monetarists led by Milton Friedman, who now seem rather old fashioned because they too wanted to do something rather similar.

Those monetarist economists wanted central banks to set policy on autopilot, which they defined not in terms of inflation but in terms of an anchor for the level of prices; "just fixing the money supply" was all that they thought was necessary to provide such an anchor. They no longer relied on the gold standard to provide the necessary restraint. But nevertheless they did not feel that any finely tuned policy interventions would be required. By contrast, the New Keynesian approach to policy is active and interventionist. The fundamental reason for advocating activism is the same as that for having a driver in a car—without a driver a car tends to go off the road. Keynes taught us that economies are not self-regulating.

These central bank policies were accompanied by the acceptance of more open international capital accounts in the international monetary system that replaced Bretton Woods, by more deregulated domestic financial systems, and by a belief that fiscal policy should not be adjusted on a discretionary basis in any attempts to control the economy. What emerged was a strategy that appeared to be serving the United States and Britain extremely well, right up until the recent Global Financial Crisis. During the mid-2000s, policymakers smugly congratulated themselves as having brought about the "Great Moderation" of low inflation and low unemployment.

The new inflation-targeting system came to make important use of the international mobility of capital that had grown up since the end of the Bretton Woods era, allied with the new system of floating exchange rates. Indeed, this new inflation-targeting system came to be one in which movements in the exchange rate, prompted by international movements of capital, were an important part of the overall macroeconomic policy process. If a particular country were to suffer from a shock that raised its inflation rate, then its monetary policymakers would need to set higher interest rates, and the nominal exchange rate of the country would thereby appreciate. This action would reduce exports by the country, which would add to the reduction in demand caused by the increase in interest rates, and that would strengthen the downward effects of the higher interest rate on the rate of inflation. The currency appreciation also would cause domestic expenditure to be directed toward imports and away from domestically produced goods, which would further reduce the demand for home goods and so further help with the reduction in inflation. In addition, the appreciation of the currency would also cause imports to become cheaper: cheaper imports would be an additional way in which an increase in interest rates reduced inflation. But when inflation had returned to its target level, then the interest rate could be returned to its original position, close to the level of interest rates in the rest of the world.

It came to be realized that movements in the exchange rate were an important part of the way in which aggregate demand is stabilized in this floating exchange-rate system. Suppose that a country were to suffer from, say, a reduction in the demand for its goods, because its domestic consumers wished to spend less. Then, if inflation were under control, its monetary policymakers would wish to counteract this shock by lowering the interest rate to prevent the demand for its goods from falling. But in a world with a high degree of international capital mobility, holders of internationally mobile funds would see that this was likely to happen and so would withdraw their funds, causing the exchange rate to depreciate of its own accord, without any policy action. Depreciation of the exchange rate would increase exports and reduce imports, which would cause demand to increase and offset the effects on demand caused by the fall in consumption. If financial capital were highly mobile internationally, and if international investors really understood what was going on, then movements in the interest rate below the world level would only need to be temporary, during the time it took net exports to adjust to exchange-rate changes. This analysis comes from the Mundell-Fleming model first proposed at the IMF in the 1960s. It revamps and develops the model of internal and external balance that Keynes and his colleagues developed during the Second World War, discussed in Chapter 3.

It shows how, with floating exchange rates, monetary policy can engineer an exchange rate that will bring about the expenditure-switching component of the policies required to establish external and internal balance. In such a world, policymakers are able to bring about the necessary external adjustment by engineering the appropriate adjustments of the exchange rate. This policy framework is a modern version of the model of internal and external balance of Keynes, and Meade and Swan, which we explained in Chapter 3 and which is presented in more detail in the Appendix.[5]

The collapse of the Bretton Woods system and crisis of the 1970s that followed it led to a very different response in continental Europe, consisting a macroeconomic, a microeconomic, and an institutional response. Taken together, these components appear to have enabled European policymakers to avoid learning the lessons about macroeconomic policymaking that we have just described, lessons that had been learned in the United States and Great Britain.

There was no reform of macroeconomic policymaking in most countries in the EU during the 1980s. Instead, attention was concentrated on the reconstruction in Europe of a rather loose system of pegged but adjustable exchange rates—known first as the "snake" and then as the "snake in the tunnel." In this rather chaotic system, macroeconomic imbalances persisted, and a series of adjustments went on well into the 1980s, coupled with a combination of high inflation, high unemployment, and in some cases (in particular in Belgium and Italy) an alarming buildup of public debt. The buildup of debt was a sure sign of disequilibrium.

The spectacular exception to this trend was provided by West Germany, where the German central bank—the Bundesbank—had always exerted anti-inflationary discipline with an iron fist, and where fiscal discipline was firmly established. Gradually a view grew in the rest of Europe that other European countries could latch themselves onto Germany by forming the European Monetary System, and that by doing so they could assume the anti-inflation credibility of the Bundesbank.

This wish for monetary integration was coupled with a related motive, which grew out of European skepticism about the workings of free financial markets. There was much disquiet in Europe about the volatility of exchange rates that had emerged in the decade following the collapse of the Bretton Woods system. It was believed that this fluctuation posed a threat to the free market in trade within Europe and to the heavily protected agricultural pricing system. It was widely believed that such volatility could be greatly reduced if countries pegged their exchange rates to the Deutschmark. Furthermore, many people in Europe found the transaction costs of different currencies within Europe annoying, if only for matters as trivial as tourism between France and Spain.

As a result of this view, the European Monetary System was established in the 1980s, setting Europe on the path to monetary union. Initially this new, more integrated macroeconomic policy system enabled policy discipline to be introduced in France, paving the way for a successful decade in that country. This decisive shift in policy regime took place, somewhat ironically, under President François Mitterrand, who was forced by market reactions to abandon his attempt to implement a more socialist set of economic policies. The outcome was a remarkably successful few years, as France built a new system of monetary management around the *franc fort*. The same happened in the late 1980s for Italy, which became committed to the task of becoming a founding member of the monetary union. Italy's moves in this direction were partly spurred on by the rapid progress of Spain (which joined the EU much later than Italy). Britain joined reluctantly in 1988, but only after much public conflict among its economic policymakers.

In the early 1980s, the EEC called on a French visionary, Jacques Delors, to lead a committee of enquiry whose task was to propose further steps toward growth by microeconomic means. Delors belonged to the generation that followed Monnet, and he shared Monnet's vision of the growth-inducing possibilities that would come from a better-integrated Europe. As a result, the Delors Commission published a white paper in 1985 that set out how the Common Market could be relaunched: it identified hundreds of measures that could be taken to properly complete the process of trade liberalization. The white paper was well received. In particular, it was embraced by Britain, led by Margaret Thatcher, who saw the prospect of greater access to other markets in Europe, along with the strengthening of competition, as advantageous for British producers.

The result was the launch of the European Single Market on January 1, 1993, and the adoption of the Single European Act, a treaty that reformed and strengthened the decisionmaking mechanisms of the EEC. This new approach led to positive trends in integration, such as moves toward a greater harmonization of laws and standards. It also led to negative trends, such as prohibitions on Member States to outlaw discriminatory behavior.

The other European response to the decade of crisis was institutional. Beyond the Common Market, the process of institutional integration in Europe had been rather slow. In the 1960s, that integration progressed with the establishment of executive bodies in the EEC: the European Commission and the European Council of Ministers. But further institutionalization of the European Economic Community had to wait until pressures emerged following the collapse of the Bretton Woods system. In 1973, Britain joined the EEC only after a heated and divisive internal debate. The European Council was formed in 1974, and the European Parliament was created in 1979. Over time, the EEC gradually evolved into the EU, with the signing of the Maastricht Treaty in 1993. Starting from the original 6 countries who joined the European Coal and Steel Community in 1950, the EU has grown in size by the accession of new member states to have 27 members.

These responses to the crisis of the 1970s—macroeconomic, microeconomic, and institutional—were interlinked in several ways. One link came from the connections between microeconomic and macroeconomic views. As we have said, it was widely believed by the pioneers of the European Single Market that a system of fixed exchange rates among European countries was essential if the integration of the European economies was to proceed in the way they envisaged. This European view has always differed from that held in the United States and Canada, which for many years have had currencies that float against each other. This situation apparently has not impeded the integration of North American markets. Indeed, policymakers in Canada have always thought that their country needed a floating exchange rate with the United States, because at times the latter has needed to adopt monetary policies that have been highly inappropriate for Canada. This raises the question of why Europe was not happy with a Canadian-like model in which the currencies of other countries in the EU would float against the Deutschmark.

One reason is that there is an important difference between the European and North American systems, in that the United States is the center of the North American economic system. It is therefore politically possible for a peripheral economy like that of Canada to float its exchange rates against the dollar. It would not have been so easy for France to float its exchange rate against the Deutschmark. Perhaps the imperatives of the single European market described above have made that outcome impossible. As a result, the role model for European economic integration in the 1980s was not so much

that of United States and Canada, but instead the rather successful formation of a Deutschmark bloc in Northern Europe. For example, the Netherlands last adjusted its Deutschmark parity in 1983, after which an agreement
among the social partners (a very European phrase) in the Netherlands
ensured the conditions for currency stability. Rather more remarkably, given
its very high debt, Belgium ended up with a similar Deutschmark-pegged
arrangement. Of course, a system of countries joining an asymmetrical currency union pegged to the Deutschmark with Germany at the center would
have carried very different political connotations from a monetary union.
We discuss below, in the later context of German unification, just how difficult this might have become.

But crucial to the outcome was the belief of European policymakers that
a fixed-exchange-rate system would be necessary if the European single market was to prosper. The central idea was that, for success of the single
market, large productive firms would need to invest in a number of countries to spread their operations throughout Europe and thereby become
more efficient. But it was widely thought that this would not be possible if
doing so would cause such firms to bear exchange risk. For example, risk of
this kind would clearly be present if Airbus jets were assembled in Toulouse
using components made in other European countries. The desirable frag-
mentation of production of the final aircraft caused by making parts of
the plane in different parts of Europe would necessarily expose Airbus to
exchange-market risk. Such risk was considered to be in principle un-
manageable, because the time scales of the necessary investments would be
so long. It was thought that such exchange-rate risk would be an impediment to the required long-term, productivity-enhancing investment in the
single market.

The shared objective of the EEC from the beginning was the development
of a common market offering free movement of goods, services, people, and
capital within Europe, which, as we have seen, led to the creation of a single
market. Nevertheless, the EEC struggled to enforce this single market in the
absence of strong decisionmaking structures. Persistent protectionist atti-
tudes meant that it was difficult to remove intangible barriers through the
mutual recognition of standards and the establishment of common regulations. Moreover, capital movements among some Member States remained
restricted until the late 1970s and 1980s.

There are good reasons for this confusion. The political integration process faced a fundamental dilemma from the beginning, one that has paral-

leled, at the EU level, the dilemma faced all along by Britain. Is the European Community merely about the single market and the integration of trade in Europe? Or is it, more broadly, about the deeper integration of European economies? Even more fundamentally, is it a project whose ultimate ambition is the one articulated by Schuman: the creation of a politically integrated Europe?

Countries have differed fundamentally in their answers this question. The British approach has always been a minimalist one in areas other than trade liberalization and competition policy. There have been some other exemptions to this rule but only partial ones, like those related to Europe-wide cooperation on defense, through the partially overlapping, but distinct, Western European Union.

For France—which, like Great Britain, was a major global power two hundred years ago—the ambition has always been much greater. The French have seen the European economic integration project as a means for France to regain greater political power. French strategy has always been very straightforward: France should support the project. As has already been noted, this project has gradually required the construction of institutions to manage the integration process. And France expected to be able to use these institutions as a vehicle for the projection of French power, thereby preventing domination of the European political space by Germany.

German strategy has always been quite different from that of France, even though many Germans share the ultimate objective of a political federation in Europe. Mindful of its history in the Second World War, the German approach has been to delay the creation of institutions for the management of the single European market. The objective of this delay has been to ensure that sufficient political integration has already taken place that would enable these institutions to be managed through a Europe-wide democratic process. Ultimately, the German approach has been more democratic than that of France. The French approach has a much more technocratic character. As we shall see, the German approach was more cognizant than the French one of the need for democratic political support for the project of monetary unification that emerged.

Nevertheless, for a while, all seemed to be going well. Then came the shock of German reunification, which created huge fiscal demands on West Germany. There was an enormous number of things to do in Eastern Germany. Infrastructure was entirely out of date, and so were factories. Many of us remember the Trabant, the East German car that blew out huge clouds of smoke if it tried to budge. West German fiscal problems were made much worse by Chancellor Helmut Kohl's decision to reunify the two German monetary systems at a one-for-one exchange rate between the East and West. This decision made the East totally uncompetitive; it needed not just huge investment in infrastructure but also welfare payments for unemployed workers. The necessary payments meant that all of a sudden West Germany was experiencing a huge fiscal expenditure—and a booming economy as a result.

In the face of this huge fiscal deficit, the Bundesbank sharply raised interest rates. Other countries in the European Monetary System had to follow Germany's lead, which had undesirable effects in these countries. Britain, in particular, was already in recession. The country was being governed by a demoralized Conservative Party, exhausted by more than a decade of Thatcherite rule. Everyone knew the Conservatives wanted to win the election in 1992, and the economic circumstances being inflicted by membership of the European Monetary System were likely to make this impossible. The country was too uncompetitive, just as it had been under the gold standard in 1931, especially with higher interest rates pulling the economy down further. The action of the Bundesbank in raising interest rates led to vociferous anti-German comment, especially as British voters realized that monetary policy in the so-called "European" Monetary System was being decided entirely on the basis of the needs of Germany.

Ultimately it was just a matter of time until Britain was forced out of the European Monetary System—although the Bank of England defended the currency long enough for George Soros to make many billions of dollars at the expense of the British taxpayer. Britain withdrew from the Exchange Rate Mechanism on September 16, 1992. There was a valiant last-minute attempt to raise British interest rates to extraordinary levels—to 15 percent—to try to defend the pound. But ultimately the beliefs of financial markets that such a policy would be impossible to sustain proved dominant.

Italy was ejected from the European Monetary System the day after Britain. Quite soon Sweden was thrown out too—but not until the high interest rates used to defend the Swedish currency contributed to the bankruptcy of the entire Swedish banking system. There were significant attacks on France in the year which followed. It became clear that the European Monetary System could not remain as it was. Europe needed to go back to floating exchange rates or forward to monetary union. It faces a similar choice today:

its monetary union will either go backward—it will break up—or it will go forward to a real monetary union.

In 1992, there was a widespread wish to go forward in France. The long-running political objective of the French would, it was thought, be greatly enhanced if France could join Germany and the Bundesbank in controlling macroeconomic policy in Europe. Furthermore, the French experience of their ejection from the European Monetary System reinforced their view that market volatility was the enemy. A year after the French were thrown out of the European Monetary System, the exchange rate of the French franc against the Deutschmark had returned to a position more or less equal to where it had started, demonstrating to French policymakers how damaging market sentiment could be.

By contrast, opinion in Germany was deeply divided. There were many in Germany who were strongly against the creation of a monetary union, believing that the credibility of monetary policymaking in both Germany and Europe as a whole would be greatly damaged if the authority of the Bundesbank was surrendered. Furthermore, these people saw a risk of excessive fiscal expansion by weaker members of any future monetary union and were worried that these members' debts and obligations would fall upon Germany. This group was determined to delay any move toward monetary union until after sufficient progress had been made toward political integration within Europe. In particular, they wanted to make sure that any attempt by the weaker countries to place fiscal demands on Germany could be managed through a democratic, Europe-wide political system. As a necessary first move, they sought the kind of fiscal discipline that exists in federal states, such as the United States, Canada, and Australia, in which the central federal authority imposes fiscal discipline on the states within the union and can do so in a democratically legitimate manner.

By contrast, industrial interests in Germany were strongly in favor of rapid moves toward monetary integration. They had been damaged by the appreciation of the Deutschmark in the 1970s and 1980s, and they saw the global system of floating exchange rates as very much against the interests of their export-oriented industry. Their ambition was to continue the fixed-exchange-rate system in Europe, in which their ability to improve labor productivity at a rapid rate and control wage demands would give them a growing competitive advantage, both in and outside Europe, enabling them to grow. This conflict in German opinion continues to this day. Back in early

1992, nobody in Germany saw quite how much the ambitions of the second group to grow at the expense of other regions in Europe would end up imposing fiscal burdens on Germany of the kind that the first group had so clearly feared.

In the end Germany's hand was forced by France. This happened when the opportunity for Germany to prevent monetary union was effectively sabotaged by the bargaining power that had been given to France by the fall of the Berlin Wall three years earlier. Many people in Europe in 1989 had been frightened at the prospect of a reunified Germany, especially in France, given the history of Franco-German conflict. The United States and Great Britain were also worried and supported France, because they too feared German dominance, given Germany's past. In the end, the French extracted a bargain.

The deal was that Germany could gain French support for reunification of the East and West in 1990, so important to the German people, only if France's ambitions for monetary integration in Europe were supported by Germany, giving France the enhanced political influence that it sought. The rest of the world—in particular, Great Britain and the United States—were comforted by the prospect that French influence would tie Germany firmly to the task of European integration, binding it into a Western European base rather than allowing it to become an independent power and power broker in Central Europe. When the European Monetary System collapsed two years later in 1992, there was no way in which Germany could have resisted the moves toward EMU, given the international support that the country had received for its reunification in 1990. This German surrender to the French position was led by Chancellor Kohl, who shared the French vision of a politically integrated Europe and believed that Germany could be made to bear the responsibility of such a union. Little did the French realize that nearly twenty years later, the threat of fiscal burdens on Germany, so much feared by one part of the German elite—and by so much of the rest of the German population—would put Germany's commitment to the European integration project so deeply at risk.

The formal arrangements for the monetary union were set out in the Maastricht Treaty of 1992. Given British history, it is no surprise that Britain obtained an opt-out clause. This clause enabled Britain to stay out when the monetary union was first formed, but to join if and when it chose to do so. Public opinion around Europe was very suspicious of the deal worked out by high-level diplomats. Without adequate explanations, British apprehensions were shared less intensively around Europe.

EMU was finally established in 1999, after a seven-year period of preparation. Initially the union consisted of 12 members; the number has since grown to 17. Until three years ago, it appeared that the establishment of the euro had been highly successful. Many member states enjoyed the benefits of belonging to a currency union, notably the high growth rates that resulted. The area was cushioned against economic shocks, and disruptions due to intra-European exchange-rate realignments were a thing of the past. Financial market integration continued apace, although it was stronger in wholesale and securities markets than in retail banking and short-term corporate lending, There were wide divergences in growth rates within the Eurozone, and even serious divergences in the competitiveness levels and balance-of-payments positions of the union's economies, but these appeared to be manageable. Europeans felt they had finally emerged from the turmoil that followed the end of the Bretton Woods system almost three decades earlier.

Then came the Global Financial Crisis of 2008, described at length in Chapter 4. It emerged as hugely important that Britain had chosen to stay outside the monetary union, enabling the country to devalue its exchange rate when the crisis struck. Suddenly, for those in EMU, it became apparent that the divergences in growth rates, competitiveness, and balance-of-payments positions were significant. It now appeared that they were symptoms of a monetary union that had become fragile and as a result, had become vulnerable to the shock of the financial crisis. In the first half of 2010, EMU began to unravel, beginning with financial turmoil in Greece. Then difficulties gradually spread throughout the Eurozone until the middle of 2011, when the crisis exploded. By this time, the Eurozone had become a very dangerous place, threatening the stability of the entire world economy.

The European crisis can be seen to have two causes. The common currency was established on the basis of a faulty analysis of how a monetary union was meant to operate. In addition, there was inadequate recognition of the degree of political support that was required for a common currency. It was believed that the cart-before-the-horse deal struck between France and Germany, in which France gained a monetary union in return for Germany achieving reunification, was sufficient to hold the Eurozone together. This hope was maintained even though many in Germany believed that Europe was not yet politically ready for the creation of such a Eurozone.

We support these assertions by describing in detail the failings in the planning process for the euro area. We claim that those planning the union failed to understand the ideas about internal and external balance that lie at the heart of this book. Then we highlight the inadequacy of the political support for the EMU project. And finally we show how these two failings came together and fed upon each other in a way that has become particularly unhelpful to the future of the Eurozone.

Before continuing, we need to make clear that in this chapter we are discussing the position of countries in the Eurozone *relative to each other*. The absolute position of countries in the Eurozone—and that of European inflation, employment, output, and growth—is managed by the ECB. As we show, Europe-wide outcomes have been well managed by the ECB. We return to these absolute European positions when we examine the global situation in Chapter 6.

The development of the Eurozone since the early 1980s is clear in Figures 5.1 and 5.2, which show Eurozone financial balances for Spain and Germany. The example of Spain helps explain what happened in most of the European periphery. Only Greece is really different.

We stated in Chapter 1 that the gap between domestic investment and domestic savings is equal to the sum of government savings and foreign savings (where government savings equal tax receipts minus the sum of government expenditures and interest payments by the government, and foreign savings equal the sum of imports plus interest payments made abroad minus exports, that is to say, the deficit on the current account of the balance of payments). In Figures 5.1 and 5.2, positive values on the curves show surplus outcomes and the accumulation of assets, and negative ones indicate deficits and the accumulation of debts. Bars show the balance on current account. Because a deficit in the current account indicates foreign savings are positive, downward bars represent positive foreign savings. Investment is not shown in the graphs, because it did not change as much as the various kinds of savings, and we do not go far wrong if we simply assume that investment was constant and ignore it.

The experience of Spain since 1980 is shown in Figure 5.1. Before the formation of EMU in 1999, Spain had two episodes in which government savings fell and private savings rose, but in each case the movement was limited, and in each case the changes tended to cancel each other out. In the decade after the formation of EMU, private savings fell hugely relative to its

Percentage of GDP

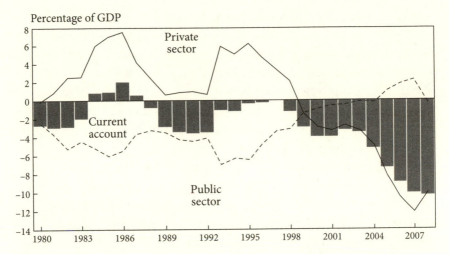

FIGURE 5.1   Spain: sectoral balances
Source: Oxford Economics / Haver Analytics.

Percentage of GDP

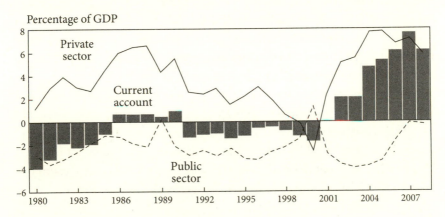

FIGURE 5.2   Germany: sectoral balances
Source: Oxford Economics / Haver Analytics.

level in the earlier episodes, and this fall was not offset by a rise in govern-ment savings. Instead, foreign savings offset the decrease. Foreigners bought the private debt generated by private actions. After Europe adopted the euro, the swings of savings became larger, causing domestic and foreign private debts to rise.

Germany, as shown in Figure 5.2, looks almost like a mirror image of Spain. The private sector saved abundantly in the 1980s and decreased its savings only gradually during the reunification process in the 1990s. The government —the public sector—ran deficits during the 1990s to finance reunification. Borrowing from abroad was minimal, but it was persistent, as Germany appeared to be uncompetitive with its trading partners. After the formation of EMU in 1999, private savings skyrocketed, in conjunction with an offset by an ever-increasing flow of financial investment abroad. Near the end of this period, these changes were augmented by a rapid increase in government's savings. As a result, Germany had a growing surplus on current account; the resulting accumulation of foreign assets financed the Spanish boom.

Because Germany's economy is larger than Spain's, we cannot match the series in Figures 5.1 and 5.2; and Germany provided loans to other countries as well as Spain. But the interaction between Germany and Spain looks ominous. Each country is out of external balance, albeit in opposite directions.

We first need to ask why the current account of the balance of payments between member countries is an objective of policy in a monetary union. The balance of payments between Tuscany and Sicily is not an objective of policy in Italy. So why should it be in Europe?

Such a requirement for current account balance is clearly not a monthly or annual requirement. As countries experience different shocks, their economic activities may speed up or slow down. If speeding up in a country causes an increase in inflation, the resulting loss of competitiveness is supposed to set in train a natural equilibrating mechanism that brings the pace of growth in the country back to a level once again well adapted to the country's needs. Interest rates under the common monetary policy were not involved, because they were common across EMU until recently. Current account balance is a condition that must hold in the longer term, because each country— and its government—must not build up too much debt. Foreign debts build up when a country's current account deficit is large for a number of years in a row. Public debt is built up when a country's government runs a significant deficit for a number of years. Markets will finance such debt buildups for a while, but at some point (perhaps rather late and rather suddenly), they will question whether politics in the country can deliver the sort of adjustment needed to set its debt back on a declining trend. In the following, we concentrate on foreign debt, although public debt is also important.

If a country earns less than it spends for many years because it is uncompetitive, it will be out of external balance, and it will accumulate foreign debts to pay for its imports. Tax revenues will shrink, and the government's budgetary position will become difficult. There will be political pressures on the government to spend more to counteract the loss of activity caused by the loss of competitiveness, making the fiscal position worse. Financial markets will begin to fear that the country's government might default on its debt, and a sovereign risk premium will emerge. By contrast, a different situation exists within a country, for example within Italy. Sicily and Tuscany are bound together in a fiscal union within Italy. This means that a sovereign risk premium does not develop in Sicily. It is clearly is—or ought to be—an objective of policy to prevent such a risk premium from emerging within the Eurozone.

Sovereign risk premiums were essentially zero until 2008; all countries using euros borrowed at the same interest rate. Then, after the onset of the Global Financial Crisis, these risk premiums became larger and larger, and finally in mid-2011, enormous. This happened not just for Greece but also for Ireland, Italy, Portugal, and Spain. (Together with Greece, these countries have become known as the GIIPS.) Short of the kind of fiscal union that exists between Sicily and Tuscany, the balance of payments of European countries remains an object of policy, because balance-of-payments divergences lead to a risk premium on public debt.

In 2011, participants in financial markets became worried about a second risk that can follow from a balance-of-payments deficit within a monetary union. They became concerned about whether the competitive position of the GIIPS will ever improve enough for the private sector to repay its debts if the country remains within the Eurozone. Competitiveness is the product of prices and the exchange rate. If the exchange rate is fixed, all adjustment must be accomplished by deflation. This takes markets beyond the fears about sovereign risk: financial markets begin to fear that the country will need to depart from the monetary union. As a result, country risk emerges, alongside sovereign risk. It is clearly an objective of policy to prevent this happening as well.

Participants in financial markets also began to worry about a third kind of risk—financial risk. They have become concerned about how the downturn in the GIIPS is weakening the positions of banks in these countries. It has become an open question whether the financial positions of banks in the GIIPS will ever improve if these countries remain in the Eurozone. This takes markets beyond fears about both sovereign and country risks. Financial markets have, since 2011, begin to fear that, for the position of the country's banks to improve, the country will need to depart from the monetary union to improve the competitive position of its producers, who have borrowed from its banking system. This fear has been worsened by the fact that the banks in these countries hold debts of their own governments, which have been weakened because of the rise of sovereign risk. Furthermore, the fears have become circular; financial markets have come to fear that the governments in such countries—weakened by the rise in sovereign risk—will become unable to act as a lender of last resort for the country's banks. As a result, financial risk has also worsened, as well as sovereign and country risks.

This financial risk is a double-edged sword, because much of the funding of the banking sector in a monetary union comes from sources outside the member country. As a result, the debts that banks in the country have incurred with foreigners become more burdensome if the country departs from the monetary union and creates its own depreciated currency. As we discuss in Chapter 6, that action went disastrously wrong in the 1997 Asian financial crisis when currency collapses, first in Thailand and then elsewhere, led to collapses of banking systems across Asia—in South Korea, Indonesia, and Malaysia. Once a country in a monetary union has begun to experience a significant current account deficit, it is right to fear that its financial system has become risky. If the country remains in the monetary union, then growth may not resume, and so it will be difficult for borrowers to repay banks. But if the country departs from the monetary union, then the banks' own borrowing becomes crippling. Either choice looks risky.

Until 2008, all three of the risks we have described—sovereign, country, and financial—had disappeared in the Eurozone. This is why nominal interest rates across the Eurozone converged on the interest rates in Germany. Indeed, policymakers ceased to be concerned about the balance-of-payments positions of Eurozone countries. And financial markets had similar views. Financial markets held the opinion that governments of countries in the Eurozone would pay their way in the long run, especially as the Stability and Growth Pact—which we discuss below—was in place to ensure good fiscal behavior. And financial markets also believed that private sector borrowings would be repaid, except in the few difficult cases that normally lead to the occasional bankruptcy in any country. Thus it appeared that it was satisfactory for banks in the north of Europe to lend large sums to Spain and Ireland to finance property booms, because it was believed that growth in Spain and

Ireland would continue and that those who had borrowed in these countries would by and large be able to repay their loans.

Moreover, what now seems like a rather strange metaphysical belief emerged. This article of faith was that national balances in the Eurozone had been somehow abolished simply because the countries in the Eurozone shared the same money. The idea of an external deficit between the members no longer seemed to make sense, in much the same way that it does not really make sense to talk about an external deficit between Sicily and Tuscany.

None of the beliefs described above is now held with any conviction, particularly the last one! Sovereign and currency risks are discussed on the front pages of daily newspapers, as is financial risk. The crucial point for us is that it now seems that a country in the Eurozone will only be able to avoid these different kinds of risks if the current account deficit of its balance of payments does not stray too far off track. Imbalance in the balance of payments leads, in due course, to an excess of foreign debt and to sovereign, currency, and financial risks. This is why the current account of the balance of payments between member countries really does need to be an objective of policy in the monetary union. It could only cease to be so if there were a sufficient degree of political integration for the sovereign risk, currency risk, and financial risk to be permanently banished.

Furthermore, the inability to move exchange rates within a monetary union (assuming that the union does not disintegrate) may now lead to such a slow process of adjustment of external imbalances and such a long period of slow growth that it may put in question the sustainability of the whole adjustment process of national economies in the Eurozone. Today, we are back in a situation comparable to Britain's crisis in the European Exchange Rate Mechanism in 1992. We may even be approaching conditions like those of the British crisis of 1930 that the Macmillan Committee attempted to address. This makes sovereign risk, currency risk, and financial risk all the more difficult to dispel.

We can understand the forces behind the emerging current account imbalances with the aid of the model introduced in Chapter 1 and developed in Chapter 3 and the Appendix. As we discussed in Chapter 1, there are two indicators of our current distress, unemployment and the balance-of-payments position. Economic policy has two objectives: full employment without inflation, and a sustainable balance-of-payments position. We have often referred to these two objectives as internal and external balance. We now return to these two objectives of policy to understand the problems within the monetary union. We want to know why one region in Europe grew rapidly and had too-high inflation along with a deficit on the current account of the balance of payments, while the other region experienced the opposite. As pointed out in Chapters 1 and 3 and the Appendix, two things determine whether these two objectives can be obtained at the same time, namely, the level of domestic demand for goods and the level of competitiveness of the economy.

The current problems in Europe can be boiled down to a very simple representation, or model, which can be used to set out the key difficulties. The following model is a generalization of the one-country model mentioned above in that it involves the interaction between countries, and so helps us to understand what is happening within the Eurozone.

For this purpose, let us imagine Europe as having two regions (rather than its actual 17 members), which we will still call "Germany" and "Spain." In such an imaginary Eurozone, there are three objectives of policy: internal balance in each of Germany and Spain, and external balance between them. In our imaginary world, an external imbalance for Germany—say, a surplus—would necessarily result in an external imbalance for Spain—a deficit—unless Europe, as a whole, were to run a surplus or deficit with the rest of the world. Acting as economic theorists, we put that possibility to one side for the moment to get to the simplest ideas possible. We come back to consider these broader ideas in Chapter 6.

In our imaginary Europe of two countries, there are three policy instruments available. Each country can use its own domestic demand, which can be influenced by the country's fiscal policy. (Remember that, in this chapter, we are discussing the relative position of countries in the Eurozone. In the Eurozone, both countries face the same interest rate set by the ECB, and we do not consider monetary policy.) So that is two policy instruments: domestic demand in each country. There is also, third, the level of competitiveness between the countries, which can be adjusted. An improvement in the competitiveness of Spain will increase its exports to Germany and reduce its imports from Germany. (This can be thought of as a worsening of Germany's competitiveness, which will reduce its exports and increase its imports.)

Competitiveness is the product of the exchange rate and the ratio of prices in each country. This product is called the real exchange rate to distinguish competitiveness from the nominal exchange rate you can look up in a newspaper. Clearly, the competitiveness of Spain can be improved in one of two ways. The easier, less painful, way would be to change the exchange rate, that is, to devalue the currency. This instrument is ruled out in EMU: there is no way to change the exchange rate within the Eurozone. The second instrument to improve competitiveness is to change relative prices. This can be done by Spain deflating, that is, reducing demand and activity and forcing down prices—the kind of strategy that Keynes discussed with Montagu Norman. This of course is far harder. It can also be achieved by Germany increasing demand and activity and raising prices—but Germany may be unwilling to do this. So adjustments of competitiveness in a monetary union are difficult to bring about.

In the world in which the number of objectives is equal to three—internal balance in both countries and external balance between them—the two countries need to agree about their objectives for external balance. As a result, it is a world in which the countries need to agree about the competitive position that rules between them. Keynes thought that it was important for agreements about competitiveness to be overseen by the IMF. European policymakers are also coming to think that an agreement about competitiveness is a necessary part of the new European policy process.[6]

It is straightforward to think about how this imaginary two-country European system would work. Suppose that Germany has internal balance so that resources in Germany are fully employed, and also that Spain has internal balance so that resources in Europe are fully employed. We can then work out what the level of competitiveness would need to be between Germany and Spain. If Germany were too competitive, then it would sell too many exports and buy too few imports, and there would not be external balance between Germany and Spain. Similarly, if the competitive position of Germany were too weak, then Germany would be in external deficit, and Spain would be in surplus. The appropriate competitive position between the two countries lies in between these two extremes.

Given that the competitiveness is at this level, then fiscal policy needs to be used in Germany to ensure that its internal balance is achieved. If at the ruling level of competitiveness, exports and imports were in balance, but Germany had excess demand for its domestic goods and was not in internal balance, then government expenditure would to need be cut or taxes increased. And vice versa. As a result, we can work out what the level of government expenditure and taxation must be in Germany to ensure full employment there.

In a similar way, we can ask what fiscal policy needs to be applied in Spain, so that it is also at a position of internal balance. If Spanish exports were equal to imports at the ruling exchange rate, but there was excess demand for goods in Spain, and so Spain was not in internal balance, then government expenditure in Spain must be cut or Spanish taxes increased. And vice versa. Thus we can work out what the level of government expenditure and taxation must be in Spain as well.

Hypothetically, we can think of what is required for a situation of internal balance in both countries and of external balance between them. As a result, to return to our earlier discussion, we know both what the competitive position needs to be between the countries and what the fiscal position should be in each of the countries. Note that fiscal policy needs to do the "heavy lifting" in this simple economy. Monetary policy does not exist for the adjustment of relations between euro countries. Fiscal policy then must adjust, along with competitiveness, to achieve both internal and external balance. To avoid conflicts between these two goals, the two countries must agree on external balance.

This is a policymaking system in which international cooperation, concerning the external balance objective and the level of competitiveness necessary to achieve it, needs to be at the center of the stage. The countries must agree on the surplus or deficit that they want to rule between them—it is no use if both of the countries are seeking to run a balance-of-payments surplus (for example, to encourage domestic industry), because that would only be possible by running a surplus for Europe with the rest of the world. Once they have agreed on this objective, they need to agree about the level of competitiveness to be established between them. But, subject to this, the countries should be free to follow their own domestic fiscal policies, in pursuit of their objectives at home.

Why then is such an agreement necessary between Germany and Spain, when it is not necessary between Tuscany and Sicily? Because Tuscany and Sicily are regions within a single country, transfers are made between them by fiscal policy as well as by borrowing. Support from one region to another is in the form of expenditures or tax relief, and accounts are kept of the flow of funds but not the accumulation of assets. There are no internal debts from one Italian department to another. There may of course be informal obligations, but these are political forces that affect the direction of fiscal policy rather than bonds that need to be serviced.

When fiscal policy is inadequate to achieve the desired allocation of resources, population mobility comes into play. Labor migrates from regions of excess supply to those of excess demand. Workers easily move north within Italy and west within Germany. There are far fewer barriers to labor mobility within countries than between them. Language, customs, and laws all are far more similar within national boundaries than across Europe as a whole. Labor mobility restores internal balance. On the wider European stage, labor mobility ameliorates but is not large enough to achieve Eurozone balance.

Let us return from the world of our simple theoretical model to the actual outcomes in Europe. The economic policy system in the Eurozone had four very clear components. But this economic policy system turns out to have been extraordinarily irresponsible. We shall see that what went wrong was that the components of this policy system did not ensure internal and external balance for countries within the Eurozone—something that we have stressed as critical. We first carefully set out these four components of the policymaking system and then examine them to see how little sense they have made when taken together. In doing this we also see how little European policymakers remembered about what Keynes had learned in the 1930s and 1940s.

The first big component of Eurozone policymaking was that the newly created European Central Bank was given the task of managing the Eurozone economy as a whole. Unlike the US Federal Reserve, the ECB has only one explicit target, inflation, whereas the Fed has two, inflation and full employment. The ECB was to manage the economy by setting up a regime based on inflation targeting, something like what was already functioning well in the United States (without that formal name) and Britain or Sweden. It would target inflation for the Eurozone as a whole, aiming for an inflation rate at or below 2 percent per year for the entire region. At the same time—under its so-called Second Pillar—it was meant to keep some peripheral vision over the financial aggregates as a check on whether monetary policy was becoming vulnerable down the line to pressures that were not yet evident in the price level—a somewhat diluted heritage of the Bundesbank's concern with monetary aggregates.

This policy regime for the ECB meant that the bank normally would raise the interest rate when inflation was excessive and cut it when inflation was too low for the EMU region as a whole. It would do this in the way described earlier in this chapter. It might even follow something like the famous Taylor Rule in response to inflation throughout the EMU area. As already discussed, such an approach to policy is markedly different from what would have been done by Keynesian policymakers, who would have put an emphasis on fiscal policy in control of the economy. In this setup, fiscal policy of the separate European economies would not play a role in European macroeconomic management.[7]

The second component of the macroeconomic policy regime in EMU concerned the role of fiscal policy. As already noted, it was decided that fiscal policy would not play a part in managing the performance of the Eurozone economy. Of course, each national government would play a part to ensure the provision of public goods, like health services and education, in its territory. Each government would also make payments to the unemployed and other recipients of welfare. It would need to levy taxes to enable it to do these things without running up large debts. Nevertheless, the only macroeconomic aspect of fiscal policy would need to be—it was thought—to ensure that the level of taxes more or less matched the level of public expenditure in the long run, so that public debt did not end up being too high. Of course, such an approach to policy would require that, in the shorter term, this level of public debt did not grow too fast. It therefore required control over public deficits.

Public debt and deficits had been severely out of control in Europe in the 1980s and 1990s, before the Exchange Rate Mechanism crisis of 1992. As a result, policymakers were determined to use the creation of the monetary union as a means of helping prevent this. Article 104c of the Maastricht Treaty, which set out the basis of EMU, stipulated that public deficits were not to exceed 3 percent of GDP except in exceptional circumstances and that public debt was to be gradually brought down toward a target level of 60 percent of GDP. This article demanded that "Member States . . . avoid excessive government deficits." It called on the "Commission [to] monitor the development of the budgetary situation and of the stock of government debt in the Member States with a view to identifying gross errors."[8] Substantial excesses over reference values (3 percent of GDP for the deficit and 60 percent for the debt) were specified in the protocol on the excessive deficit procedure annexed to the treaty. The reference values did not amount to binding rules in the sense that their breaching would lead to automatic sanctions. Nonetheless, Article 104c foresaw that the council eventually could impose sanctions if a Member State persisted in failing to correct its situation.

There was a further agreement in 1997, based on a proposal by the German government, to reinforce these fiscal provisions of the Maastricht Treaty. The Stability and Growth Pact (or SGP, as this agreement came to be called) provided a commitment by EMU countries "to respect the medium-term budgetary objective of positions close to balance or in surplus."[9] This would allow EMU countries to deal with normal cyclical fluctuations while keeping their government deficit below the reference value of 3 percent of GDP. In essence, the SGP was designed to transform the 3 percent reference value specified in the Maastricht Treaty, which remained untouched, into a hard ceiling. Given German fears concerning the fiscal risks that a monetary union might create, it is no surprise that this proposal for the SGP came from Germany.

The approach to fiscal policy embodied in the SGP assigned a particular task to fiscal policymakers, and in that respect it aimed to place fiscal policy on autopilot, independent of deliberate policy decisions, just like the approach to monetary policy aimed to do in the control of inflation. According to the SGP, fiscal policy is assigned the task of ensuring a satisfactory outcome for the level of public debt. But, beyond this, fiscal policy was is given no other macroeconomic responsibility.

The SGP ruled out fiscal policy as a tool to achieve either internal balance or external balance. Without either monetary or fiscal policy, individual countries were left without any tools to achieve such balance. In the theoretical exercise we just went through, the two countries had three possible policy instruments. The SGP ruled out the first one; EMU of course ruled out devaluation. This left only the final instrument, internal inflation or deflation.

The SGP therefore had significant implications for the third component of the macroeconomic policymaking regime in EMU: the understanding that policymakers had of how wage bargaining and price setting would be carried out in the Eurozone. It was believed by policymakers that those in the private sector would understand the discipline that had been imposed on them by their membership in a monetary union. This understanding also involved an assignment of responsibilities: wages and prices in each country *should*—it was asserted—be set in the knowledge that the country needed to remain competitive relative to the other members of the union. How this was meant to work was made clear by Otmar Issing, a prominent member of the Bundesbank in the 1980s and 1990s, who became highly influential in the ECB during the first ten years of EMU. Issing's view stressed the need for wage and price setters throughout the monetary union to be aware of the need to be competitive, and to cut costs, to ensure that the firms for which they work were competitive in their local markets and in the global marketplace.[10]

With fixed exchange rates, member countries lacked monetary policy. Without being able to devalue, these countries gave up the easy way to achieve external balance. No easy tools were available to affect the relative competitiveness of countries, and there was no way to arrest a drift in competitiveness that could destabilize the system—unless and until higher risk premiums and a loss of export revenues brought the cycle to an end, quite possibly with a hard landing.

Two interesting examples of successful convergence are to be found in the cases of Belgium and the Netherlands. In Belgium, once a hard peg to the Deutschmark was established, a tripartite wage-setting system was highly successful at dampening movements in average wages in light of trends in the three major (and intra-euro) trading partners. In the Netherlands, this experience was broadly paralleled after the 1983 Wassenaar agreement, which also established a hard peg; but interestingly, in the mid-1990s, the Dutch authorities became complacent and allowed an asymmetric boom and serious overheating to develop. Once realization dawned, wage setters and the fiscal authorities then exercised the kind of discipline that was needed within EMU and brought the economy back into internal balance. The experience under a hard exchange-rate peg—of fiscal and wage discipline in highly indebted Belgium and of sharp ex post adjustment in the booming Netherlands—seemed to provide evidence that sovereign states could live with the rigors of a full monetary union.

The fourth and final component of the macroeconomic policy system established in the Eurozone followed from the nature of the financial system that was built in this region. Those who established the Eurozone aimed to create an integrated, competitive European financial system within the Eurozone, operating in the European Single Market with a Single Banking License. They thought that no currency risk would exist for the separate countries in the Eurozone. And they also thought that no default risk would exist for the separate sovereigns in the Eurozone—given that sovereign states were bound by the SGP.

As a result, interest rates would converge across the Eurozone. Europe's founders thought that this would be good for the European banking system and for those who wanted to borrow money in Europe. In such a stable European financial system, financial regulation could remain safely delegated to the separate nation states. And the authorities in each nation state could safely manage financial supervision. They would also provide lender-of-last resort financing to banks headquartered in their respective countries as and when this proved necessary, and each country would eliminate financial risk in this way. The creators of the euro saw no reason to pre-negotiate a Europe-wide lender of last resort for European sovereigns and no reason to prepare for a lender of last resort for European banks, or for crisis management or bank resolution, or bank recapitalization, at the level of the Eurozone.

We now go over the four components of policymaking that we have set out, examining which of them worked and which did not. One component of this economic policy system worked well, but the others turned out to be woefully inadequate. The macroeconomic management of Europe as a whole by the ECB has been admirably successful, both in the period before the Global Financial Crisis and during the early stages of the crisis. Inflation remained firmly under control during the Great Moderation. And in the early days of the crisis, interest rates were slashed to help mitigate the downturn and liquidity was injected as needed. The inflation-targeting strategy of the ECB remains firmly in place, which we believe is a good thing.

But when we turn to the other three components of the European policy system, almost everything possible has gone wrong. Fiscal policy did not successfully accomplish its objectives. In the exceptional circumstances of the Global Financial Crisis, all observers were glad that initial policy response was one in which the SGP was overridden. Huge fiscal deficits were caused by discretionary policy actions, by allowing tax revenues to fall as the recession developed, and by not immediately increasing tax rates to keep revenues up. Even before the crisis, the SGP was flagrantly disregarded. Both France and Germany disregarded the pact in the mid-2000s; the essence of the SGP was neither fully understood nor correctly implemented. As we shall see, this has had devastating consequences for countries that entered the monetary union with high debt levels, and also for countries whose output has fallen and tax revenues collapsed since the onset of crisis, throwing them into fiscal turmoil. Greece was not alone in disregarding the SGP, though it was admittedly the worst offender.[11]

In addition, the third component of the policy strategy has not worked as desired. The adjustment of competitiveness within Europe has clearly not happened in the way intended. The European Commission recognized this in its assessment after EMU had existed for ten years:

> There have been substantial and lasting differences across countries in terms of inflation and unit labor costs. The tendency for persistent divergences between euro-area Member States has been due in part to a lack of responsiveness of prices and wages, which have not adjusted smoothly across products, sectors and regions. This has led to accumulated competitiveness losses and large external imbalances.

Again, Greece was not alone in its plight, but it is probably the worst case.[12]

Finally, the understanding of what would happen financially in the Eurozone following greater financial integration in Europe turned out to be disastrously wrong. Hopes for a successful integration of the financial systems of the Eurozone member countries were initially well rewarded, and risk premiums for the peripheral countries disappeared. But these understandings unraveled under the pressure of the European sovereign debt crisis. Large risk premiums emerged, as discussed above. That the European financial system had become so tightly integrated turned into one of its problems, because a policy framework was not in place to deal with this integration.

To begin to understand what has gone wrong, consider what has happened to competitiveness. Figure 5.3 shows just how serious the competitiveness problem has become. Germany entered EMU in an uncompetitive position in 1999 and had many, many years of slow growth and low inflation. As a result German costs fell relative to those in the rest of Europe for a full ten years, causing the German real exchange rate and competitiveness to steadily improve relative to other countries in the union.

By contrast, the countries of the European periphery—Greece, Italy, Ireland, Portugal, and Spain, the GIIPS—entered EMU in highly competitive positions in 1999. These countries experienced excessive growth in domestic demand and inflation over the first ten years of EMU, with steadily worsening competitive positions.

Figure 5.3 shows a failure to ensure sustained convergence of the economic performances of the EMU Member States. There have been substan-

Real exchange rate

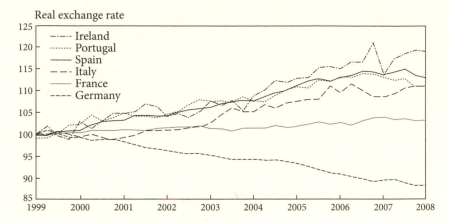

FIGURE 5.3   Real exchange rates
Source: Oxford Economics / Haver Analytics.
Note: 1999 = 100, measured as unit labor costs.

tial and lasting differences across countries in terms of inflation of prices and labor costs. The tendency for persistent divergences among Eurozone Member States has been due in part to a lack of responsiveness of prices and wages, which have not adjusted smoothly across products, sectors, and regions. This has led to accumulated losses of competitiveness. It has also been due in part to the totally inadequate response to this difficulty, created by the European macroeconomic framework.

Some loss of competitiveness was beneficial (in economic jargon, an equilibrium phenomenon) in the booming peripheral economies, and it was indeed needed in the Eurozone to slow down these country-specific booms. But neither fiscal policy nor bank supervisory policies leaned against the wind to moderate these swings and balances in competitiveness. In some cases the policies poured gasoline on the fire and allowed competitiveness, for example, to deteriorate to a point where truly massive wage-cost adjustments (of 15 or 30 percent, or more) would be required to bring economies back to a longer run state of internal and external balance. Nor did risk premiums in capital markets rise early or rapidly enough to flag the pending tensions in financing long-lasting imbalances. These imbalances had been generated by low interest rates in the banking system, by the budget, or by both, and they would be difficult to correct after such large divergences in competitiveness had emerged.

This was not meant to happen. In a common currency system like EMU, the adjustment process was meant to bring national conditions back in line with those in other Member States. In such a common currency area—as we have seen—a centralized monetary policy is imposed. As a result, higher inflation in the GIIPS relative to that in Germany would not have caused higher interest rates, if, on average, inflation in the whole of the Eurozone is close to its target, because the ECB reacts to the average rate of inflation across the whole of the zone. That the ECB did not respond in this way means that there was no monetary policy response to the problem depicted in Figure 5.3. Nevertheless, the gradual increase in costs in the GIIPS, caused by higher inflation there—which caused goods produced in these countries to become uncompetitive—was meant to depress exports, stimulate imports, worsen the current account of the GIIPS, and bring their booms to an end. These changes were meant to stop the GIIPS from becoming more and more uncompetitive.

But large current account deficits emerged in Southern Europe, as shown in Figure 5.4. This is the quantity side of the real exchange rates shown in Figure 5.3. Capital imports raised real exchange rates in the GIIPS. But the worsening of their competitiveness did not have the moderating effect imagined. The boom and inflation went on and on right up to 2008. The countries remained out of internal balance for a sustained period of time, and as a result, their external imbalances became worse and worse.

The idea that convergence would happen was like an appeal to rational expectations. Producers and consumers in each country were assumed to understand the long-run implications of their actions and to modify them accordingly. The assumption was even stronger than the usual assumption in an economy with only one consumer and producer. In a real economy, individual firms and people would have to understand and to coordinate their activities with others who also understood what was needed. There was coordination in Belgium and the Netherlands, as described earlier, but there was no coordinating event in the gradual processes of wage and price determination in Southern Europe.

The self-correcting mechanism in the design of the euro may be fine for the long run, but in the short run it ignored bubbles stimulated by low interest rates. The European experience here has similarities to the housing booms in the United States in 2003–6 and in China starting in 2011.

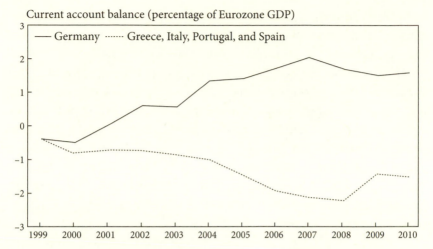

Current account balance (percentage of Eurozone GDP)

— Germany ······ Greece, Italy, Portugal, and Spain

FIGURE 5.4   Current account balances
Source: Krugman (2011b).
Note: This figure omits Ireland so that it represents the countries of Southern Europe.

The reverse should have occurred in Germany. The low level of inflation there—which improved German competitiveness—produced an increase in exports, a reduction in imports, and an improvement in the current account. That was intended to trigger an increase in expenditures in Germany, which was meant to increase relative inflation in the country and stop it from becoming excessively competitive relative to the other countries. Figure 5.4 shows that a large current account surplus did emerge in Germany, but it did not have the moderating effect internally. The boom in Germany went on and on, making the country more and more competitive and continuing until recently. Germany's current account surplus has been continually improving.

The conventional view is that the equilibrating process would work satis-factorily in the way put forward by Issing, which we described above. This process would ensure intercountry adjustment in EMU. This conventional view was carefully discussed in detail in a paper by the European Commis-sion in 2006. This, in retrospect, framed the adjustment questions in the right terms (which was not a feature of other official documents at the time)—recognizing that losses of competitiveness in Spain and other coun-tries reflected a macroeconomic process that would need to be unwound over time, and warning that unrecognized overshooting of fiscal cycles in Germany and elsewhere was in part a by-product of that process. However, the paper reached policy conclusions that now look wildly optimistic about the stability of the Eurozone adjustment process. In hindsight, it is clear that the crucial failure of analysis concerned the serious loss of competitiveness that was occurring in some countries, where (unlike in the Netherlands, or indeed, Ireland) wages were and would remain downwardly rigid. This implied that imbalances in these countries (notably Greece, Portugal, and Spain) would need to be financed over a long adjustment period, which became even less plausible after the Lehman Brothers shock to global risk premiums and the highly specific episode of loss of fiscal control and reporting in Greece.[13]

It is clear that policymakers did not have in mind our model of the need for both internal and external balance. For a while, the view prevailed that the systematic divergences in competitiveness were occurring not as part of an adjustment mechanism in the Eurozone but because of longstanding issues about progress in enhancing the flexibility of European markets. This view agreed with more widespread pessimism in Europe that modernization of European production methods had been too slow, and that a European strategy was necessary to promote adoption of new ideas and methods of working. The aim was a rather grand vision to make Europe the most competitive and dynamic knowledge-based economy in the world, capable of sustainable economic growth with more and better jobs and greater social cohesion. A Lisbon strategy was adopted after a 2000 summit in Lisbon that was in intended to deal with the low productivity and stagnation of economic growth in the EU through the formulation of various policy initiatives to be taken by all EU Member States. The broader objectives set out by the Lisbon strategy were to be attained by 2010.

Few of the goals of this strategy had been achieved by 2010. During the intervening ten years, a totally unconvincing, but widely held, view was that the improvement in supply side flexibility being sought in the Lisbon process would somehow help correct the divergence of competitiveness displayed in Figure 5.3 and so help remove the current account imbalances shown in Figure 5.4. It was suggested that this Lisbon agenda might help bring pressure on uncompetitive regions to adjust their costs and prices in a way that reduced the divergence. But a moment's thought will reveal that this idea was completely ridiculous, because it was never made clear how the required pressure might be brought to bear more in the GIIPS than in Germany, in whatever way was required. In fact, it was Germany that adopted the Lisbon agenda. It was certainly not adopted in Italy under Silvio Berlusconi or in Greece.

We now narrow our focus to ask how European monetary and fiscal policies have dealt with the emerging imbalances in EMU. We start with monetary policy. In the Eurozone the GIIPS faced the same interest rate as other member countries, including Germany: their higher inflation did not lead to higher interest rates. Figure 5.5 shows that the result was lower real interest rates in the GIIPS. What happened as a result of this has been succinctly described by Paul Krugman:

> As I see it, the underlying eurozone story is pretty clear and simple. After the creation of the euro, investors developed a false sense of security about lending to peripheral economies; this led to large capital flows from the core to the periphery, and corresponding current account imbalances.[14]

Capital inflows enabled increases expenditures, which strengthened the boom in these countries and made inflation worse. The opposite was true in Germany. High real interest rates and outflows of capital, organized by the

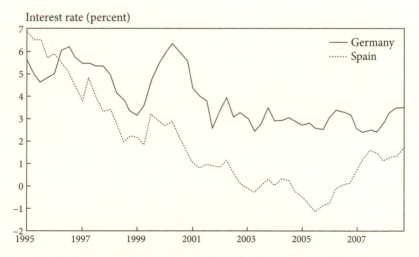

FIGURE 5.5   Real long-term interest rates
Source: Oxford Economics / Haver Analytics.
Note: Values have been deflated with the GDP deflator.

German banking system, meant that German savings were not used at home but flowed to the European periphery. German expenditures remain low, keeping inflation below the Europe-wide target within Germany. Conversely, expenditures in the GIIPS were increased, leading to inflation in those countries. These divergent inflationary pressures worsened the competitiveness problems shown in Figure 5.3 and led to the imbalances displayed in Figure 5.4. The problem went on and on for nearly ten years.

Did anyone notice what was happening during this decade? Most people were celebrating the years of stability, but a few observers identified this kind of problem lurking in the monetary union. This contrarian view became known in Britain as the Walters critique after Sir Alan Walters, the economic adviser to Prime Minister Thatcher, who was highly critical of Britain joining the European Monetary System in the 1980s. According to the Walters critique, as the European financial system integrated, an economy in the European Monetary System would be forced to maintain a level of nominal interest rates converging to that in the region as a whole. But if that country had a boom and higher inflation—as the GIIPS did in the 2000s—this would reduce real interest rates, because the real interest rate is equal to the nominal interest rate minus the rate of inflation. Figure 5.5 shows that this is exactly what happened in the decade after EMU was formed. But, said Walters when talking about the European Monetary System, such lower real interest rates would stimulate the booming economy, exacerbating the inflation problem. As a result, he said, such a system would be unstable. His criticism applies just as readily to EMU as to the earlier European Monetary System.[15]

Many macroeconomists, including most in the EU, argued against Thatcher and Walters in ways that now look ridiculous and have severely damaged the reputation of macroeconomists. For example, Miller and Sutherland disputed Walters on the grounds that wage and price setters would come to view the discipline of the monetary union as credible, inflation in the booming country would be brought under control, and the competitive position of the economy would stabilize rather than getting worse. The lack of competitiveness in the booming country would begin to have an important negative effect on foreign demand for the countries' exports. The lack of competitiveness would cause domestic demand to move away from domestic goods and services, and toward imports. These outcomes would cause unemployment to begin to rise, dampening inflation, and putting downward pressure on unit labor costs in the production of a whole range of products in the country that had been booming. In retrospect this view looks ludicrously optimistic, and as Figure 5.3 shows, the process that Miller and Sutherland envisaged simply failed to materialize.[16]

Keynes understood the difficulty identified by the Walters critique. He opened his testimony at the Macmillan Committee in 1930 by explaining how he understood the workings of the gold-standard adjustment mechanism. As described in Chapter 3, he argued that there was a two-step process, consisting of a signal that something needed to be done to correct an imbalance and actions taken as a result of the signal. In the context of 1930, the signal was given by the interest rate. Within the Eurozone, the interest rate is controlled by the ECB—there are no separate interest rates for individual countries. Keynes made it abundantly clear that a country that was uncompetitive and suffering a reduction in net exports—that is, an external imbalance—would need to raise its interest rate to attract capital. That would, said Keynes, cause spending in the economy to fall, unemployment to rise and wages to fall, and the economy to become more competitive again. In the absence of this communication, an imbalance would continue until financial markets took alarm, and individual country interest rates rose in the context of financial panic.

Had the mechanism Keynes described been at work in the Eurozone, it would have moderated the boom in the GIIPS, caused inflation to be lower in these countries, and checked the cumulative movement in competitiveness, which lay at the heart of the problem. But the integration of the European financial system in the Eurozone and the competitive pressure opened up by the single European market prevented this mechanism from developing. It did so for reasons that many people judged to be good ones at the time, because they were in favor of opening up the European financial market and improving its competitiveness. Moreover, the authorities in Ireland and Spain (where public debt was initially quite low) did not recognize the huge process of overshooting—in the form of property booms—that was under way in the private sector and imposed few measures to slow the rapid and externally financed expansion of bank lending that was its financial counterpart.

Thus market risk premiums, national fiscal policy, and indeed macro prudential policies failed to play a sufficiently strong role in leaning against the wind during these domestic booms. They did not constrain the external imbalances (which had to be financed during the upswing and subsequent adjustment period) or the rapid rise in wages (which would need to be reversed).

This is an example of the kind of microeconomic thinking we criticized in Chapter 3. A macroeconomic understanding of the difficulties revealed by the figures in this chapter was needed, the kind of understanding provided by our model. But, just as Alfred Marshall would not have understood the Keynesian revolution—and just as Marshall's pupil Dennis Robertson failed to understand it—European policymakers failed to grasp the macroeconomic implications of their microeconomic policy of liberalizing financial markets in the Eurozone. These policymakers failed to understand that if the gold-standard mechanism of the kind propounded by Keynes to the Macmillan Committee was not working—because they had liberalized capital flows among countries in the Eurozone—then some other adjustment mechanism would be needed to bring the countries back to internal and external balance. And there was no other adjustment mechanism. Indeed, the conduct of fiscal policy in the Eurozone turned out to be the exact opposite of the kind of adjustment mechanism that was needed. It is remarkable that the dismal lessons of the gold standard in the interwar period were not heeded in the calm deliberations of the 1990s.

Another theory that was disregarded was that of optimal currency areas. American economists had used this theory to oppose the plans for a common European currency, as Walters had opposed it from Britain. They based their arguments on theories claiming that certain conditions needed to be satisfied for a currency area to succeed. One argument was that there must be extensive labor mobility for a currency area to be durable. If one part of the area suffered an adverse shock, then people had to be able to move away from that location into another part of the common area to spread the costs of the shock around the common currency area.[17]

This argument obviously referred to the variety of languages, nationalities, and cultures that made up the Eurozone. This diversity was contrasted with the single language of the United States and the free mobility of Americans. However, it ignored conditions at the time the currency area of the United States originated in the late eighteenth century. True, most everyone spoke English, but state loyalties were as strong as they are for current European nationalities. It was only over time that labor became as mobile as it was during the twentieth century.

A substitute for labor mobility in the theory of optimal currency areas is fiscal integration. Again, the United States is the reference point. As described in Chapter 1, the United States was formed to enable the federal government to tax individuals as opposed to Member States. This structure started a system of taxation that provides a potent way to socialize local losses. When a specific location suffers an adverse shock, its tax revenues fall, even though federal expenditures do not. This contrast provides a cushion for each locality in the currency area.

The European Monetary Union, according to this critique, lacked both labor mobility and fiscal integration. It therefore was vulnerable to local shocks. The Europeans dismissed these arguments as sour grapes and even jealousy on the part of American economists. Instead of designing fiscal policy to ensure that adjustment within the Eurozone happened in a way that cushioned shocks, fiscal policy was proudly set up within the framework of the SGP to point in exactly the opposite direction. Planners were afraid that countries might misuse the system, and they did not consider how a currency will work when everyone is playing by the rules. In their effort to avoid one disaster, they set up an unworkable system without internal correctives and produced another disaster.

Many observers focus on the fact that Greece ran a fiscal deficit and argue that this is the reason that inflation occurred in that country. As a result, they seem to believe that fiscal laxity in Greece was the reason for the loss of its competitiveness. That Greece ran its fiscal deficit—and the Greek civil service employed Goldman Sachs to help them lie and cheat to conceal it—makes this story seem all the more persuasive. Portugal also ran a big fiscal deficit, and the story fits Portugal too, even though Portugal did not lie and cheat.

But this is not true of Spain, Italy, or Ireland. Greece and Portugal had an unsound fiscal stance (in terms of the debt-to-GDP ratio) well before the 2008–9 financial crisis, but Spain, Ireland, and Italy all had sound fiscal stances. To understand the implications of this contrast, note that the combined GDP of Greece and Portugal is somewhat over $500 billion, whereas the combined GDP of Spain, Ireland, and Italy is more than $3.5 trillion, seven times as large. The larger economies now in trouble were following sound fiscal policies according to the SGP before the crisis. Even though fiscal policy was sound in these countries, there were excessive private expenditures financed by extravagant bank lending, which resulted from the integration of the European financial system. Furthermore, bank lending was excessively cheap in real terms—real interest rates were lower in the GIIPS than they were in Germany for Walters-critique reasons. Moreover, the rapid growth in output meant a rapid rise in tax revenues, so that even though fiscal positions were sound, the fiscal positions were actually ones in which government expenditure was growing fast, fueling the inflationary problems even further. In these countries, it was excessive private sector expenditure that led to inflation. These countries were not in internal balance, and fiscal policy was making the problem worse.

The European response to the crisis has been based on the assumption that fiscal profligacy was the villain. This may have been so for Greece. But it was not the case for the other members of the GIIPS. And fiscal policy should have acted against the unsound expansion in private expenditures that was caused for Walters-critique reasons to help pull these countries back toward internal balance. But it did not do so, because the SGP stipulated that it was appropriate not to do this. The outcome was not just that the diagnosis was wrong; the prognosis was wrong as well.

These errors may seem astonishing in retrospect, but they must be seen against the backdrop of two powerful currents of ideology in play at the time. The first was a new paradigm in regulation, emanating from America, which saw markets as fully efficient and their instabilities as being mainly a by-product of government distortion. The second was a strongly held view among the Eurozone elite, especially in the central bank: the national balance of payments had been abolished following the creation of EMU, so cross-border financing had ceased to be an issue. External imbalance just was not a problem. The two views compounded one another. They led to complacency about the distortions involved in a credit-driven buildup of private imbalances in Ireland and Spain, and they led to complacency about the ability of capital markets to provide a graduated set of signals where imbalances, including external imbalances, needed to be corrected. In addition, these views distracted from the possibility of a nationally based feedback mechanism between guarantees of the banking system and the level of public debt.

The ideology also prevented national leaders from enlisting their constituencies in discussions of the implications of the new currency union. We described how some prominent economists went astray in their analysis of Eurozone problems as they developed. Ordinary people must have had even more difficulty realizing that the prosperity of the euro's first decade was built on an exceedingly fragile base. The architecture of the Eurozone was created by European leaders without popular support; there is no popular consensus supporting needed reforms.

We should be under no illusion about how difficult it is to manage such a macroeconomic system. Ensuring a satisfactory balance-of-payments outcome for a country like Spain is a difficult task. In reality this is true at present for all countries on the European periphery. Countries in a monetary union cannot change their exchange rates and so cannot change their level of competitiveness as an act of policy. As we displayed above, competitiveness has steadily drifted in the one direction over the full ten years in which EMU has been in existence. The monetary union began with Germany in an uncompetitive position, but once adjustment began, it continued well beyond the level that was appropriate. In such circumstances, the leaders of the dominant power in Europe—Germany—did not possess sufficient understanding of the balance-of-payments difficulties experienced by peripheral countries.

In the early parts of the past decade, just after EMU was established, Germany had an uncompetitive economy, as shown in Figure 5.1. But fiscal discipline ensured that Germany moved too far in the opposite direction. Germany was out of external balance, ran growing export surpluses, and remained below internal balance, thus experiencing low inflation. This overreaction is the essence of the Walters critique. Fiscal policy was procyclical in a way that enhanced problems by massively cutting expenditures and increasing taxes after 2003. Both these policies offset the effects on demand of improving competitiveness.

By contrast, the peripheral economies (Greece, Ireland, Italy, Portugal, and Spain) were—if not initially, then soon—out of external balance with growing import surpluses and out of internal balance with inflation. Fiscal policy was actively procyclical in stimulating government demand and cutting tax rates as tax revenues rose. Both effects amplified the effects of worsening competitiveness. This was not always evident at the time, to the extent that (in Ireland and Spain particularly) calculations of cyclically adjusted balances gave far too benign a view of the actual fiscal stance during the financial boom—a phenomenon well documented by Jaeger and Schuhknecht at the IMF in 2004 and indeed in contemporary work at the ECB and the European Commission. The high level of demand in these countries caused a high rate of inflation there, as predicted by the Walters critique, and the loss of national competitiveness in the booming economies reached far more extreme levels than might normally be predicted under a smoothly working adjustment mechanism in a monetary union.[18]

Thus, overall, low inflation in Germany and high inflation in Spain and the other peripheral countries gradually propelled this European system away from equilibrium. The momentum created by the wrong relative inflation rates in the two countries pushed the adjustment of competitiveness well beyond its equilibrium position, allowing a severe external balance to develop. Fiscal policy made this much worse. Apart from Greece, the fiscal position in the GIIPS allowed internal demand to remain too high and the internal imbalance to continue.

Since the financial crisis, this policy system has come to impose on these peripheral countries an obligation to deflate demand below full employment to reestablish balance. Fear of exactly this kind of difficulty explains why, as we discussed in Chapter 3, Keynes put forward a plan for a Clearing Union in the initial proposals for the international monetary system that he made in 1941. Such a union would act for the world like a national central bank acts in a country; it would act as a lender of last resort and would lend to countries that have balance-of-payments difficulties. These difficulties might, thought Keynes, be long lasting, and his proposal was designed to help countries to deal with this. George Soros has recently been arguing for a similar approach to policy for the ECB in Europe.[19]

We can understand Keynes' concerns using our model. Now, ten years after the formation of EMU, Spain and the other peripheral countries are uncompetitive. Any correction of these uncompetitive positions will only be gradual. Then, even if demand was kept high in Germany, the austerity now needed in Spain to prevent external debts from growing further will mean that output in Spain must be kept below its capacity level to depress imports for many years. In other words, it would not be possible for Spain to have internal balance.

This concern suggests that such a European system might lead to a position of perpetual depression in Europe, similar to the postwar depressions in the region after the First World War. In the presence of pressures that cause the peripheral deficit-laden countries in Europe to contract in the way just described, there might not be any way of reaching internal agreement in EMU about the relative competitive positions of member countries. This difficulty arose in the world in the 1960s when both Germany and Japan were unwilling to appreciate their exchange rates. And of course, this the same fear that has been expressed recently about the behavior of China in the world today, which we discuss in the next chapter. In such circumstances, no amount of discipline on the part of the peripheral countries in EMU will produce an outcome in which they are able to remain at full employment and correct their external positions. Many now believe that this absence of symmetry might thereby create perpetual pressures toward deflation in EMU.

The problems in EMU are just like those that Keynes observed for the gold standard. It is very difficult to adjust the competitiveness of countries without movements of the nominal exchange rates. Furthermore, difficulties in EMU are worse in several ways than those observed by Keynes. As noted above, real interest rates have tended to augment differences in growth rates among countries ever since the establishment of EMU, and these differences have led to cumulative divergences of competitiveness. Keynes made it clear that the country in an uncompetitive position needed to raise its interest rate to attract funds and to depress its level of activity, pushing in the direction of adjustment. Things worked in exactly the opposite direction in the Eurozone. With nominal interest rates shared throughout the zone—because of the tight integration of the financial system within the Eurozone—real interest rates in the country in difficulty actually moved in the wrong direction. A country in external difficulty, suffering a fall in its exports, as with Germany during the first five years of the first decade of the century, should undergo a recession, which would cause wages and prices to fall. But this actually caused real interest rates to rise, deepening the depression. The opposite happened with the GIIPS. For them, a boom caused inflation, depressing real interest rates and thus accentuating the boom.

In addition, fiscal policy made things worse, operating in a contractionary way in Germany and an expansionary one in the GIIPS. Keynes said that without the corrective mechanism of interest rate policy, some other corrective mechanism was required. Keynes suggested fiscal policy. He would most likely have advocated a contractionary fiscal policy for a country in external deficit (to stand in for the higher interest rate that his interest rate response mechanism would have brought about under the gold standard) and an expansionary fiscal policy for a country in external surplus (to stand in for the corresponding lower interest rate of his response mechanism).

This contrast shows just how bad the macroeconomic policy system under EMU has been.

The solution to all these problems has to be a grand bargain with several parts. It can be seen as the cooperative solution in the Prisoner's Dilemma, following the lead of the Marshall Plan almost seventy years earlier. The easiest way to see the structure of such a cooperative solution is to return to the simple model of a Eurozone containing only Germany and Spain. The solution needs to accommodate macroeconomic expansion by both countries to alleviate the push of German exports on Spain and allow Spain to grow toward internal balance. This of course is the opposite of current policies.[20]

As we said earlier when introducing the model of two countries, there needs to be an agreement between Germany and Spain on the desired external balance between them. The ordinary presumption that each country "should neither a borrower nor a lender be" (Polonius) may be the obvious arrangement, but obvious does not mean optimal. Economic history is full of long-run borrowing and lending as developing countries grow with the aid of capital imports or—in the context of export-led growth—the aid of capital exports. Because the two countries are in the Eurozone, the key is for them to agree on a desired balance. German exports concentrate on industrial goods, whereas Spanish exports are centered on tourist and vacation services. These quite different compositions of exports may offset each other exactly, but it is more likely that the complications of determining the desired level of each results in resource flows one way or the other.

Once the desired external balance is agreed on, then fiscal policy can be used to attain internal balance in each country. Monetary policy cannot be used, because the interest rate is the same in the two countries when country risk is not an issue. Therefore, fiscal policy is the instrument to use to approach internal balance. German fiscal policy needs to be expansive to promote domestic consumption and reduce the German export surplus. Even at this very simple analytic level, this conclusion is clear. It flies in the face of the SGP, and of present views in Germany about the need for austerity.

Spanish fiscal policy is a more subtle issue. There clearly are unused resources in Southern Europe, indicating that an expansive fiscal policy is desired. However, expansive consumption is likely to increase imports, worsening the external balance. In other words, domestic expansion must minimize the resulting rise in imports. It is not possible to go further at this level of analysis to see how this will affect the total fiscal stance; the composition of fiscal policy also is important. The unemployed resources provide a presumption that Spanish fiscal policy will be more expansive than it is now, but care must be taken to preserve the agreed-on external balance.

Beyond this, an adjustment of competitiveness is necessary. There has been much discussion of the need to cut costs and prices in Southern Europe —what has been described as an "internal devaluation." But the adjustment of competitiveness cannot be brought about only by deflation in the periphery. There also needs to be, for a period of time, a higher level of demand in Germany than that leading to internal balance, so that there is some upward inflationary pressure in Germany. This has further implications for the necessary fiscal position in Germany. Furthermore, to bring this adjustment of competiveness about, the ECB, which determines the common interest rate, needs to move into a mildly inflationary mode to facilitate the shift of resources required to implement all these changes in fiscal policies. It is far easier to make the needed adjustments in relative prices if the overall trend of prices is up rather than down. Inflation targeting should be maintained, as it worked well before the Global Financial Crisis, but a period of above-target inflation for Europe as a whole should be allowed to make the adjustments of the peripheral countries easier. This change is not structural; it simply allows above-target inflation during an adjustment process. (Such a policy of above-target inflation has been followed in Britain since the crisis to enable its competitiveness to be improved, although for slightly different reasons.) It is nevertheless a big step for a central bank to contemplate a looser rein on prices, even temporarily.

Returning from our simple two-country model to current conditions, we need to acknowledge that all is not yet stable enough to contemplate these shifts in fiscal position and relative competitiveness without short-run financial obstacles. The macroeconomic adjustments described above will take time. During this process of adjustment, the banks in the countries in difficulty will need protection, and the governments in these countries will need to be able to go on borrowing, until internal balance is restored and growth resumes. Instead, Europe currently lives in fear of another financial meltdown.

There was a large scare in late 2011. Facing the currency risks described earlier in this chapter, money has gradually been withdrawn from the banks of the European periphery and redeposited in Germany; not yet a genuine

Southern European bank run, but creeping toward the edge of such a run. At the end of December 2011, the ECB started the biggest injection of credit into the EMU banking system in the euro's thirteen-year history. It loaned nearly €500 billion to 523 banks for an exceptionally long period of three years at an interest rate of just 1 percent, and by far the largest amount (€325 billion) was tapped by banks in Greece, Ireland, Italy, and Spain. Then at a summit on February 29, 2012, the ECB provided 800 Eurozone banks with a further €529.5 billion in cheap loans. These are staggering sums of money.

But problems remain for banks in the GIIPS. In June, the Spanish government was required to go beyond the injection of credit and to inject huge sums into the Spanish banks, weakening the fiscal position of the Spanish government. At a major summit on June 28, it was agreed that the recapitalizations of banks might be undertaken at the European level by the European Financial Stability Facility (EFSF), and, from 2013, the European Stability Mechanism (ESM), although details remained to be resolved. This agreement is important, because it means that the responsibility for bank debts will become a Europe-wide responsibility. This was an important step forward from the previous position. As described earlier in this chapter, the Eurozone was set up on the understanding that banking problems would be resolved by the national government where the banks are located. As a result, the financial collapse of banks in a country threatens the solvency of the national government, leading to a vicious circle of interacting solvency crises of banks and governments. Cutting the link between the two is therefore a key to creating a more stable financial environment in the Eurozone.

Two related problems remain. First, the EFSF and ESM may not be large enough. At the time of writing, a sum of only €500 billion had been agreed on. Germany, France, and other Member States may need to underwrite larger debts than this.

Second, and more important, the ECB must be able to be a lender of last resort if investors get spooked again. And it will need to act in that capacity for European governments as well as banks, supported as needed by the EFSF and the ESM. This must be accompanied, in due course, by the issue of Eurobonds, which enable separate European governments to borrow in a way that is supported by all European governments. Only then will it be possible to securely remove the varied risk premiums facing peripheral EMU member governments that we described earlier in this chapter—sovereign, currency, and financial risks. This is what Soros and many others have been advocating. As long as these risk premiums remain, it will be impossible to restore internal balance in the GIIPS and return them to growth.[21]

To have the resources to act this way as an emergency solution, the EU needs taxing powers within its constituent countries to support such actions by the ECB, the EFSF, and the ESM. Only then will such actions be fiscally affordable. Of course, such powers would take the EMU firmly in the direction of political union. Such a move—which many of the founders of EMU desired, but which they thought could be approached gradually by means of a monetary union—has now become essential. Now, paradoxically, the monetary union seems unlikely to survive unless, very rapidly, such a greatly enhanced political union is brought about. This system would closely resemble an integrated economy.

This solution described above is a total package: all the required elements need to be done together. To summarize, there are three components. First, fiscal positions must be adjusted, with fiscal expansion in Germany and other northern countries compensating for austerity in the GIIPS. Second, relative competitiveness must be adjusted. Both these things will take time. Third, governments and banks in the GIIPS must be able to borrow during the period in which adjustment takes place. Risk premiums on borrowing must be forced down during this adjustment period, back toward zero. It was right that these risk premiums should be forced down in the monetary union, as happened until 2008. What we have seen is that this is only possible if there are other policies in place that give rise to external and internal balance.[22]

Negotiations for such a major package of changes will be difficult in the complex Eurozone of 17 countries. Countries will have to be willing to compromise with one another to reach agreement and to respect the concerns of others. Germany must be reassured that the countries in Southern Europe will not demand so much support that they take advantage of the Germans, who will need to guarantee the system during adjustment. In the particular case of Greece, there is a real question about whether the government and tax system is secure enough to make long-run commitments about taxes and spending. By contrast, the GIIPS countries need to be reassured that Germany will agree to the fiscal adjustments described above. They certainly need to know that Germany will not push for austerity so severe as to keep the GIIPS below internal balance for the foreseeable future. Germany, Spain, and Italy must provide explicit or implicit commitments for one another.

Germany, the putative hegemon in the Eurozone, must take the lead in promoting this cooperative solution. At present, the necessary fiscal parts of this package are being opposed by some parts of the German policymaking community. At one level, it appears that there remain forces in this community who fear that Italy, Spain, and other GIIPS countries will display inadequate fiscal discipline. As a result, they are unwilling to commit to Germany agreeing to the taxing power described above. But, much more important than this, it appears that many in Germany oppose the package we have described, refusing to accept the need for internal and external balance as a framework, and instead promoting austerity and competitiveness as a solution to the problem. But as we have said, the package is a package: without the necessary fiscal adjustments in both the periphery and Germany, and without the relative adjustment of competitiveness, it is clear to us that the Eurozone will unravel.

How this might happen is, of course, hard to predict. But we think it possible that risk premiums will remain high, meaning that sovereigns and banks in the GIIPS will be unable to borrow. Perhaps then a bank run will occur, something too large to be stopped by the EFSF, the ESM, and the ECB. We think a spectacular crisis would then erupt.

There are also massive challenges in the GIIPS countries. Policy elites and citizens in these peripheral countries wish to stay in the Eurozone partly because they fear the crisis that would come with an unraveling. But they will face an huge political backlash in trying to implement enormous cuts in wages and in social welfare, cuts that Figure 5.3 has shown must be made to correct the competitiveness gap in EMU. Greece and Italy have already had major public protests, and austerity is already being resisted in France and Spain. And these countries will need to accept the kind of political integration with Germany that is required.

We need to be clear. We believe that if the overall package described above is not accepted, then the Eurozone will unravel. The costs of a euro breakup will be staggering. Even if only Greece leaves the Eurozone, the outcome will be bankruptcy of the Greek banking system, and widespread defaults and insolvency as Greek citizens became unable to honor loans contracted in euros. If Greece is ejected, rather than exiting voluntarily, contagion would spread. A disorderly default and exit by Spain and Portugal could well follow. This is because it would become clear that EMU is not really a monetary union but is simply a fixed-exchange-rate system from which countries can be forced to exit by speculative pressure. This is what happened in the East Asia crisis, which we discuss in the next chapter.

Germany and other competitively strong countries in Northern Europe would find such an outcome disruptive, because their banks would suffer. Financial institutions in the new Deutschmark area would have liabilities in the new Deutschmark that may well have increased in value, but also assets in euros that would require rescue. And the remaining Eurozone would probably, in the end, split into separate national currencies. Such a process of breakup will put huge pressure on the EU and could quite possibly precipitate tragic conflict of the kind that dominated the past century. Such an outcome could as well also drag down much of the North American banking system and parts of the rest of the global banking system, creating another world global crisis that might last for many years. The case for avoiding breakup is strong.

Nevertheless, ensuring survival will be difficult and may turn out to be impossible. Any solution that ultimately emerges in which the euro is preserved will almost certainly need to include lending to the GIIPS by the IMF. Even if political opposition in Germany can be overcome, the amount of funds needed by the ECB, the EFSF, and the ESM probably will turn out to be too great for these institutions to supply. We discuss the role of the IMF in the next chapter.

In the end, some crucial choices will need to be made if a solution is to emerge. A solution will require that the burdens of adjustment fall on both the peripheral countries in EMU on the one hand and on its core, including Germany, on the other hand. That is to say, the GIIPS will need to accept austerity measures. The ECB must act as a lender of last resort for the GIIPS, both banks and sovereigns. And Germany will need to bear a large proportion of the tax burden to support this activity by the ECB. In addition, Germany must pursue a more expansionary fiscal policy. And competitiveness must be adjusted. These are all political decisions, and agreement on them is now necessary if EMU is to survive.

SIX Restoring International Balance in the World

WE EXTEND OUR STORY FROM THE PROBLEMS OF EUROPE to those of the world in this chapter. This is a complex endeavor, the culmination of our intellectual journey. It will take three demanding steps to understand the complexity of world economic relations.

Our first step concerns the relations between China and the United States. These relations resemble those within Europe to an alarming degree. In the case of Europe, our concern for internal and external balance pointed to two possible solutions: a cooperative solution sends us on a path to internal and external balance for all countries, whereas a noncooperative solution is unpleasant. The same conclusions hold in the case of China and the United States, with one caveat. In Europe, it is clear that Germany must act as a regional hegemon to lead the way to a cooperative European solution. It is less clear who can promote cooperation across the Pacific Ocean, as both China and the United States are contending for hegemonic status.

In this chapter, we demonstrate that cooperation yields benefits to all participants, as discussed in Chapter 5. In the world context, it is harder to locate the gains than it was in the Eurozone. The two cases of fixed exchange rates in Asia and Europe are tied together primarily through the United States. Asia is linked to the United States by the fixed rate between the renminbi and the dollar; by contrast, the euro floats relative to the dollar. We need to understand how external balances are managed under flexible exchange rates to expand our analysis to the world economy.

In our second step we therefore turn to analyze the relations between the United States and Europe. These are somewhat different, because the euro floats against the dollar. The euro-dollar exchange rate is no longer a policy variable; it is now determined by market conditions. It has become endogenous, in the jargon of economics. The analysis of two countries with a floating exchange rate between them is rather different from what we have discussed for countries on the gold standard or for those in the Eurozone. The added flexibility of a floating exchange rate provides more opportunity for a favorable outcome. Under the reasonable assumption of perfect international capital markets, interest rates are unified in Europe and America, and the exchange rate adjusts to allow prosperity for all. With perfect capital markets, the question of international debts disappears in the short run. But it becomes relevant again in the long run if countries allow their external debts to get out of hand.

Our final step is to put these two analyses together. To do this, we consider what we might call the "three-body problem" of the world economy. How can East Asia, the United States, and Europe all coexist harmoniously? The interactions among these bodies cannot be symmetrical, as the exchange rate between the United States and China is fixed, whereas that between the dollar and the euro is not. This asymmetry makes the three-body problem quite awkward, but we will lead the reader through it carefully. The conclusion from our analysis is that cooperative global policies are needed for global growth. There are many potential problems. Starting with interest rates at the zero lower bound means that monetary policy is severely constrained. China may not be able to change its economic policies quickly and abandon its export-led development strategy. Europe may not expand as much as it could. The United States might then be forced to continue as the legatee market until financial observers conclude that American debt has become unserviceable even at low interest rates. At that point, we predict another global financial crisis.

We end this analysis of attempts to cooperate with a choice, as with the analysis of Europe in Chapter 5. There is a cooperative solution that leads the way to the resolution of the imbalances described in Chapter 1 and analyzed here. However, the prospect of continuing economic misery is all too real if we cannot achieve enough cooperation.

We begin our analysis with background about the international economy immediately after the Second World War, the industrialization of East Asia, and the ensuing East Asian financial crisis of 1997. That crisis provides an important backdrop to the contemporary relationship between the United States and China.

The world split into three camps in the decade after the Second World War. The First World consisted of Europe, the United States, and the former Anglo-Saxon colonies of Australia, New Zealand, and Canada. The Second World was made up of communist countries and was led by the Soviet Union and by China, where Chairman Mao Zedong came to power in the late 1940s. The Third World included postcolonial regimes in South Asia (including India, Pakistan, and Indonesia), in Latin America, and in Africa, and also the occasional country like Thailand, which had never been colonized. Japan did not fit easily into any of these three camps.

The First World and Japan were the only places that had been reached by the Industrial Revolution and that great process of rising living standards, which had begun in Britain in the late eighteenth century. We discussed this process in Chapter 2 and described how it spread to the United States in Chapter 4. Europe, exhausted in 1945 by two world wars, saw its task as re-creating the great period of expansion that had existed in the late nineteenth century—the possibility that Keynes saw had been prevented by the Versailles Treaty twenty-five years earlier. This vision led to the reconstruction of Europe with Germany at its center, a project initially led by the United States in the way we discussed in Chapters 4 and 5. The project was joined by a group of countries that had also been part of the British Empire—Australia, New Zealand, and Canada—and it was also joined by Japan. It was a huge task.

The Second World saw itself as a separate from this First World project. That group of countries was dedicated to building a communist future along Marxian lines. This was also a huge enterprise. But economic growth stalled in the 1980s, and communist Europe collapsed spectacularly with the fall of the Berlin Wall in 1989 and the disintegration of the Soviet Union a year later. The great reforms of China emerged at the same time.

The Third World saw its future as separate from the First World and from the communist world as well. The Third World future would be based on self-reliance and independence from both of the other camps. There was much optimism that this third way might prosper. It seemed for a while that a future for this group of countries might be provided by the inward-looking industrialization model being established in India. This enormous new nation would build goods for itself, using steel from mills that had been built by Soviet engineers. It would do this in a way that was separate from the Second World and that did not encourage the growth of Western-style capitalism. Infrastructure had been left behind by Britain, India's former colonial power, and new skills would be provided by an educated middle-class that built on centuries of cultural sophistication. Indian markets would be heavily protected from foreign competition.

There was a similar rise of anti-imperialism as a way of doing things in Latin America, a growth-promoting policy also based on the idea of industrializing for the home market, in which domestic production was protected from global competition. Allied to these new ways of developing in South Asia and Latin America was another route provided by African socialism and led by developments in Tanzania. But this Third World dream also ran out of steam, because inward-looking industrialization turned out to be spectacularly inefficient. It collapsed in the early 1980s with the Latin American debt crisis, when the period of extensive American loans with low real interest rates during the inflationary 1970s came to a sudden end.

The golden age in the First World also came to an end in 1971. The macroeconomic crisis of that year led to the collapse of the Bretton Woods system. In Chapter 5, we discussed the gradual process by which macroeconomic policy was reconstructed in a move to inflation-targeting regimes. The initial moves toward such regimes were led by Paul Volcker in the United States and Margaret Thatcher in Britain, who together instituted the tight monetary policies needed to bring inflation under control. The high interest rates resulting from these policies in the early 1980s caused the Latin American debt crisis, which delayed the spread of the great process of economic expansion to the Third World for another decade.

High-growth outcomes had begun to emerge in a new region of the world by the mid-1980s: East Asia. This new development became the "Asian miracle" by the mid-1990s. That miracle happened as yet another part of the world adopted the model of economic growth—outward-looking industrialization—that had originated in Britain in the nineteenth century and had been adopted, notably by Germany and then Japan, after 1945.

Germany had carried out this outward-looking process of development over a period of nearly a hundred years, a time in which German society and politics focused on developing best-practice ways of producing modern industrial goods for the world: cars, other transport equipment, machine tools, cameras, and other technologically advanced products. The country developed an education system suited to the task of training people for work in such industries. German politics became dedicated to the hard work required to rebuild Germany in this way after the Second World War. Internationally, this vibrant German industry was dedicated to serving the global market through exporting. Domestically, the population saved to make it possible to invest in the future of industry and to produce goods for world markets.

Something similar happened in Japan. This country had been totally isolated from the West until the 1860s. After being forced to open their economy, the Japanese systematically set out to learn from the industrialized countries in the late nineteenth century. This happened first in Britain—the earliest leaders of Japanese industry were trained at the University of Glasgow —and then in the United States and Germany. Japanese exports, which were initially regarded in world markets as substandard, gradually came to set the pace. By the 1970s, the Japanese car industry, transport industry, and other heavy engineering industries were world leaders. And, just as in Germany, these products were sold to world markets, and the domestic population saved to make this possible.

This model of export-led growth was adopted by East Asia in the mid-1980s. The extraordinary transformation of East Asian economic life happened first in the trading centers of Singapore and Hong Kong. These places were soon followed by two large countries, South Korea and Thailand, each with populations of around 40 million, and by Indonesia, an enormous string of islands with a population of nearly 200 million. Together these countries became known as the Asian Tigers. Fifteen years earlier, it would have seemed surprising that an Asian miracle should happen in these places, rather than in India, whose hoped-for development was to be based—as we have observed—on an inward-looking model of industrialization like that in Latin America.

In each of the East Asian miracle countries, institutions were created that gave protection to domestic industry from foreign competition, and many of the protected industries initially concentrated on supplying the domestic market. But protection from imports for domestic industries and financial support in the form of industrial subsidies was only made available on the understanding that the firms that grew up eventually would produce goods for export to the global market. And, as this happened, savings, and investment, grew to unprecedentedly high proportions of GDP, making it possible to create the capital equipment that would enable production to grow. In line with this growth in the capital stock, populations moved from rural agricultural settings to towns and cities, as had happened earlier in Britain during the Industrial Revolution, in America in the nineteenth century, and again in Europe and Japan after the Second World War.

The entry of these Asian Tigers into to the global economy created new challenges for global macroeconomic management. Almost all the emerging market countries—including those in East Asia—continued to maintain a system of fixed exchange rates. When they began their industrialization, they did not have sufficiently open capital markets to make use of floating exchange rates. The post–Bretton Woods floating exchange rate had only emerged in the United States and Europe in the late 1960s, after many years of growth and financial development, and there had not yet been sufficient experience of these things in East Asia. Furthermore, policymakers in East Asian countries continued to have a significant fear of floating their exchange rates, a fear which parallels that held in Europe, as described in Chapter 5. They continued to run pegged-exchange-rate systems, in which their currencies were tied to the dollar. This system has become known as Bretton Woods II. That some of the world operated in this manner has been particularly important since the East Asian financial crisis of 1997–98.

We describe the Bretton Woods II system in some detail. But first it is helpful to say something about the East Asian financial crisis. This financial crisis of more than fifteen years ago bears a similarity to the crisis that has emerged in advanced economies in the past four years. It also set the stage for the contemporary relationship between the United States and China.

The underdeveloped nature of financial markets in East Asia—particularly of equity markets—meant that firms needed to borrow from the banking system during the East Asian miracle. As a result, investment in the rapidly growing export sectors was highly leveraged. When, starting in Thailand, the growth of exports slowed in 1996–97, firms found themselves unable to cover the interest payments on their outstanding debts. The East Asian crisis struck on July 2, 1997, with a speculative attack on the Thai baht, which led to a drastic fall in the currency to only about 60 percent of its previous value. The result was widespread bankruptcy, which gradually spread into the banking and financial system. As has happened in the current Global Financial Crisis in the United States, Britain, Ireland, and more recently, Spain, the Thai government needed to take over bankrupt banks to keep the financial system afloat. This rescue caused a rapid increase in public debt.[1]

Similar events took place in South Korea, and the Korean won fell to around 60 percent of its value by Christmas 1997. Other Asian currencies fell violently late in the year, and the Indonesian rupiah fell to a quarter of its previous value. The speculative attacks were launched because of foreign investors' concerns about both industrial and banking solvency. But because so much borrowing was denominated in foreign currency and was not hedged, the falls in exchange rates provoked the bankruptcies that investors had feared. These bankruptcies provoked in turn a series of massive financial failures among the banks that had lent to the bankrupt firms.[2]

The overall effect of all this turmoil was to cause a huge collapse in investment, which fell by around 10 percent of GDP across Thailand, Indonesia, South Korea, and Singapore. The outcome, at least initially, was a conventional Keynesian recession. Consumption fell along with income as investment plummeted.

The fall in economic activity led to the usual collapse in tax revenue. Fears grew that fiscal systems would be unable to bear the cost of large-scale bank rescues, and sovereign debt came under attack as well. Thus, not only did a financial crisis and a currency crisis break out, but also, as a result, a sovereign debt crisis erupted. As we discussed in Chapter 5, this same mix of three types of crisis is being played out in Europe at present.[3]

The IMF played a large part in resolving the crises that emerged in Asia. It moved quickly and lent large sums to Thailand, South Korea, and Indonesia. There was widespread criticism of the IMF's behavior before and after the crisis, criticism that is worth recounting. The IMF required an aggressive tightening of both fiscal and monetary policies in the countries that sought IMF programs. As the IMF subsequently acknowledged in its own review of the crisis, its programs placed too much emphasis on tightening budgets in countries that were already running prudent fiscal policies. This criticism was repeated in the evaluation of the IMF's performance during the East Asian crisis that was carried out by its Independent Evaluation Office. Stanley Fischer, then the Fund's First Deputy Managing Director, argued that this approach was driven by a need to boost government savings to support the current account of the balance of payments and to provide for the impending cost of bank restructurings, based on a policy that erred on the side of being too tight, in order to send a clear signal to markets. Once the scale of the economic downturn became apparent in East Asia and current account balances improved, Fischer noted that the IMF programs were loosened.[4]

In addition, monetary policy was drastically tightened in an attempt to defend currencies. Of course, there is an inevitable trade-off between the need to raise interest rates to moderate exchange rate depreciations and the need to lower interest rates to ease the stress on both the banking system and corporations that depend on domestic credit. But many observers argued that the tightening was too forceful. The tightening of both fiscal and monetary policy that the IMF recommended at the time stands in marked contrast to the actions of the IMF and of national policymakers at the time of the current Global Financial Crisis. In the present crisis, governments carried out aggressive stimulus packages starting in early 2009. They acted individually and collectively, coordinating at the G20 summit in London in April 2009. Asian policymakers remain bitter about the behavior of the IMF fifteen years ago. This resentment has been compounded by the obvious contrast between the way in which the IMF behaved then and the way it behaved during the recent crisis, when it has been much more accommodating of countries' needs.[5]

The IMF did not have a mandate to declare standstills on external debt payments during the Asian crisis. In corporate bankruptcies, standstills force creditors to share in the burden of the crisis and agree to reasonable debt rescheduling. In the context of a currency crisis, a standstill mechanism would similarly "bail-in" foreign private sector creditors and then make rescheduling possible to reduce debt to sustainable levels. That a standstill was not imposed in Thailand, South Korea, or Indonesia enabled creditors to race to get their assets out of these countries. Negotiations with creditors in South Korea and Indonesia ensured some rollover of existing short-term lending with effects somewhat like that of a standstill; the trouble was that this was done too late and not systematically enough. Elsewhere, nothing of this kind was achieved.

Because the IMF lacked a mandate to impose standstills, it instead lent countries large amounts of money in an attempt to allay the concerns of foreign creditors and to stem capital flight—a tactic that caused its programs to soar in size. By this means the IMF saved East Asia from catastrophe. The IMF's Independent Evaluation Office writes, "No single national government, nor any private sector institution, could have played this role as effectively." But the IMF simply bailed out the Wall Street banks that had lent to East Asian countries rather than encouraging them to extend their Asian loans. It did not bail out East Asian governments. Instead, the IMF loans made it possible for governments to rescue corporations and the banks that had lent to them. This in turn rescued the banks on Wall Street that had lent money to East Asian banks. As a result, the burden of the debts owed to Wall Street banks was shifted onto public balance sheets in the form of loans from the IMF. In effect the burden was shifted onto the shoulders of taxpayers, who have gone on bearing the burden of this debt. Of course, this is the same process that was repeated in the current crisis and described in Chapters 4 and 5.[6]

The inability to encourage private creditors to expand their portfolio has continued to be a difficulty in the European financial crisis in 2010–12. Anne Krueger, Fischer's successor at the IMF in 2001, proposed a bankruptcy or standstill procedure for countries: the Sovereign Debt Restructuring Mechanism. The US Treasury and financial markets both opposed this proposal on the grounds that it would create unrestrained debtor moral hazard. Under what came to be known as the Taylor Doctrine (after John Taylor, the US Treasury Undersecretary for International Affairs, who also devised the Taylor Rule), the US government argued that countries should be left on their own to negotiate with their creditors. But this approach is only feasible when the number of external creditors is small.[7]

To help remedy this problem, the United States supported the introduction of collective action clauses in bond contracts with commercial creditors. These clauses prevent rogue creditors from holding out in restructuring negotiations to extract a premium from the bond issuer; they work by enforcing a restructuring if a prespecified minimum proportion of creditors have agreed to its terms. However, they do not provide a framework to guide the allocation of losses between borrowers and lenders, which is necessary in any restructuring. In the absence of a clear means of sharing these losses, it remains impossible to renegotiate debt owed to commercial creditors, as the current financial crisis in Europe is demonstrating.

Faced with debt-servicing problems, debtor countries need to borrow from official sources (including the IMF, whose debt is senior to other external liabilities and is not schedulable) to repay private sector creditors. Because private sector creditors believe that this will happen, the Taylor Doctrine approach continues to promote creditor moral hazard. It has made dealing with the problems in Europe all the more difficult, as our discussion in the previous chapter showed, even though the approach was put forward to minimize moral hazard on the part of debtors.[8]

Recovery in much of Asia, notably in Thailand, South Korea, and Malaysia, came through sharp nominal and real exchange rate depreciations. These depreciations stimulated a rapid growth in exports, replacing the missing domestic demand. The result was a rapid recovery from the crisis, resulting in a period of strong growth during the early 2000s. The currency depreciations were a central part of the means of recovery. There is a tremendous contrast with the difficulty of recovery from the European crisis, which we discussed at length in Chapter 5.

This review of the East Asian crisis sets the stage for a discussion of the rise of China. China of course is far larger than any of the Asian Tigers caught in the 1997 crisis. It began its process of industrialization through export-led growth in the 1980s and had become a significant presence on the world scene by the late 1990s. China did not devalue at the time of the crisis, maintaining its peg to the dollar. However, it underwent a significant period of deflation, starting from 1998 and continuing until 2002. The deflation led to a steep depreciation of the Chinese real exchange rate, even though the means of bringing this about was different from that used by the smaller Asian Tigers. China's currency peg was strictly maintained subsequently and locked in the resulting gain in competitiveness. This effect was further enhanced by rapid technological progress promoted in part by foreign direct investment. The Chinese competitive position came to be hugely improved, leading to rapid growth of Chinese exports.[9]

The distinctive feature of the decade of growth in East Asia following the East Asian crisis involved the transformation of the strategy of export-led recovery into one of export-led growth. Rapidly growing exports allowed all these countries, especially China, to solve their development challenge of generating sufficient productive employment to absorb a vast quantity of surplus labor coming into their cities from the agricultural sector.

A key question concerns why this strategy of rapidly increasing sales to world markets was preferred over an alternative, which might have relied on building up investment and consumption at home. Several reasons for this choice have been advanced. The first of them is that public policy encouraged a buildup of reserves to guard against the future: a public sector strategy of self-insurance against the possibility of future crises. This explains policy in the first few years, but it is not a satisfactory story for a longer period. High gross savings rates in Asia, particularly in China, reflected slow-changing structural and demographic characteristics, including relatively weak social security and pension systems. With the important exception of China, domestic investment rates among the Asian crisis countries remain substantially below their pre-crisis levels, even a decade after the crisis, partly because of underdeveloped financial markets. And several major emerging market countries in Asia, in particular China, deliberately pursued an export-led growth strategy because they can sell into existing global markets for products using best-practice global technology without having to build domestic markets. Several recent studies have shown that the growth record of developing countries who are net exporters of savings is consistently superior to that of countries who are net importers.[10]

It is helpful to have a simple macroeconomic model of what the world looked like after the East Asian financial crisis. We want to understand the way the world worked when it contained some countries operating a pegged exchange rate system like that which operated in the Bretton Woods system, a system that has become known as Bretton Woods II. To do this, it is helpful if we aggregate all the high-income G20 countries into a single country, which we call the United States, and the rest of the world's economies into a single East Asian economy, which we call China. We adapt the simple two-country model of Europe presented in Chapter 5 to help us think about the global economy. Of course, the world contains many more countries than does Europe, but the underlying ideas can be explained in our imaginary world in which there are only two countries. Our analysis of this model will be the first step in our three-step analysis in this chapter.

As we pointed out in previous chapters, economic policy has two objectives: full employment without inflation and a sustainable balance-of-payments position. We have referred to these objectives as internal and external balance. We now want to use our imaginary model of the world to understand how it was it that, during the decade following the Asia crisis, both regions of our imagined world came to have satisfactory output levels and economic growth while a growing external balance opened up between them. As we pointed out in Chapter 1, two things determine whether these two objectives are obtained: the level of competitiveness of the economy and the level of domestic demand for goods.

The growth in the international mobility of capital of the kind that has happened ever since the collapse of the Bretton Woods system did not require countries to balance their international accounts year by year, because it made borrowing possible. But when international debts become large, the holders of foreign bonds may worry whether the host country will be able to service its debt. If they decide that the borrowing country may have trouble doing so, they may try to sell their holdings, possibly precipitating a debt crisis. Something like this happened for Greece in 2010, and subsequently for the other GIIPS, as we described in Chapter 5. Similar problems remain in the wider world when part of this world subscribes to a Bretton Woods II philosophy.

In the simple model of Bretton Woods II that follows, we think of the world as pursuing only two targets—the level of output (or output growth) in the United States and the level of output (or output growth) in China. We describe what happens when the balance of payments has not been treated as a target, and we focus on the reasons imbalances have emerged. We then show what is needed to correct these imbalances.

Two policy instruments exist at the world level in our simple model. The first of these is the exchange rate between China and the United States, which is not floating but is set by Chinese policymakers, because they operate policy in a Bretton Woods II manner. The second policy instrument is the level of world interest rates, which is set in New York. Open international capital markets ensure that this interest rate prevails at similar levels everywhere in the world, even if not at the same level. Note that this model differs slightly from its twin in Chapter 5 by considering monetary policy rather than fiscal policy as the second instrument. This is because there are irrevocably fixed exchange rates within EMU, and it is not possible for policymakers to set different interest rates in different countries; fiscal policy becomes necessary in order to make the adjustments of demand within the Eurozone that we were discussing in Chapter 5. By contrast, in the global economy since the collapse of the Bretton Woods system, monetary policy has become central to economic policymaking, as we have explained. We add fiscal policy in due course; it is of central importance in thinking about how to correct the resulting external imbalances.[11]

In our imagined world, we thus have a setup in which the exchange rate is set as the policy instrument in one region—China—and the level of interest rates is set in the other—the United States. We now show how these instruments were set to ensure both internal balance in the United States and in China in the decade after the East Asian crisis.[12]

There are two possible policy instruments and two policy objectives in such a world. Just as in the two-country model discussed in Chapter 5, we need to think about these things together. It is important to remember that changes in China's exchange rate will—in the absence of inflation—cause a change in its level of competitiveness. Depreciation of the renminbi relative to the dollar will cause an improvement in the competitiveness of China; it will also cause China's exports to the United States to increase and its imports from the United States to fall. This train of events will cause China's economic activity to rise. It will have the opposite effect on the United States.

In this situation, each country could use its own macroeconomic policy in the pursuit of its own objective of internal balance. To increase employment in China, policymakers there could depreciate their exchange rate to make their economy more competitive, encourage exports, and discourage imports. Conversely, to reduce employment in China, policymakers could appreciate their exchange rate. In a similar manner, to increase employment in the United States, policymakers in New York could reduce the interest rate to encourage domestic consumption and investment. And to reduce employment in the United States, they could increase the interest rate.

However, this is not the end of the story. The exchange rate set by the Chinese policymakers has an influence on employment in the United States. A more depreciated value for the renminbi causes the United States to export less and import more, and so tends to reduce US employment. Even though China operates capital controls, the integration of international capital markets across borders makes it difficult to insulate China from the lower levels of interest rates that are set in New York. Thus the interest rate, set by US policymakers in New York, will tend to influence the level of employment in China, unless its effects can be eliminated by capital controls. A lower world interest rate tends to increase employment in China, and vice versa.

The simplest way to think about how this imagined two-country world works is to apply it to what actually happened after the East Asian financial crisis of 1997–98. East Asian economies initially had a low level of domestic demand. They utilized depreciated currencies to become more competitive and raise their level of output—that is, they relied on export-led growth for their recovery from the crisis. China was the exception to this pattern; it achieved a more competitive position by means of domestic deflation and through importing foreign technical skills by means of foreign direct investment. As we described above, East Asian countries have continued to rely on export-led growth.

A low level of domestic demand in China—representing the slow recovery of domestic demand across East Asia after the financial crisis—meant that, if China was to continue to achieve full employment of resources, its exchange rate needed to be devalued. But that took demand away from the United States. As a result, to keep demand at the appropriate level in the United States, the global interest rate, set in New York, needed to be reduced relative to what would have been the outcome if interest rates only responded to domestic developments. This turned out to be convenient for the Fed, because at the time the dot-com boom was in progress. It was possible to prevent the emergence of an inflationary boom in the United States without interest rates having to be increased as much as would otherwise have been necessary. But the situation changed after the dot-com crash at the end of 2001. That crash meant that the United States needed a lower interest rate to ensure that growth was sustained and to achieve internal balance. The reduction in the interest rate became known as the "Greenspan put." And, as described in Chapter 4, these lower interest rates were coupled with tax cuts and then with the expenditure on a war in Iraq. Of course, the low interest rates generated pressure to set very low interest rates in East Asia and China—pressure that led to higher spending there, which was partly resisted by capital controls

This simple story reveals the reason for the external imbalances that have emerged in the world since the East Asian financial crisis. The policies we have described—a depreciated real exchange rate in East Asia, and low interest rates coupled with lax fiscal policy in the United States—meant that the United States began to run a current account deficit with the East Asian region.

Remember that East Asian countries were unwilling to appreciate their currencies at this time, which would have been required if the dollar were to depreciate against East Asian currencies. Such a depreciation would have helped demand in the United States to recover after the dot-com crash, but it did not happen. This is why the US interest rate needed to be reduced so much after the dot-com crash. These policy decisions—no appreciation of the renminbi (and so no depreciation of the dollar) and therefore lower American interest rates to increase domestic demand in the United States—also meant that China could grow through exporting. These decisions ensured that, although growth was sustained and internal balance maintained in both countries, the need for external balance was not respected. As the

2000s continued, the current account imbalances worsened. Those increasingly large global imbalances were a direct consequence of the policies chosen to pursue internal balance in both countries.

The situation became even more difficult around 2004. East Asian countries had fully recovered from the financial crisis of 1997–98. These countries had to prevent their low exchange rates, coupled with the extremely low level of world interest rates, from causing excess demand after they had recovered from the financial crisis. This was partly achieved using monetary restriction by raising interest rates above the world level behind a barrier of capital controls. Such outcomes go beyond what can be captured by our simple model, although we can think of them as enabling China to go on living with its depreciated real exchange rate, even though the United States had lowered interest rates so much. This policy action enabled Chinese growth to continue through export growth, and further worsened the global imbalances.

The outcomes could have been different. An outcome could have been achieved in the early 2000s that encouraged both internal and external balance in both the United States and China. It is worth remembering our discussion of the interactions between Germany and Spain in Chapter 5. In that earlier discussion, it was possible to work out in our model what the real exchange rate would need to be between Germany and Spain to be consistent with both internal and external balance in each of the two countries. We then worked out what the fiscal position would need to be in Germany (and in Spain), and in particular, we showed how this position needs to be looser in Germany. Here we can think in a similar way.

More appreciated currencies in East Asia and increased internal demand in East Asia in the early 2000s, coupled with a more depreciated dollar, would have meant that the interest rates in the United States did not need to be so low to achieve internal balance, because some of the recovery from the dot-com crash would have happened by means of an improving current account position. The US current account deficit was, at the time, around 4 percent of GDP, a level that was historically unprecedented at that time. A reduction of a large proportion of this external deficit, brought about by means of a depreciation of the dollar, would have helped to moderate the post-dot-com crash without the need for policy to resort to such low interest rates.

John Taylor suggested that interest rates were set too low from 2002 onward. He has argued that US interest rates need not have fallen as much as they did, and could have been raised again much more rapidly than they were, if the US policymakers had followed something much more like his Taylor Rule when they set interest rates. However, a recommendation that policy follow a preset and unchanging Taylor Rule if the dollar had not fallen significantly would have created a recession, possibly leading to deflation. It certainly would have ended the Great Moderation. The cut in interest rates was precisely engineered to avoid this recession and to enable the Great Moderation to continue. Perhaps a contractionary squeeze would have been desirable. But it is also hard to see how, with inflation under control, Greenspan could have announced that "this is the recession you need to have," just after September 11, 2001, and have brought about a deliberate departure from internal balance. If the dollar had been able to depreciate, things might well have been very different.[13]

The policy outcomes in the United States and elsewhere were jointly determined. Global imbalances are the consequence of the way that full employment was pursued in the two regions. The global imbalances are not simply the result of savings by China and Chinese policy. Nor are they caused only by the operation of the Greenspan put. Policymakers in both the United States and China jointly caused the global imbalances as they each pursued their own full employment objectives. It is clear that this system did indeed lead to global imbalances. As we discussed in Chapter 4, it also helped to create the financial fragility that led to the Global Financial Crisis, even though it sustained growth for the next few years. The policies required to reestablish external balances along with internal balances are discussed at the end of this chapter.

We have stressed the connections between the story of China and the United States and that of Europe in Chapter 5. The parallels are both substantive and methodological, and the same reasoning illuminates the policies needed in these two areas. To complete our analysis, we need to tie these stories together. The natural way to do this is to recall that the United States is intimately involved with Europe and therefore provides the link between the two areas. The link is complex, because even though some countries operated a Bretton Woods II system, others operated a floating exchange rate system. The advanced countries in Europe stabilized exchange rates among one another, but they maintained a floating exchange rate vis-à-vis the rest of the world.

We therefore observe the following asymmetric arrangement. In East Asia and Europe, countries are operating a fixed exchange system among themselves. This is a Bretton Woods II system in Asia, and it is the European Monetary Union in Europe. The United States is linked to both systems but in different ways. Given the fixed exchange rate between China and the United States, the United States is part of the Bretton Woods II system there. But because Europe has continued to operate inflation-targeting regimes on monetary policy while allowing the exchange rate between itself and the United States to float, the relations between these two regions have continued to be like the post–Bretton Woods setup described in Chapter 5. We need to think of that post–Bretton Woods system as being one in which interest rates in the United States and Europe are set to ensure full employment of resources in both regions, and the floating exchange rate between the two regions adjusts to ensure that the interest rates that emerged are similar.

This asymmetric relationship makes the world economy difficult to understand. However, we need to make this effort, because the analysis helps us understand how changes in the China–United States relationship will affect the United States and Europe. Although it is revealing to understand the similarity between the analyses of Chapter 5 and this chapter, they do not exist in parallel universes. They coexist in the same world, and we need to make the effort to understand the world economy as a whole.

It may help to see the current discussion as a recapitulation of the European history recounted in Chapter 5. We saw there the end of Bretton Woods and the ensuing chaos in exchange rates. This phase was transitory in Europe, but a flexible exchange rate between the euro and the dollar was maintained. We did not follow the story of the euro's foreign relations further in Chapter 5, other than to note that the ECB did a commendable job of stabilizing the European economy and the value of the euro between its creation in 1998 and the current Global Financial Crisis. We need to inquire a bit more deeply into the workings of flexible exchange rates to integrate the discussions of this chapter and the preceding one.

We invite you into the kitchen, as we did in Chapter 1, to explain how fixed and flexible exchange rates differ. This visit will reveal even more sharp corners and bright lights than the earlier one. Those readers who are not interested in the technical details can skip the analysis and rejoin the discussion on p. 229 where we say "The Great Moderation came to an abrupt end. . . ." That is where conclusions are drawn from the following analysis.

We are about to start some complex economic reasoning to explain how the world economy fits together. We are considering three regions, and the links among the regions are not symmetrical. The models are not more difficult than before, but the amount of reasoning may be daunting to non-economists. The problem, in brief, is that the nominal euro-dollar exchange rate is not fixed. It is determined by the market, not by policy. The result is that countries lose a policy tool, making their situation simpler in one sense and more complex in another.[14] The rest of the discussion depends on this difference, but the main thrust of the argument should be clear.

We start our discussion of the world with three regions by considering what happens in a model of the world in which there are just two countries with a flexible exchange rate between them—this time the United States and Europe. Each country in this world aims for stabilization of inflation and, subject to this being achieved, for full employment of its resources. It uses its own interest rate policy in the pursuit of these objectives. Our analysis of this model is the second step in our three-step analysis in this chapter.

In the floating-exchange-rate world after Bretton Woods, it came to be thought that the balance of payments between countries—between the United States and Europe in our simple example—was not an objective of policy because international capital markets had become so highly integrated and exchange rates were floating. It was thought that all that mattered was the long-term solvency of a country, because in the short term the country would be able to borrow sufficient amounts to cover any liquidity needs on international capital markets. Private sector holders of financial capital in a system of floating exchange rates would, it was thought, always move the exchange rate to a point consistent with the long-term solvency of the country. If financial markets did not move the exchange rate in the way just described, then investors would work out that the exchange rate was at an inappropriate level and so would have to change in the future. The exchange rate would then be under pressure to change to a level consistent with what the private sector holders of capital considered necessary for the future solvency of the country.

In these circumstances, each country can be thought of as having just one target: a full employment level of output. The balance of payments can be put to one side because of capital mobility and floating exchange rates. It is possible to accept the idea that the exchange rate will change to a level consistent with what the private sector holders of capital think necessary for the future solvency of the country. Unlike current conditions in Europe, or indeed unlike in the Bretton Woods II system, the exchange rate is free to help bring about any needed adjustment. External balance ceases to be a problem in these circumstances.

This is a global system—albeit an imaginary one with only two countries—in which there are now only two objectives: the requirement that there be full utilization of resources in both countries (that is, internal balance in each country). There clearly are two instruments in this system, given that each country has control of its own interest rate. So this appears to be like a two-instrument, two-target system.

Interest rates cannot remain greatly different from each other in different countries with a high degree of international mobility of capital. If they differed, large international movements of capital would result from seeking the highest return, which would lead to large exchange rate swings. It must be the case that the exchange rates between countries move to ensure that the interest rates in different countries turn out to be approximately the same. Thus there is really only one monetary policy instrument for the whole system—the global interest rate—but an additional "free" variable exists: the floating exchange rate between the countries.

This is a two-target, two-instrument system of a special kind in which the exchange rate between the two countries in the model responds to the two instruments in a very particular way, a way suggested by Mundell and Fleming. Nevertheless, thinking of the system in a two-target, two-instrument manner can be helpful. There are two targets—full employment of resources in each country—and the interest rate in each country. It is useful to think about the relationship between these targets of policy and the instruments that can be used to influence them. How this works can again be seen as an adaptation to two countries of the one-country, Swan-diagram model, which is described in Chapter 3 and in the Appendix.

There are two possible policy instruments in such a world. Each country could use its own macroeconomic policy—its interest rate policy—in the pursuit of its own objective of internal balance. But we have to wind up with an outcome in which interest rates are the same in both countries to avoid large flows of international capital. We argued above that the exchange rate would move in such a way as to bring this about, and we now explain how that might happen. To see this, it is important to remember that in the absence of inflation, changes in a country's exchange rate cause a change in its level of competitiveness. Thus a depreciation of the euro relative to the dollar improves the competitiveness of Europe, increases its exports to the

United States, and reduces its imports from the United States. This causes Europe's economic activity to rise and has the opposite effect on the United States.

The simplest way to think about how this imagined two-country world works is to think about it in two stages. Assume first that the United States and Europe both have a level of activity that is below full capacity by a similar amount. Then the monetary authorities in both countries will want to cut the interest rate by a similar amount. Conversely, if both the United States and Europe have a level of activity that is too high and threatens to cause inflation, then the monetary authorities in both countries will want to increase the interest rate by a similar amount. Because the interest rate in both countries moves by roughly the same amount, then these policy actions are unlikely to cause any change in the exchange rate between the United States and Europe. So far, so straightforward.

Now suppose that the United States has a level of economic activity that is too high and that Europe's is too low, both by a similar amount. Then the monetary authority in the United States would wish to raise the interest rate, and that in Europe would wish to reduce it. Capital will flow out of Europe to the United States, which, with a floating exchange rate, will cause the euro to depreciate relative to the dollar. But we have argued above that such an exchange rate change will cause economic activity to fall in the United States and rise in Europe. The exchange rate will move to the level at which it redistributes just enough demand for goods away from the United States and toward Europe to cause the monetary authorities to be happy with setting the same interest rates for both regions. It follows that monetary policy and the outcomes for the euro-dollar exchange rate are jointly determined.

This system operates in a very different manner from the workings of the Bretton Woods II system discussed above. In that system, one country set the exchange rate and the other set the interest rate, with each country aiming to achieve internal balance. And with a system of fixed exchange rates, policy needs to correct both the level of internal demand and the exchange rate; that is, both expenditure-changing and expenditure-switching policies are needed. In our case, there are floating exchange rates. Each country sets its interest rates, again with the objective of achieving internal balance, and the exchange rate moves as part of the process of bringing this about.

Policy outcomes in the two countries are jointly determined. In the United States, given the exchange rate and holding everything else constant, policymakers set the US interest rate to ensure full employment, that is, to reach internal balance in the United States. In Europe, given the exchange rate and holding everything else constant, policymakers will set the European interest rate to ensure full employment for Europe. But open international capital markets mean that the two interest rates end up being the same, brought about by movements in the exchange rate. If European policymakers need to set a higher interest rate than currently held for the region to achieve internal balance in Europe, then capital would flow out of the United States and into Europe, causing the euro to appreciate relative to the dollar and making Europe less competitive and the United States more so. Such an exchange rate movement would only cease when the appreciated euro so reduced demand in Europe and stimulated demand in the United States that the interest rate that European policymakers wished to set was exactly the same as that set in the United States.

There is no longer any constraint imposed on this system by the need to ensure a satisfactory external balance between the regions. And an external balance can be corrected in such a system by the use of fiscal policy, and floating exchange rates help in the correction of such a deficit. None of the difficulties arise of the kind that we have described for Europe, or between the United States and China. In a country with such an external deficit, fiscal policy can be tightened, leading to a reduction in domestic demand. It is the task of monetary policy to lower the interest rate in such circumstances. But that causes the currency to depreciate, in the way described above, attracting foreign demand to the domestic country to the point where the external balance is corrected. The foreign interest rate adjusts downward. The world ends up with internal balance in both countries—as desired—but it helps the domestic country become more competitive and corrects the external imbalance between the countries. This may seem like a complex story. It is designed to show why the difficulties that we have described for Europe and for the Bretton Woods II system do not arise in this floating-exchange-rate world.

This is a system in which policymakers in both the United States and Europe can achieve the objectives they desire, and the mechanism of the floating exchange rate is part of how they achieve this. No cooperation between policymakers is necessary to ensure that they are able to do this. Max Corden once described this outcome as an international monetary nonsystem, where "nonsystem" was used as a term of praise.[15] In fact there was a brief flurry of interest in international macroeconomic policy cooperation in the early 1980s, when inflation remained a problem. There was a concern that a country might try to use tight monetary policy to lower inflation by appreciating its exchange rate, thereby getting cheaper imports, and exporting inflation to other countries by making its exports more expensive. It was thought that cooperation might prevent this. But the concern went away as the world's inflation problem disappeared in the 1990s.[16]

We now turn to the system of three regions, the United States, East Asia, and Europe. Our analysis of this model—the three-body problem—is the third step in the three-step analysis in this chapter. In such a world, the relationships between East Asia and the other regions are of the kind described by a Bretton Woods II system. By contrast, in the relationship between the United States and Europe, each region operates an inflation-targeting monetary policy, and the exchange rate between Europe and the United States floats.

Let us sketch out the three-region version of this model. In such a model, although two different interest rates are set in the United States and Europe, the exchange rate between the regions adjusts to ensure that these interest rates turn out to be similar, in the way discussed above for the post–Bretton Woods nonsystem. But for East Asia the exchange rate is set as a policy instrument, and the interest rate is the same as that in the United States, because of open international capital accounts. Let us use "China" as shorthand for East Asia in what follows—so that our three regions are the United States, Europe, and China.

There are now three objectives of policy, namely internal balance in each of the three regions. There are three instruments: the American interest rate (set in New York), the European interest rate (set in Frankfurt), and the renminbi-dollar exchange rate (set in China). As noted above, our move to a three-region world means that there is also an additional exchange rate, the euro-dollar exchange rate. As in the two-country nonsystem, this is a floating exchange rate. The exchange rate between the United States and China now influences output in all three regions, as does the exchange rate between the United States and Europe. As before, output in each region depends on the level of output in the other two regions through trade relations between the regions. Finally, open international capital markets mean that the interest rate in Europe is equal to that in the United States and is similar to that in China. But this is a Bretton Woods II system, embedded in a wider world.

Since the renminbi-dollar exchange rate is fixed, the external balance between China and the other regions remains an issue of concern as well as the level of output in each region.

The three instruments can now be manipulated in this system to ensure that the levels of output in the three regions achieve their full employment levels, providing that the dollar-euro exchange rate moves in the way required to ensure that interest rates in the United States and Europe are the same. That the renminbi-dollar is a fixed exchange rate policy instrument, coupled with the assumption of open international capital markets, ensures that the interest rate in China is similar to that in the United States, apart from the (limited) effects of capital controls.

We used this model to examine what happened after the East Asian crisis when there was a reduction in demand in East Asia. In these circumstances, the Chinese authorities depreciated the renminbi against the dollar. This took demand away from both the United States and Europe, and it meant that the monetary authorities in both of these regions needed to cut their interest rates in exactly the same way as happened when we were discussing the Bretton Woods II system earlier. The trade balance and the current account surplus of the East Asian region improved, and that of both the United States and Europe worsened.

What happens to the euro-dollar exchange rate depends on asymmetries in the world. It is possible to imagine circumstances that are so symmetric that the euro-dollar exchange rate does not need to change at all. That would be the case if the reduction in demand for European goods caused by the improvement of competitiveness in China was exactly matched by an increase in demand for European goods caused by the fall in the world interest rate. What happens to the trade balance of Europe also depends on the relevant asymmetries. If the system is as symmetric as in the case just imagined, then the improvement in the Chinese trade balance will be at the expense of both the United States and Europe. This story shows how global imbalances can emerge. As in the simple Bretton Woods story narrated earlier, these imbalances need to be corrected.

We can use this model to consider what happens if Europe as a whole saves more. In Chapter 5, we discussed how such an increase in European savings happened as a result of the kind of tight policy practiced in Germany throughout the past decade up until the financial crisis. We also discussed how such a high-savings policy is now being carried out in Europe, as a result of the austerity being imposed on the GIIPS. The effect of such an increase in savings is to cause the interest rate to be reduced in Europe and the euro to depreciate relative to the dollar. Thus the US interest rate also needs to be reduced by the American policy authorities; the outcome is both a depreciated euro and lower interest rates in both Europe and the United States. Europe runs a current account surplus, and the United States runs a current account deficit.

What will happen to the renminbi-dollar exchange rate will also, in this case, depend on the asymmetries in the world. It is possible to imagine circumstances so symmetric that the renminbi-dollar exchange rate does not need to change. That would be the case if the reduction in demand for Chinese goods, caused by the improvement of competitiveness in Europe, was exactly matched by an increase in demand for Chinese goods caused by the fall in European and United States interest rates. In that case, the Chinese authorities would not need to change their exchange rate against the dollar to ensure that the full employment of resources in China was preserved.

Putting these two stories together gives a picture of full employment (and growth) in all three regions, but with global imbalances. Low demand in China causes a current account surplus between China and the rest of the world. But Europe's high savings means that Europe does not run a deficit. The surplus of China is mainly maintained at the expense of the United States. This is the story of the US deficit.

This narrative is an analytic description of how the world worked from just after the Asian crisis in 1998 until the onset of the Global Financial Crisis in 2008, a period that became known as the Great Moderation. Outcomes during this period earned that label because things seemed to be going so well, even though the United States current account deficit emerged. In such a mixed global system, no international cooperation was needed to ensure the continued full employment of resources in all three regions, just as was the case in the Bretton Woods II system, and just as was true in the international monetary nonsystem of floating exchange rates. It was still a "nonsystem" in the language of Max Corden (which we used earlier to describe the relationships between the United States and Europe), and this nonsystem was still a "good thing." The interest rate in this world was set in the United States and Europe, and the exchange rate between the United States and Europe adjusted to ensure that there were similar interest rates in the two regions. But the exchange rate between the renminbi and the dollar was manipulated as a policy instrument in China. This mixed regime en-sured that output could reach its target level in all three regions. In reality, such a mixed regime meant that global growth could take place in all three regions. That was why the term "Great Moderation" seemed so appropriate. During the time of the Great Moderation, it seemed that there was incoher-ence in the international monetary system; one part of the world had float-ing exchange rates and the other did not. But until 2008, the macroeconomic outcomes of output growth (and inflation) were on track.

However, this world system gave rise to a large US current account defi-cit. It also led to very low global interest rates that helped create the financial fragility, resulting in the Global Financial Crisis. Much of the income gains went to the financial sector in many countries, as shown for the United States in Chapter 4. The measured growth looks more like a transfer to the rich be-cause taxpayers have since then been asked to pay off the debts assumed by their governments during the crisis.[17]

The absence of an international reserve currency system—and the fact that international reserves were held in dollars—was not an obstacle to such satisfactory growth rates. As a result of the low level of demand in East Asia (denoted as China in our model) and the resulting East Asian current account surpluses, East Asia was building up its holdings of international reserves. In effect, East Asia was prepared to hold ever-increasing amounts of US debt, something that General Charles de Gaulle of France once called an "exorbitant privilege." This was a consequence of how the Great Modera-tion worked.[18]

The Great Moderation came to an abrupt end with the arrival of the Global Financial Crisis. The task of policymakers now is to safeguard the world's recovery from that crisis, just as policymakers in 1944 ensured that the Great Depression did not recur after the Second World War. The global economy is now markedly different from that which ruled during the time of the Great Moderation. It faces a raft of challenges, which we explore in some detail.

The crisis quickly caused the largest downturn in global economic activ-ity since the time of Keynes' speech at Savannah, Georgia, at the launch of the Bretton Woods system in 1946 (quoted in Chapter 3). Indeed, it was the largest downturn since the onset of the Great Depression fifteen years before that time. The initial policy response to the crisis by world leaders displayed a remarkable degree of international cooperation. This was put into effect at the G20 Summit in London in April 2009. Cuts in interest rates and the enormous fiscal expansions agreed to at that summit played a significant part in preventing the financial crisis from becoming another Great Depression. This kind of cooperation would have been applauded by those who gathered at Bretton Woods in 1944.[19]

Recovery from the crisis has been under way since late 2009. This recovery has created a need for macroeconomic cooperation of a rather different kind from that exhibited in London in April 2009. The task at that time was to stimulate the world economy on a broad front to prevent a collapse of the global economy—something on which it was easy to achieve agreement. The task now is to sustain global growth in much more difficult circumstances than prevailed before the crisis. Fiscal policy has reached its limit in many countries. The world continues to have the same three objectives: the growth of output in the United States, Europe, and East Asia. But global interest rates hit their zero bound in late 2008, which has made the situation profoundly different from the one described above. There are no longer three policy instruments available to meet these three policy targets. And the problem of global imbalances remains. Sorting out the resulting policy challenges requires cooperation of a kind that was not necessary during the Great Moderation. That is the task facing the world.

The challenges to policy are as follows. The economies in the advanced countries in the G20 are still deleveraging, with corresponding declines in private spending. Political instability in the Middle East and other circumstances have led to high oil prices—for a period well over $100 a barrel. Chapter 5 described how the EMU crisis in Europe has led to urgent fiscal cuts in the GIIPS and beyond (in India and Belgium), but no compensating rise of spending in Germany. In many of the other OECD countries, including the United States and Japan, financial markets and policymakers are focused on reducing public deficits and debt. Finally, and crucially, in East Asia, an adjustment is happening only gradually, due to the slow rise of consumer spending in China. Demand continues to be sustained by export surpluses, which are taking demand away from other G20 countries.

We continue to use our simple model to examine what has happened since global short-term interest rates reached their zero lower bound. We begin with our imaginary two-region version of the world, in which the two regions are the United States and China (representing East Asia). We use this model to display the consequences of low domestic demand in East Asia, in a world in which there is a zero bound.[20]

Imagine what would happen if the demand in the United States fell drastically because of the Global Financial Crisis, and demand from China continued be low. Suppose that the United States and China both would require a level of interest rates lower than the zero bound to ensure full utilization of resources. This captures the problem that the world has found itself in since the end of 2008.

It is important to recall that we live in a world in which the monetary system is that of Bretton Woods II. In our imaginary world, this corresponds to a situation in which China fixes the renminbi-dollar exchange rate. Because, in our imaginary world, the objective of China is to ensure full utilization of resources in China, this means that it must seek a larger depreciation of the renminbi-dollar exchange rate than it would need if it had been possible to lower the world interest rate enough to sustain global demand. As a result, the outcome will be one in which there are unemployed resources in the United States. Thus, in this case, an inadequate level of demand in both the United States (because of deleveraging and for other reasons described above) and in China (because of its wish for export-led growth) is coupled with an exchange rate policy that gives China what it wants. China is able to ensure that the renminbi is depreciated enough to ensure full employment of resources in China, clearly leading to inadequate demand for goods and to unemployment in the United States.

Of course, this model is very stylized, and one can think of alternative policy instruments—most obviously fiscal policy—that might help to sustain domestic demand in the United States. But such a policy strategy might not be available if there is a need for fiscal policy adjustment to ensure debt sustainability.

The US Federal Reserve and central banks around the world are now relying on a new instrument in these circumstances: quantitative easing. This policy involves a central bank buying government and corporate bonds with newly created money to lower the *long-term* interest rate and thereby help stimulate demand, even though it is not possible to lower short-term interest rates. In principle this practice pushes up global aggregate demand and could help deal with the global demand-deficiency problem. But so far, this policy instrument is of uncertain effectiveness. Businesses and banks are deleveraging, and their response to quantitative easing remains small.[21]

When we consider the existence of the third region, Europe, the problem becomes more serious still. Achieving a satisfactory level of output in Europe conflicts with the objective of doing the same in the United States. When there is a zero lower bound and demand coming from East Asia is inadequate, then the depreciation of the renminbi—which enables a high level of output to be preserved in China, and more generally in East Asia—not only leads to a reduction in demand and output in the United States. It also does so in Europe.

It is not possible to reach a definitive conclusion about what will happen in these circumstances. Europe has already engaged in huge amounts of monetary easing and may well do more. The effect of this will be to cause the European exchange rate to depreciate in a way that will divert to Europe the insufficient residual demand for goods (after China has fixed its exchange rate to ensure full employment for itself), rather than to the United States. But that might well be resisted by the United States, perhaps by even more quantitative easing there. We thus see a tendency to provoke a currency war between the United States and Europe.

We can now analyze what is happening with the aid of our simple model of internal and external balance. To analyze this thoroughly, we would need a more complicated model, but we can reveal some important features.

There are two issues at stake. First, consider only internal balance. With three objectives—internal balance in three regions—and an inadequate set of policy instruments, we can see that global policymakers are clearly in danger of not being able to achieve what they desire, which is to ensure that the recovery be sustained and so to ensure that the world moves back toward internal balance. Many countries, including China, various East Asian countries, Germany, and Britain, are attempting to pursue export-led growth, each trying to achieve internal balance by growing at the expense of the others. But not all countries can have export-led growth. Policymakers and financial markets are refusing to realize this. Each country—properly— thinks of its own interests, rather than thinking of the world as a system. But this kind of thinking is in danger of producing a world that does not add up. This is a Prisoner's Dilemma.

Second, the need for external balance is making this problem even worse. In Europe, the GIIPS are unable to adjust vis-à-vis Germany. As we have seen, for Europe as a whole, this difficulty pushes the region in the direction of inadequate demand, and so either toward recession or the pursuit of growth achieved by exports through currency depreciation, making it harder for the rest of the world to move in the direction of internal balance. For the wider world, the United States is unable to adjust vis-à-vis China (and more generally against all of East Asia) because of the pegged renminbi-dollar exchange rate. As we have seen, this pushes the world as a whole in the direction of inadequate demand, as the United States is unable to expand demand to compensate for its balance-of-payments deficit. The United States cannot do what happened at the time of the Greenspan put, by expanding demand through lower interest rates. Although quantitative easing is being pursued, it is not adequate. And fiscal expansion is constrained.

In sum, there are difficulties enough in keeping world demand sufficiently high to achieve internal balance. The difficulty of ensuring that external adjustment moves in the direction of external balance is making the problem even more formidable. In other words, it worsens the Prisoner's Dilemma.

The United States can ameliorate this Prisoner's Dilemma if it refrains from raising taxes and expands its stimulus spending beyond what is planned. In these circumstances, the global growth trajectory would be better sustained, at least in part. But a global growth trajectory sustained in this manner will necessarily lead to a continuation of global imbalances. Such a resolution of the dilemma may look acceptable for a while. But the resulting global growth trajectory will bring the prospect of a delayed global adjustment, because such a strategy will fail to resolve the problem of global imbalances. After another few years, the external debts of the United States may become pressing, and the dollar may well need to fall significantly further, something that has been resisted because of the inability of the renminbi-dollar exchange rate to move sufficiently. But once the dollar begins to fall, holders of dollar assets may have to sell en masse, because international currency traders are highly leveraged. They share this attribute with the leveraged borrowers who supported the purchase of mortgage-backed securities in the run-up to the Global Financial Crisis. This leveraging may well lead to a full-blown dollar crisis. The medium-term implications of this approach are therefore grim.

In addition, the US Federal Reserve is likely to respond to this Prisoner's Dilemma with further aggressive quantitative easing to keep US long-term interest rates low and push the dollar down sooner rather than later. But if the dollar falls soon against the euro, Eurozone nations will ensure that the

ECB continues to resort to quantitative easing to push the euro down and safeguard European growth, leading to the prospect of a global currency war, to which we already alluded. Therefore, these quantitative easing strategies may together push us into another global low-interest rate bubble. That outcome will be bad for China, and for East Asia generally, for whom the current level of interest rates is already too low.

What lies at the heart of the global problem? The first cause of the continuing global crisis is fiscal. The difficulties of sustaining internal balance are now being augmented by worldwide moves toward fiscal consolidation. Of course, fiscal consolidation is important, but it is happening at the wrong time. Consolidation is making it harder to achieve internal balance in countries where it is happening. Immediately after the onset of the financial crisis, governments acted to keep up aggregate demand and prevent the financial crisis from turning into another Great Depression. They did so by increasing expenditure, cutting tax rates, and, in particular, allowing tax receipts to fall as output fell and not putting up tax rates to offset the effect on revenues. As this happened, the public sector deficit increased. In many countries, including particularly the United States and Britain, the public sector deficit remains enormous. The buildup of public sector debt has exploded. Effectively, the public sector has supplied enough assets to be held by the household sector as it increases its savings and by the financial sector as it deleverages out of its holdings of risky assets. In the medium run, this fiscal position must be reversed.

In the long run, there is a risk that this fiscal correction will not happen and that a sustained global recovery might be jeopardized by continuing fiscal laxity. A continuation of sustained fiscal deficit is likely to cause interest rates to rise and subvert the global recovery. If it is accompanied by a fear of longer-term fiscal insolvency, such a position may, ultimately, lead to a fiscal crisis. The case of the United States is perhaps the most worrying of all the large G20 countries. The United States needs a coherent strategy of long-term deficit reduction to stabilize its level of public debt and begin gradually to bring down the level of this debt. But such a strategy is not in place. Furthermore, current discussion in the United States seems incapable of separating short-term fiscal needs from the paramount need of long-run fiscal consolidation. Those who wish to keep fiscal policy expansionary in the short run—for example, Paul Krugman—are attacked for not understanding the need for long-run consolidation. But those (in the Republican party) who insist on immediate fiscal cuts in pursuit of the long-run consolidation objective run the danger of preventing fiscal policy from doing what it needs to do in the short run.[22]

Many economists are now wondering whether, in many parts of the world, there is adequate institutional capacity to operate an adequate fiscal policy system. Long-term fiscal plans need to ensure that there is fiscal solvency. To ensure such long-term solvency and yet create sufficient short-term flexibility to allow a return to internal balance requires fiscal policy design of a wholly new kind, with which the world is only just beginning to grapple.

Timing is crucial. The question of concern here is whether fiscal policy-makers are coming under pressure from markets to cut the deficit too fast, given the other events happening in East Asia and Europe, which we reviewed earlier in this chapter. If that is true, then it is possible that fiscal rebalancing may make it all the more difficult to achieve the desired objective of global rebalancing with growth.

The planned fiscal reductions in Europe are large. The British plan is for a reduction in demand of 1.6 percent a year, over five years—a total of 8 percent of GDP. In France and Italy, the planned consolidations are 4 or 5 percent over five years. For Germany, the numbers are much smaller. But very large cuts are planned in Portugal, Italy, Greece, and Spain.[23]

In Japan, a large consolidation is planned. In the United States, the stimulus package is being withdrawn (it is this to which Paul Krugman has been objecting). But conversely, the United States as yet has no long-run consolidation package on the table. The US position is perhaps as bad as anywhere, in that there may be too-rapid removal of the stimulus in the short run but no coherent fiscal stabilization plan for the long run.[24]

Long-run fiscal problems exist in many countries, including the United States, Japan, Britain, France, and India. There is a risk that these fiscal problems will be dealt with too rapidly. An overly rapid fiscal correction will add to the pressure on global aggregate demand coming from East Asia and Europe, which we have already discussed. These conditions will make it all the more likely that global growth will be difficult to achieve.

The second cause of continuing global malaise lies at the core of the argument of this book: the difficulty of achieving adjustment toward external balance, both in Europe and the wider world. We identified the critical issues in Europe in Chapter 5. Germany is forcing a speedy and unprecedented degree of austerity adjustment on the GIIPS. But Germany is not ensuring a correspondingly rapid expansion of demand at home. Instead, it is using its competitive position to ensure that it grows rapidly by means of an export surplus. The external surplus of Germany, caused by an overly competitive position and inadequate internal demand, is making it impossible for the GIIPS to achieve either internal or external balance. The GIIPS are unable to move their competitiveness in the required direction because of the inability of exchange rates to move within EMU. This explains why the rest of Europe is so keen to see the euro fall against the dollar. We have also identified a parallel East Asian problem in this chapter. The external surplus of China and other East Asian countries, caused by an overly competitive position and inadequate internal demand, is making it impossible for the United States and Europe to achieve either internal or external balance. These two regions are together unable to move their competitiveness in the required direction because of the way in which the renminbi is pegged to the dollar.

We used our model in Chapter 5 to show what was needed for a rebalancing to work within Europe. This required both an improvement of the competitive position of the GIIPS relative to Germany and an expansion of demand in Germany relative to that in the GIIPS. Something very similar is required globally. Global rebalancing, in a way which does not put the global recovery at risk, requires both an improvement of the competitive position of Europe and the United States, relative to both China and other East Asian countries, and an expansion of demand in these East Asian countries relative to that in the United States and Europe.

As long as East Asia—and in particular China—continues at its own slow pace of adjustment and maintains an undervalued exchange rate, the United States may be tempted to proceed with quantitative easing, provoking quantitative easing in Europe. This bad global outcome must therefore be seen as a necessary consequence of the deliberately slow adjustment being carried out by the Chinese authorities. Not only is such a strategy not in the global interest, it is also not in China's interest. It is in danger of pushing China into a bubble, which the Chinese authorities would find extremely difficult to manage. This difficulty is already being observed in China.

Why is adjustment in China and the rest of East Asia not happening more rapidly? We have already described in some detail the reasons policymakers in East Asia, and in China in particular, decided to pursue the strategy of export-led growth. Moving away from such a strategy is now a central objective of Chinese policy. But such a strategy is fraught with tremendous political difficulties. Vested interests are now locked into investment that supports manufacturing production designed for export. Such a rebalancing strategy also involves stimulating demand in the eastern region of China, partly by the use of fiscal policy, and there are political difficulties in the face of such a strategy.

There is also a structural explanation of the Chinese imbalance. Savings in China are high and domestic demand low partly because of the high level of profits in the old state enterprises and in the rapidly growing private sector. These profits are not being distributed to the household sector in a way that could stimulate the required increase in consumption, but are instead being used to fund investment. A large fraction of the Chinese fiscal stimulus has been used to finance large increases in public infrastructure investment rather than to finance increases in consumption.[25]

An adjustment process in China focused on investment is not sustainable. The extra investment will create extra capacity to produce output. If that capacity is to be fully utilized, then demand must grow further. If exports are to remain curtailed, and private savings remain high in this way, then the only way to increase demand is to increase investment yet further. This process may create an unstable upward spiral that will eventually collapse.

A complementary argument focuses on costs rather than on demand. A key determining factor of China's imbalances is the repressed costs and prices of a number of factors of production, not just labor. There are heavily distorted markets for labor, capital, land, resources, and the environment. These repressed factor prices are implicit subsidies for producers, investors, and exporters. Such subsidies boost growth but at the same time lift investment and exports. Previous policy efforts to resolve imbalances have focused mainly on administrative measures, which have not been sustainable. A more fundamental solution to the imbalance problem will require more market-oriented reforms of the markets for factors of production, with the liberalization of prices for labor, capital, land, and resources.[26]

These two explanations are complementary, because a sustainable rebalancing will require *both* an increase in domestic consumption and an increase in domestic costs relative to those abroad. Both these arguments suggest that any rebalancing will be slow, however much it is in the interests of policymakers to move in this direction. The longer it takes, the longer

Chinese policymakers will to continue to seek an outlet for their growing production through exports, pushing the world back toward the unsustainable outcome that contributed to the global imbalances. It appears that for domestic political reasons, China may not be in a position to engineer the rapid recovery in consumption and the demand-driven appreciation of the renminbi that this would entail. Simulations of such gradual adjustment using the IMF's global economic model suggest that adjustment will be sluggish and infer that Chinese net exports will continue to subtract nearly 1 percent of world GDP from the level of demand facing other countries for more than the next five years.[27]

Furthermore, the required appreciation of the renminbi may be difficult to bring about. Until recently it was thought that the Chinese currency was 30 or 40 percent undervalued. Appreciation of the nominal and real exchange rate has proceeded strongly since then, although there is no clear understanding of the proportion of the gap that has been closed, given the rapid rate at which technical advance is happening in China.[28] The remaining gap cannot be corrected in a large immediate movement without bankrupting firms geared to producing for export. A gradual appreciation of the real exchange rate is required. But such a gradual appreciation would offer opportunities for speculative benefit, creating the possibility of large capital inflow in search of capital gains. These could bring the appreciation forward, creating the possibility of a reverse currency crisis in which the renminbi *appreciated* greatly. Any attempt to moderate such capital inflow by setting lower interest rates in China would be vulnerable to the possibility that this would stimulate excessive growth in domestic demand in the form of investment.[29]

Making a successful move in the required direction of currency appreciation seems to necessitate sufficient restrictions on capital movements to prevent capital inflow from destabilizing the process. It is possible that liberalizing the financial system in China to encourage an increase in holdings of foreign financial assets by Chinese residents might create a counterbalancing capital outflow that could offset any capital inflow. Movements of the currencies of other Asian countries will become much easier if the Chinese currency appreciates.

Thus in East Asia—particularly in China—circumstances are likely to both hold back the growth of domestic demand and dampen the adjustment of relative prices. Thus East Asia continues to have an interest in seeing demand recovery happen through a growth in the demand for its exports. This is making it impossible for the United States and Europe to move together toward internal and external balance.

Putting the pieces of this story together, it is clear that global policies need to sustain global growth. In addition, there is a desire to use policy to ensure global rebalancing. We have reviewed the prospects for growth and rebalancing, and have seen that there are three significant risks.

The first risk is that adjustment in East Asia will be gradual, and that, in the interim, East Asia will seek to sustain demand by continuing to run large export surpluses. The risk is that East Asia will do this by maintaining overly competitive exchange rates. The strain on the rest of the world may be eased gradually by China's domestic inflation, which will appreciate its real exchange rate. If this happens China's positive balance of trade will erode and eventually disappear, reducing the strain on the rest of the world economy.[30]

Spence is optimistic that China will reorient its economy toward domestic demand. He sees this process as a normal maturation of middle-income nations—of which China is by far the largest. Starting with Britain, industrializing countries have relied on export demand to absorb their expanding supplies of goods. Eventually, domestic demand rose to absorb their productive capacity, and the continuation of international trade allowed countries to exploit their comparative advantages and benefit even more from their productivity.[31]

We worry that this grand transition of development will not happen quickly enough to avoid economic crises along the way. Germany has not yet made this transition; we described in Chapter 5 the difficulties and risks that current German policies impose on the Eurozone. In that context, we are not sanguine that China will leap over Germany in this race to economic maturation. Only time will tell whether the Chinese reforms anticipated by Spence occur rapidly enough to prevent more financial crises. The example of Germany—no longer a middle-income country, highly productive in a wide range of economic activities, and yet not ready to support domestic consumption over exports—is hardly encouraging.

The second risk is that expenditures will not grow rapidly enough in Europe, that a competitive Germany will seek to restrain domestic demand, while a European periphery in crisis will be forced to restrain demand. The risk is that Europe will seek to sustain demand by running export surpluses as a region, and that it will seek to continue to do this by maintaining an overly competitive exchange rate.

The third risk is that Britain, Japan, and other such countries will seek to make rapid fiscal adjustments and to sustain demand by pursuing export-led growth, seeking to do this by engineering competitive exchange rates.

The reason that fiscal consolidation contributes to this problem, even though fiscal consolidation is in the long term necessary, is that fiscal consolidation does not cause a change in the *relative* levels of expenditures. A reduction in fiscal expenditure in countries with balance-of-payments deficits and an increase in fiscal expenditure in countries with balance-of-payments surpluses would do this. But fiscal consolidation on its own only causes a fall in spending in countries undergoing austerity. There is no compensating rise in spending elsewhere. As a result, it causes a fall in the *absolute* level of spending.

To ensure a satisfactory global rate of growth requires that other demand grows fast enough at the world level to compensate for the effects of fiscal consolidation and an inadequate growth of demand in China and Europe. In the absence of this, fiscal consolidation adds to the global problem of inadequate demand. The world faces a choice: either there is enough private sector growth to compensate for the fiscal tightening or the policy moves contemplated will lead to an outcome that does not rebalance the world economy but instead leads to stagnation.

We can summarize the narrative of this chapter as follows. The Prisoner's Dilemma can be described as having three possible outcomes:[32]

1. A cooperative outcome in which there is
   - sufficient increase in spending in surplus countries,
   - sufficient cut in spending in deficit countries, and
   - adjustment of real exchange rates, and so of relative prices, both in Europe and between East Asia and the rest of the world, to bring about expenditure switching.

   This solution would enable the world to meet all three growth objectives, that is, to move toward internal balance in all three regions. It would also enable the world to gradually rebalance demand and commence correction of external imbalances between the three regions at the same time.

2. A leader-and-follower outcome in which there is
   - insufficient increase in spending in surplus countries,

- fiscal retrenchment in deficit countries, except for the United States, and
- continued spending by the United States—using fiscal and monetary means—so that it acts, yet again, as a spender of last resort.

This is a possible outcome when the risks reviewed in this book exert a strong negative influence. The United States plays the role of a follower, attempting to recreate the Great Moderation. Such an outcome makes it easier for all regions to move in the direction of internal balance at the cost of continuing global imbalances. These imbalances in turn hold out the prospect of a further crisis and subsequent adjustment of competitiveness in due course.

3. A noncooperative outcome in which there is

- fiscal retrenchment in deficit countries,
- insufficient increase in spending in surplus countries to make up for the fiscal contraction, and
- austerity forced on the United States, which no longer acts as a spender of last resort.

This is a possible outcome when the risks reviewed in this book again exert an even stronger negative influence. In such an outcome, the attempt to correct external imbalances would put internal imbalance at continuing risk in in all three regions, endangering the global recovery and leading to a sustained period of recession.

Neither the second outcome nor the third outcome is good. As we have already stated, the second outcome would threaten to turn into the third, noncooperative, outcome as American foreign debts mounted. Investors around the world are willing to hold obligations of the US Treasury now for almost no return. These bills and bonds are safe assets in an uncertain world. But if the United States continues to borrow and the red ink continues to expand, then investors may no longer find American obligations to be low risk. This could result in a soft landing as the value of the dollar declined or a hard landing where the fall was discrete and rapid. In either case, we would find ourselves in the third outcome.

This is the case in which there is a global adding-up problem: global demand is not large enough for global supply. In these circumstances, we can expect beggar-thy-neighbor currency depreciations in deficit countries, as each country attempts to go for export-led growth by means of currency depreciation. At present, Britain is pursuing this strategy—acting as a single small open economy. We can expect significant conflict if two major regions of the world—both Europe and the United States—pursue this option at the same time.

The IMF's "World Economic Outlook" warned in June 2010 against outcome 3. But it did not reveal whether, if that outcome was avoided, the future would be more like the first (cooperative) outcome or the second (leader-and-follower) outcome. Simulations suggest that the more likely outcome is the second one. No subsequent investigation has changed this view.[33]

In our final chapter we discuss the choices that need to be made and the leadership that must be shown to propel the world toward the first, desirable, outcome.

SEVEN   Using Theory to Learn from History

Economic history and economic theory have been combined in the previous pages to create a picture of how the world economy is broken and sketch some ideas for fixing it. Economic theory provides a framework for understanding the relations between internal and external balances, and economic history shows the context in which these relations assume importance. These two subfields of economics normally are seen as being at opposite ends of the economics spectrum, but they are intimately related—as are the internal and external balances of nations. Only by combining the insights from both history and theory can we learn from the past century about rare events like end-of-regime crises and about the mistakes of policy made by so many politicians over the course of these many years.

The links between internal and external balance were set out in the 1950s and summarized in a simple diagram known as the Swan diagram (explained further in the Appendix). The diagram showed that the two objectives of internal and external balance were matched by two policy instruments, the real exchange rate and domestic stimulus. The real exchange rate is the product of the nominal exchange rate and relative prices. Fixing exchange rates —in the gold standard, the euro, and the dollar-renminbi rate—blocks changes in nominal exchange rates. The only way to use the real exchange rate as a policy instrument is to change prices. But prices in the industrial world are only easily flexible upward. If the needed adjustment involves a fall in the real exchange rate, then this instrument is hard or even impossible to use. Workers do not like cuts in nominal wages, as they are suspicious that other workers are not suffering equally. Voters are resentful in economic contractions, and they often vote against governments that try to lower prices and wages. The English General Strike of 1926 and Nazi popularity in the 1920s and 1930s provide historical examples of these difficulties.

Current efforts in Europe to deflate economies, particularly in Southern Europe, are proving futile. Worse, they are aggravating an already bad situation. As in the early 1930s, pursuing this unattainable goal promises to send the world into another Great Depression. This is not the choice of any single actor in this unhappy drama; it is the result of various groups defending their own interests in the hope of doing better than their neighbors in the inevitable decline.

This kind of interaction has been the focus of many economists in the form of game theory, another postwar theoretical advance. The Prisoner's Dilemma (explained in the Appendix) shows that the current policies of countries supporting austerity correspond to a noncooperative solution to the game in which each participant makes the best of a bad situation without considering what might be accomplished by a cooperative effort. Research on the Prisoner's Dilemma has shown that players can achieve a better outcome through cooperation if they play repeatedly. There is a strategy that encourages cooperation, and the cooperative solution is stable as actors acquire confidence in the cooperation of others.

We contend that this cooperative solution is only attainable on an international scale, when a hegemonic country takes the lead. In fact, we have defined a hegemon as a country that can induce other countries to cooperate with it. Britain performed this function in the nineteenth century, and America played the role in the twentieth. The United States at midcentury extended the Marshall Plan to Europe in a simple tit-for-tat opening of the Prisoner's Dilemma. Institutions substituted for repeated play in the transition from the controlled experiments of game theory to complicated international interactions.

This kind of leadership was sadly lacking at the end of the First World War. Britain had been the hegemonic power for the nineteenth century, but it was too drained by the war and its long-run problems to lead the community of nations after the war. The continuation of blame and anger after the war ended led by a circuitous route to the Great Depression. Foreshadowing current conditions, most industrialized countries in the early 1930s pursued austerity policies. They tried to reestablish external balance as the gold standard changed from its prewar role as a facilitator of international trade and finance to a constraint on the continued prosperity of the industrial world. The absence of international cooperation led to a series of debt and currency crises that pushed the world economy into depression. We call this train of events the first end-of-regime crisis, as it marked the end of the British century and preceded entry into the new regime of American hegemony.

The economic problems of the 1930s only became known as the Great Depression after the fact. Politicians and economists struggled to understand what was happening in real time, finding the task daunting indeed. The intellectual odyssey of Keynes illustrates this confusion and presents Keynes' explanation in a new guise. He was not simply concerned with prosperity in a single economy; his justifiably famous *General Theory* was a way station on the path to understanding how the world economy could be rebuilt. Keynes did not do this in isolation; he had stimuli from his political activities and help from a collection of junior economists at Cambridge known as the Circus. Although the best-known book of Keynes provided an explanation of the depression in one country, his primary interest from the end of the First World War to his death a quarter-century later was the stability of the world economy. This interest can be traced from his dramatic reaction to the Versailles Treaty to his Bretton Woods negotiations during the Second World War. He did not live to complete his intellectual journey, and his students extended his thoughts, just as the members of the Circus did earlier. They produced the powerful summary of international Keynesian thought in the Swan diagram after the war. We have anchored our narrative to this apparently simple idea.

America was the hegemonic power of the twentieth century. It rose to the occasion during the two world wars, but only realized its potential at their end. The United States inaugurated a period of international cooperation after the Second World War that generated a golden age of economic growth for the next generation. The Marshall Plan stands at the center of our narrative as a demonstration of how a hegemon can lead others to a cooperative solution of their common problems. This cooperative solution included the formation of the IMF, the World Bank, GATT, and several European cooperative associations. It led to a generation of vigorous economic growth that was an amazing contrast to the continued strife and then depression that followed the previous world war.

The development of this cooperative framework led through a tangle of economic mismanagement in the 1970s and 1980s to the development of the European Monetary Union at the end of the century. Economic policies changed around 1980 in the West under Reagan and Thatcher and in the East under Deng. The new policies sustained internal balance in many countries but masked the growth of external imbalances that grew unsustainably at the start of the twenty-first century. In Europe, Germany pursued an export-led strategy supported by international lending to Southern Europe. Across the Pacific, China also pursued an export-led strategy supported by lending to the United States. The euro is scarcely more than a decade old, modeled on the great postwar efforts at cooperation and coordination. But the architecture of the Eurozone and Asian policies after the crisis of 1997 led to huge external imbalances in the next decade.

Nothing lasts forever, and the great postwar boom faded over time and finally vanished in the Global Financial Crisis that began in 2008. The crisis originated in the United States and instantly spread to Europe. Bad policies on both sides of the Atlantic made the US and European economies vulnerable to financial shocks. We find ourselves mired in the economic doldrums that increasingly remind us the Great Depression.

How can we emerge into a new period of cooperative economic growth? We explore this daunting task through an analysis of the architecture of the Eurozone. The assumption of a fixed currency in Europe aimed to reproduce the golden age of economic growth that followed the Second World War, but it actually reproduced many of the problems of Europe in the 1920s. As in that decade, the past decade resulted in countries enjoying internal balance and ignoring their external imbalances. The latter resulted in international debt, which ballooned while no one appeared to mind. The short-run challenges of the world include solving the debt problems that have emerged for various European countries since the Global Financial Crisis. Long-run problems in Europe concern the architecture of EMU, which we have described in detail.

The interaction of internal and external balance is at the center of our analysis. Policies were set in the Eurozone to achieve internal balance across all member countries. The presumption was that any external imbalances in EMU were unimportant. This assumption failed in the aftermath of the Global Financial Crisis, as good debts turned into bad ones and investors feared default. Currency crises in Europe have been averted so far, but the threat of crises like those of 1931 lurk around. It would be tragic if the parallels between the euro and the gold standard in the 1920s were followed by parallels between the next decade and the Great Depression. The SGP established before the Global Financial Crisis needs to be abandoned, not reinforced, if the euro is to survive.

European problems are complex, but they are only one part of the even more complex problems of the world economy. The fixed exchange rate between China and the United States mirrors the fixed exchange rate within EMU. It has the same problems and has resulted in the accumulation of large foreign debts owed by the United States to China. After the experience of the industrial world with the gold standard after the First World War, it seems incredible that leaders do not recall the economic history of the interwar years and have reproduced the same straitjacket that make the world economy so vulnerable. The current support for austerity policies follows exactly along the path of the gold standard in the early 1930s.

The two areas of fixed exchange rates are linked by a flexible exchange rate between the dollar and the euro. It is hard to see how such a hybrid system can deal with what we have called the world's three-body problem in Chapter 6. The simple summary of a complex analysis is that the export-led development strategy of China is forcing both the United States and Europe into a period of low demand. International imbalances lead to internal imbalances. Policies in the United States and Europe will determine how the pain is shared between these two continents. Conflict is likely between the United States and Europe as they share this pain.

Policymakers today stand before choices that will determine conditions in the world for the next decade. Taking our cue from the United States after the Second World War, we argue that international cooperation can lift the world economy out of its doldrums. Continued neglect of international imbalances will lead to conditions reminiscent of the 1930s and possibly even to military conflicts like those of the 1940s.

How can nations turn their attention from their domestic ills to cooperation with others? Only if a hegemon convinces them to do so. We stand today where the world stood in 1930. The old hegemon, Britain, no longer had the ability to lead the international community. The old hegemon today, the United Sates, appears paralyzed by domestic conflicts that make it impossible to cooperate even on a national scale. It is in no shape to command the respect internationally that would enable it to act as a hegemon. Germany, a possible European hegemon, and China also seem to have turned inward. There is no obvious hegemon at the moment.

Leaving the question of leadership aside, the content of a cooperative solution is easy to see. The problem of insufficient aggregate demand in America and Europe needs to be solved by an expansion of government spending. This means putting policies of fiscal austerity on hold and even temporarily reversing them. Debt problems of various sorts need to be managed to make this possible. Hegemonic leadership will be needed to set us on this course both internationally and in the United States and the Eurozone. The destabilizing policy of Germany needs to change into one of domestic expansion to complement expansion in the Eurozone as a whole. And the destabilizing policy of China needs to change into one of domestic expansion to complement expansion in the West. China is progressing toward this goal despite its stated policies, but the progress is slow.

We are entering a period of important decisions on both our eventual goals and our immediate steps to set us on the proper path. A straight line is not necessarily the shortest path in economic affairs, as the experience of the 1920s shows. Cooperation will be needed to solve problems both domestically and internationally in ways that are compatible with eventual prosperity, even if they do not immediately follow the fiscal austerity that will one day be required. Renewed economic expansion may well increase various kinds of debt, but this is compatible with their eventual diminution. Debts are more manageable as countries grow and if such growth generates mild inflation. Current attempts to reduce debts through austerity are doomed to failure.

The world consequently needs both cooperation and a way to make durable bargains among nations. The model here is the golden age supported by American hegemony after the Second World War and a host of international organizations. The absence of an obvious hegemonic leader makes it easy to be pessimistic that such cooperation will not be forthcoming. But perhaps the G20 organization composed of countries around the world can provide a forum for joint commitments to new policies. It is possible that leadership can emerge through the workings of this forum. In the pages that follow, we explore how this might happen.

At the beginning of the recovery from the crisis, global leaders pledged that they would work together in a cooperative way to ensure that growth was sustained at the Pittsburgh G20 Summit in September 2009. They also pledged that the international economy would be rebalanced. They put current account deficits back on the table as an issue. Even if current account balances were not to become a target of policy, ensuring satisfactory current account balances was seen as a necessary constraint on policymaking outcomes.

To push forward their agenda, global policymakers initiated a Framework for Strong, Sustainable, and Balanced Growth. This framework did not just have the aim of achieving outcomes for the macroeconomic objectives described above. It was also concerned with achieving financial stability, achieving environmental sustainability, and raising the living standards of those in developing countries. It provided a framework for a broader set of discussions about a much wider range of issues than macroeconomics alone. These wide-ranging discussions clearly have implications for global cooperation on a range of policy actions that extend beyond macroeconomics—namely, cooperation on financial policies, climate change, and development. We focus here on cooperation in relation to macroeconomic policies.[1]

In the macroeconomic area, the Framework for Strong, Sustainable, and Balanced Growth already has led to significant activity of a kind designed to bring about multilateral cooperation. The backbone of this collaborative activity has been the creation of a multilateral process through which G20 leaders have identified a set of macroeconomic objectives for the world economy, agreed on a set of macroeconomic policies that would be needed to achieve these objectives, and committed themselves to a mutual assessment of their progress toward meeting their objectives. This mutual assessment of progress has become known as the G20 Mutual Assessment Process (G20MAP).

The G20MAP has gone through a number of stages. It was decided at an early stage that the IMF would provide technical analysis to support the G20MAP. As noted above, the Framework for Strong, Sustainable, and Balanced Growth is not just about achieving satisfactory macroeconomic outcomes; it is also concerned with achieving financial stability, addressing environmental issues, and raising living standards in developing countries. The broader set of international discussions about that wider range of concerns is being assisted by technical inputs from a range of international institutions far beyond the IMF, including the Bank of International Settlements, the World Trade Organization, the World Bank, and other international institutions. But we are concentrating on macroeconomic policies and only mention inputs by the IMF into the global cooperative process.[2]

The G20MAP has been set up to deal with the issues just described. During 2011, the G20MAP carried out a detailed analysis of the policies of seven countries: China, France, Germany, India, Japan, the United Kingdom, and the United States; its overall analysis pointed out policies that would move the world toward cooperative outcome, policies precisely of the kind we identified in Chapter 6. Not all countries can pursue export-led growth at once, because it creates a global shortage of demand and a global adding-up problem. We have spelled out this problem in some detail in Chapter 6. Countries have been given the task by the G20 of ensuring that this problem is avoided.

The G20MAP is now under way. As already discussed, the IMF has carried out a detailed analysis of policies in seven individual countries and how macroeconomic policies will fit together for the world as a whole. Country leaders have already taken on the task of collectively agreeing to a set of policies that will bring about an adjustment-with-growth—rather than a low-growth or a nonadjustment—outcome.

It is possible that, as the world comes to operate the G20MAP, the international policy community might learn something from the way in which inflation-targeting regimes were constructed in many G20 countries over the past twenty years. In such regimes, central banks have come to exercise their policies in remarkably successful ways, which have been largely free from political interference. Lessons have been learned about the usefulness of transparency, accountability, and credibility in the construction and operation of these regimes. Of course, the construction of the G20MAP is a much more difficult and ambitious task than the construction of national inflation-targeting regimes, because the former is global in reach and it explicitly involves the need for global cooperation. Nevertheless, the lessons from the construction of those national regimes might be helpful in the creation of any longer lasting G20MAP.

In 1944, at Bretton Woods, John Maynard Keynes and Harry Dexter White saw a need for global support of good policies in individual countries and for a global coordination of policies. This was a rules-based system, and one in which there was a mutual assessment of national policies. Now, in the face of our present problems, we need something similar. Of course, there will be differences in the details between then and now. But, as in the Bretton Woods system, a multilateral regime is needed in which a set of rules is shared by countries to prevent the existence of fixed exchange rates from blocking necessary adjustments, as has happened recently. A formal process of policy assessment is needed, conducted in the G20MAP and managed by the IMF. Allowances will need to be made for countries to act with discretion, where necessary, and not to follow rules that are too strictly prescribed. Finally, a multilateral process of decisionmaking about policies must be established, a process that ensures that the rules are followed, and/or ensures that, when they are not followed, this is for cogent reasons that are publicly visible.

This agenda is demanding. But such an agenda appears to be necessary if global policymakers are to ensure that the recovery from the Global Financial Crisis really is sustained and rebalancing really does happen. Used this way, the G20MAP might turn out to be critical for global institution design. We may end up with an international community of policymakers and officials—both in the G20 nations and at the IMF—who are committed to resolving global macroeconomic problems and sustaining global growth. If this works, the G20MAP could come to institutionalize a newly shared responsibility for managing the global economy. Let us hope that the G20MAP can help in this process of putting the world together again.

The G20MAP would be helped by good leadership. There are many obstacles to achieving consensus as the G20 faces ever more difficult problems, and there is little doubt why this difficulty arises. The Global Financial Crisis has exposed divisions among and within countries, and a potential hegemon needs to overcome these divisions to be effective. The Marshall Plan was not passed easily, and President Truman had to put General Marshall into the forefront to blunt the inevitable opposition, as narrated in Chapter 4. Can the world find another far-sighted leader to help his or her country assume hegemonic status? We briefly consider possible leaders in turn.

Germany is the putative hegemon in EMU, but it is not yet playing the part. In November 2011, German Chancellor Angela Merkel and French President Nicolas Sarkozy together announced that Greece might end up having to leave the euro. As the European crisis escalated, a German newspaper reported that the Merkel government was inching toward accepting

Eurobonds in some form, even if her public stance remained against them, and that some of her party said there could be a trade-off of this kind in exchange for treaty changes. "We aren't saying never," a legislator from Merkel's coalition told journalists. "We're just saying no euro bonds under the current conditions." But quashing recent speculation of a softening in Germany's hard-line stance on the euro, Chancellor Merkel repeated her firm opposition to bonds issued jointly by the Eurozone countries and to an expansion of the role of the ECB. "Nothing has changed in my position," she said.[3]

Fortunately, Merkel's position softened soon after. At the end of December, the ECB started the biggest injection of credit into the European banking system in the euro's thirteen-year history. It loaned nearly €500 billion to banks for an exceptionally long period of three years at an interest rate of just 1 percent. The European Central Bank provided more Eurozone banks with a further €500 billion in cheap loans in February. These are staggering sums of money, and the loans were not prevented by Germany.

We imagine that the German chancellor looked in the rear-view mirror and saw a disastrous parallel from eighty years earlier. In May 1931, another German chancellor said that Germany would not help a European neighbor, as recounted in Chapter 2. The parallel actions—Merkel in November 2011 and Brüning in May 1931—are important for several reasons. In both cases, they made a bad situation worse. In addition, both statements spoke to domestic concerns of the chancellor, ignoring the international repercussions. Merkel was given a reprieve by the ECB that quelled the nascent European panic in 2012. But since then she has not moved fast enough on Eurobonds, and risk premiums remain impossibly high in Southern European countries. On January 30, Eurozone countries signed a German-inspired treaty designed to underpin the euro by means of tighter fiscal rules. But these rules appear designed to impose Europe-wide austerity of a kind that will prevent a resumption of growth. We cannot yet say whether the effects of Merkel's initial views will live on as Brüning's statements did. More recently, on September 6, the President of the European Central Bank, Mario Draghi, reduced the risk of a Eurozone breakup by undertaking to buy unlimited amounts of sovereign bonds in the secondary market. This move was opposed by Jens Weidmann, the President of the Bundesbank. At the time, Weidmann appeared isolated in his opposition. But it remains to be seen how firm the ECB's undertaking can be with such significant German opposition. We suspect that Germany is far from being able to solve the Prisoner's Dilemma problem in Europe in the way required of a hegemonic leader.

Joschka Fischer, who served as Foreign Minister and Vice Chancellor of Germany from 1998 to 2005, put the point brutally: "Germany destroyed itself—and the European order—twice in the twentieth century, and then convinced the West that it had drawn the right conclusions. Only in this manner—reflected most vividly in its embrace of the European project—did Germany win consent for its reunification. It would be both tragic and ironic if a restored Germany, by peaceful means and with the best of intentions, brought about the ruin of the European order a third time."[4]

The United States is engaged in a presidential campaign in which both candidates feel obliged to assert frequently that the United States is still the world's hegemon. If wishes were horses, then beggars would ride. The United States has gone into debt since 2000 to the extent that it cannot extend the kind of support needed to act as a hegemon. One candidate anticipates an expansion of US military force, supported by the very rich, who increased their share of income in recent decades as described in Chapter 4. But hegemony depends on international cooperation, not force. The military adventures of the past decade in Iraq and Afghanistan do not suggest that American military power will be well used in the future.

The United States has been largely absent from the negotiations in Europe. Even the IMF in Washington has been muted. And the United States has little power to affect economic policies in China. As described in Chapter 6, there has been much discussion of Chinese export policies, but very little action. As China maintains the exchange rate between the renminbi and the dollar, it is not clear what even a more assertive United States could do.

Finally, China appears to be more concerned with its internal problems than with the world economy. Like Germany in Europe, Chinese leaders adopt policies to maintain their support at home rather than to promote external balance. The Chinese government faces twin problems as we write. One problem is how to engineer a smooth transfer of leadership. One great advantage of democracy is that it provides for a smooth succession of leaders. The scandal surrounding the former Secretary of the Chongqing Committee of the Chinese Communist Party, Bo Xilai, has exposed differences within the Chinese ruling circle and spoiled what promised to be a placid succession of leadership. The tensions over the transfer of power appear to have unleashed Chinese xenophobia that could make it hard for the new leadership to aspire to hegemonic status.

Another problem is how to maintain economic growth in China. Growth has slowed down and the Chinese housing boom that was evident while the rest of the world was dealing with the ends of their real estate booms shows signs of collapsing. The Chinese have returned to the expansive fiscal policy that carried them through the Global Financial Crisis to help them through the current slowdown.

The Chinese economic problems may preclude China acting as a hegemon, but they may provide a palliative substitute. The Chinese balance on current account has fallen sharply in 2012. This turn inward has eased the burden on the rest of the world, as described in Chapter 6. Even without an announcement of a policy shift or a demonstration of hegemonic leadership, this diversion of Chinese production from export to domestic consumption may be the start of a sea change in the world economy. A decline of the Chinese export surplus puts less pressure on the combined economies of America and Europe. Instead of the contest to make the best of a bad lot of insufficient demand for their products, America and Europe may find that they experience growth in their domestic demand. This will promote production on both continents and may ease the political negotiations that now seem so troublesome.

We want to close on a positive note. True, the G20MAP negotiations appear to be aimless in the absence of a hegemon. But China may well be backing into acting in a hegemonic manner despite itself. It may find that policies desirable for its internal balance also promote its external balance. The closer China comes to external balance in place of export-led growth, the healthier the world economy will be. China's massive fiscal and monetary expansion in late 2008 was the world's largest single source of production and trade expansion after the collapse of Lehman Brothers. Appreciation of the real exchange rate, domestic demand expansion, and falls in the trade and current account surpluses have proceeded strongly since then. Structural factors associated with increasing scarcity of unskilled labor are likely to support continued real exchange rate appreciation.[5] Of course, China cannot fix the Eurozone or help the United States achieve internal balance. But it can provide a more hospitable environment for America and Europe to restore prosperity at home.

Alas, politics in America and Europe seems to be aimed at repeating the mistakes of the twentieth century in the first global crisis of the twenty-first. Placing the immediate focus on public debt recalls the acrimony over national debts after the First World War that encouraged the radical politics of the right and left. The pressure for austerity, reducing domestic demand, echoes the policies of the early 1930s that led to the Great Depression. And the absence of a hegemon makes it harder to come out of these troubles into anything like the golden age of economic growth that followed the Second World War. We hope that our exposition will help national leaders adopt policies that point us toward the restoration of international economic balance and prosperity.

WE EXPLAIN THE TWO MODELS WE USE in the text in this appendix. The Swan diagram is behind our discussion of the interaction between internal and external balances. The Prisoner's Dilemma supports our discussion of international coordination. We then explain how our use of these simple models fits into the modern macroeconomic framework.

THE SWAN DIAGRAM

Here we explain the model that underlies our text and shows the connection between internal and external balance for a country. This model distills a more detailed treatment of international economics and has been neglected in many studies. We explain in Chapter 3 how macroeconomics took a turn toward the analysis of closed economies—economies without external trade or capital flows—in the Great Depression. This was no accident; domestic conditions in all industrialized countries were terrible, and that was the foremost problem to be analyzed. We are now in a different world—although this book has exposed too many similarities between the Global Financial Crisis and the Great Depression—and need a different analysis.

We need to think about open economies when we analyze the modern world economic system. Like the price-specie-flow mechanism formulated in the eighteenth century, this approach deals with small countries where external balance is as important as internal. We also need to consider large economies when the external relations become important either because they get way out of balance or because they affect other countries, large and small. The explanation here focuses on a small open economy; the cases of larger economies and how they interact with one another are explained in the book as a whole.

Trevor Swan, an Australian economist whose work is not as well known as it should be, produced a simple version of the interaction of internal and external balance in what has become known as the Swan diagram. This diagram considers two markets with two variables, giving the familiar crossed-lines diagram of economics reminiscent of supply and demand curves. Swan's diagram is similar to Hicks's IS/LM diagram, which simplifies Keynes' *General Theory* into a diagram about two markets containing just two variables. Hicks said the two markets were for goods and money, and the two variables were production and the interest rate. This simple representation served to clarify the underlying complexity of Keynes' *General Theory* for many people. The Swan diagram did the same thing for what happens in an open economy.

Swan's diagram for an open economy is similar to Hicks's IS/LM diagram in an intriguing way: they both simplify crucial, but nearly incomprehensible, pieces of work by James Meade! Meade played a key part in Chapter 3, when, as a young graduate student at Cambridge in early 1931, he showed how to connect Richard Kahn's new multiplier analysis with Keynes' *Treatise on Money* in a way that made it possible for Keynes to write his *General Theory*. Meade stated that when he returned to Oxford in 1931, he took back with him in his head most of the essential ingredients of the *General Theory*. In his "Simplified Model of Mr. Keynes' System," Meade set out these essential ingredients in a baffling system of eight equations. Lurking in these equations was Hicks's IS/LM diagram. Hicks saw a draft of Meade's paper before he prepared his own article containing the diagram, and Hicks used Meade's notation in his presentation. Meade's "simplified model" is much more general than that of Hicks, and it enables one to see *much* more of what is going on in the *General Theory*. But Meade's model takes so much for granted that you can only see what is going on if you know what to look for. It was Hicks who simplified the whole story to an analysis of just two markets, the goods market and the money market. And it was Hicks who invented the famous diagram that includes just two variables: production and the interest rate.[1]

Here—for a comparison with the Swan diagram—is a reminder of what the IS/LM diagram looks like. See Figure A.1. Hicks' system is one in which the rate of interest influences the level of output (as shown by the downward-

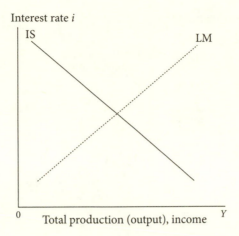

Interest rate *i*

IS

LM

0   Total production (output), income   *Y*

FIGURE A.1   The IS/LM diagram

sloping IS curve) and in which the level of output influences the rate of inter-est (as shown by the upward-sloping LM curve): both output and the interest rate are determined simultaneously. As we said in Chapter 3, that sentence summarizes what generations of undergraduates have been taught about Keynes' *General Theory*. The equilibrium is where the two curves cross in Figure A.1.

When Hicks turned Meade's not-very-simple "simplified model" into the IS/LM diagram, it was only the first of several occasions in Meade's career in which Meade set out a fully specified piece of economic theory, only to find that someone else would extract a simple, clear idea from what he had writ-ten, publish it, and then become famous. Trevor Swan did this for Meade's famous book, *The Balance of Payments*, which was published in 1951 and for which Meade received the Nobel Prize in 1977. Meade turned what he had learned from Keynes when the latter was preparing for Bretton Woods into a 300-page, hard-to-read, book, which also contained a complicated mathe-matical appendix. It was Swan who turned the main ideas of this book into a simple diagram.[2]

The Swan diagram is shown in Figure A.2 and comes from Swan's paper. It looks just like a supply and demand diagram or an IS/LM diagram—the favorite kind of image for economists. Swan showed how it could be used to understand the links between internal and external balances that are the focus of this book.[3]

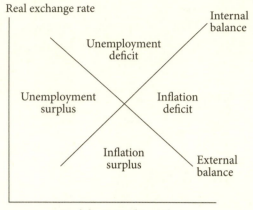

FIGURE A.2   The Swan diagram

Like the IS/LM diagram, the Swan diagram concerns just two markets, and it contains only two variables. The two markets are for domestically produced goods and for international payments; the two variables are domestic production and the real exchange rate. As with the IS/LM diagram, a quantity is on the horizontal axis whereas a price is on the vertical axis. For reasons we explain below, the Swan diagram puts domestic demand on the horizontal axis—the amount of demand for domestic goods coming from within the economy. This demand conventionally is seen as consumption plus investment plus government purchases plus net exports. Real domestic demand is sometimes known as *absorption*. We sometimes talk about this horizontal axis as domestic stimulus, which we normally regard as fiscal policy, although sometimes we think of it as monetary policy. The further to the right we go in the diagram, the greater is the stimulus is. The vertical axis is the real exchange rate, that is, the nominal exchange rate times the ratio of prices at home and abroad. For simplicity, we present the real exchange rate as the value of the home currency abroad, so a fall in the real exchange rate can be brought about by a depreciation of the currency or by a fall in costs and prices at home relative to costs and prices abroad. A fall in the real exchange rate, measured this way, means that the country is becoming more competitive relative to other countries.

The first of the two markets is domestic production. It is the familiar Keynesian definition of national production or income, normally represented by Y. Domestic production Y is equal to the sum of (domestic) consumption C, (domestic) investment I, government purchases of goods and services G, and net exports (that is, exports X minus imports M). In a simple equation:

$$Y = C + I + G + (X - M).$$

Production will be the same as income, because income includes the payments to those who produce goods and services; these payments, together with any taxes paid, will be equal to the value of what is produced. A country is in internal balance when domestic production Y is just large enough to fully use all the resources in the economy—that is, when consumption, investment, government purchases, and net exports together equal the amount of output that the economy could produce, which means that labor is fully employed.

The second market is that for international payments. It is measured as the balance on current account in the national accounts B, and it is roughly equal to exports X minus imports M. We can represent the external balance by balance of payments on current account B in the following equation:

$$B = X - M.$$

A country is in external balance when exports are just large enough to fully pay for imports, so that foreign trade is balanced, after allowing for any payments of interest that have to be made abroad and for any long-term capital inflow or foreign direct investment going to the country.

These equations already show the most important lesson of the Swan diagram: internal and external balance must be thought about at the same time. The level of domestic production Y and the balance on current account B are clearly related to each other. The first equation shows that when there are increased exports X or reduced imports M, then there is an increase in net exports $(X - M)$, which will add to demand for domestic goods and so to domestic production. But higher domestic production will increase the demand for imports, and we can see from the second equation that this will worsen the balance of payments on current account. So attempts to achieve internal balance, by having an appropriate level of domestic production, and attempts to achieve external balance, by having an appropriate level of the balance of payments on current account, must be thought about together.

The diagram shows how to do this tandem thinking. Consider first external balance. As the real exchange rate drops, a country's exports become more attractive abroad, while its imports become more expensive. If nothing else changes, the country will go into surplus. (More correctly, B will rise from its desired level. It makes the prose flow more easily if we talk as if the optimum external balance is zero. Because we are discussing changes in B, its initial size is irrelevant.) To restore balance, domestic demand will need to expand to increase the demand for imports enough to match the increase in exports from the fall in the real exchange rate. In other words, the line that defines external balance—an optimum B—slopes downward. A country is in surplus below the line and in deficit above it.

Now consider internal balance. What happens if we start on the line of balance (that is, at noninflationary full employment), and government purchases increase? If nothing else is done, a rise in demand from an expansionary fiscal policy will lead to inflation. The country will be out of internal balance. However, if the real exchange rate rises, its exports will become more expensive in other countries and their quantity will fall, and imports will become cheaper and their amount will rise. With enough information, we can figure out how much the real exchange rate has to rise for the reductions in exports and the increase in imports, taken together, to fully offset the increase in domestic demand coming from the increase in government spending. This means that the line that defines internal balance (that is, a position of noninflationary full employment) has a positive slope. To the right of the line, there is inflation; to its left, unemployment.

Now we can put these two lines together. The line of external balance is downward sloping. And that of internal balance is upward sloping. The diagram shows one can only achieve *both* external and internal balance at the point where the two curves cross. That is, to achieve both external and internal balance, one must have the right values both for domestic demand and for the real exchange rate.

It might seem that external balance occurs only when exports minus imports is zero. However, this is not the case. Countries may wish to industrialize by exporting more than they import, using what we describe in the text as an export-led growth strategy. Other countries may wish to industrialize by importing more than they export to build an infrastructure of roads, railroads, and schools that promote the growth of industry. Considering internal balance, the optimum level of domestic production—the level of domestic production at which there is internal balance—is not described in this model. It is usually taken to be as close to full employment as a country can get without inducing unwanted inflation. In fact, we normally define full employment as the highest employment consistent with stable prices.

One can make a more sophisticated model of international trade than that explained here, just as one can construct a more complex model of domestic income determination. These models are useful in many tasks; here we want insights from the simplest of models that still shows the interrelationship between internal and external balance.

In Figure A.2, we have labeled what happens when an economy is out of balance. There are two dimensions. Above the external balance line, the country is in deficit on its current account. To the left of the internal balance line, it is experiencing unemployment. Deficits need to be financed, and being in deficit means that a country has accumulated foreign debts. As we discuss further in the text, these debts can be a problem. Unemployment is a difficulty, wasting resources, degrading the work force, and even leading to political troubles. The costs of unemployment are not recorded in newspapers and annual reports like foreign debts, but they are no less real.

Countries therefore want to be in both internal and external balance, the point where the two curves cross in Figure A.2. We call that point an equilibrium in the sense that countries can approach it from any point and will stay there if possible.

We examine what happens when a country is out of equilibrium by looking at the possibility that it could be vertically out of equilibrium, that is, directly above or below the equilibrium point. As shown in Figure A.2, it then would have multiple problems. Being off both curves, it would be experiencing unemployment and an international deficit, or inflation and an international surplus. Despite the combination of difficulties, the imbalances can be cured by moving the real exchange alone. Because the real exchange rate is the nominal exchange rate times relative prices, it can be modified by changing the exchange rate or prices. We discuss this choice extensively in the text.

A country that is horizontally out of equilibrium faces a similar task. Again, it will be experiencing both internal and external problems, but in different combination than with a vertical displacement. And the policy needed to reach equilibrium is similarly simple; changing fiscal policy one way or the other will do the trick. In fact, monetary or fiscal policy will work, although only fiscal policy appears in the simple equations given above. If there is full capital mobility, as in the Eurozone today, then no single country can affect the interest rate, and monetary policy cannot be used. Fiscal policy—or more generally, absorption—has moved countries horizontally in many parts of our story. Wars typically move countries to the right in Figure A.2, creating both internal and external imbalances. Austerity, in the 1920s and again today, moves countries to the left—increasing internal imbalances while attempting to eliminate external imbalances.

Now let us consider a more complex case. To see what happens when a country is diagonally out of equilibrium, consider the case of a country that is in internal balance but has an international deficit it can no longer tolerate. This country is on the internal balance line up and to the right of equilibrium. It must reduce both its real exchange rate and its fiscal stimulus. The fall in the real exchange rate by either devaluation or deflation will stimulate exports and therefore domestic production. The fall in fiscal stimulus then will have to be large enough to offset this effect and make room for the goods that are exported and move the country toward equilibrium. Lack of coordination will generate either unemployment or inflation. The simple representation in the Swan diagram points to the central problems of macroeconomic policies in open economies. It does this in the same way that the IS/LM diagram illuminates the central macroeconomic problems of closed economies.

This model can be enlarged and extended in many ways. One way is to add assets and debts to the model. We focus our attention here on international debts, although personal and public debts are also considered in the text. Countries with persistent external imbalances accumulate foreign assets or debts. With this simple addition, the Swan diagram provides an analytic summary of the argument of this book.

Consider a country that has experienced a war or consumption boom that increased absorption for several years. This country then finds itself to the right of equilibrium in Figure A.2. Because it has been there for a while, the country has accumulated foreign debt. Now assume that the foreign debt becomes problematic as investors begin to wonder whether the country will be able to reliably service its debt. There are two policy options for the country to resolve its debt problem.

The first policy is to reduce domestic absorption; this policy is known now as austerity. It moves the country to the left in the diagram; the country has to move beyond equilibrium to achieve a current account surplus and begin paying down its debt. As the diagram shows, the cost of this policy is unemployment. How successful will this policy be? It seems unlikely to achieve its goal of reassuring investors and reducing foreign indebtedness because of the costs of unemployment. The growth in unemployment reduces tax revenues, which in turn lowers the ability of the government to repay foreign debts. It also triggers government expenditures that may conflict with debt repayment. The history of the early 1930s suggests that austerity policies intensify the problem of foreign debt instead of reducing it.

The second policy is devaluation. This moves the country down the graph; as in the previous example, the country has to move past the external balance line to generate a surplus to repay its foreign debt. As the diagram shows, the cost of this policy is inflation. How successful will it be? If devaluation causes inflation to increase so that the real exchange rate does not fall, then this policy does not work. In that case, the attempt to implement it does not move the country down in the Swan diagram. If the policy does not cause too much inflation, then the it can work. Modest inflation helps the country repay its debts, as the real value of its debt is reduced. This policy was widely employed in the past, as recounted in Chapters 2 and 4, although it is not allowed in EMU.

Another way we enlarge the model in Chapters 5 and 6 is to consider what happens to two countries trading with each other. More formally, we extend the model to large countries, where each country can no longer be considered in isolation. One country may seek to achieve internal balance by having low domestic demand and a low exchange rate, which Figure A.2 shows is perfectly possible. This strategy would give that country an external surplus. But it would mean that the other country would not have a competitive exchange rate. As viewed by the second country, the exchange rate would be high. A version of Figure A.2 drawn for the second country would show that it could only attain internal balance if it were to have high domestic demand and an external deficit—a deficit equal to the first country's surplus.

The second country may not be able to maintain such an external deficit —it may have already accumulated too many debts. It may then seek to have a different exchange rate, one that would make it more competitive. Or it may be forced to curtail its domestic demand, which would prevent it from achieving internal balance. We discuss both these cases in Chapters 5 and 6, and show that the Swan model can be extended to think about these cases.

Such a generalization of the Swan diagram to the case of more than one country enables us to analyze the problems of macroeconomic policymaking in a global context. This framework can help us think about how to resolve these problems.

THE PRISONER'S DILEMMA

Consider the choice facing the United States after the Second World War of whether to give aid to Europe as an example of the kind of interaction among people or countries analyzed by game theory. More specifically, think of it as a particular, well-known game: the Prisoner's Dilemma. There are two players in this game: the United States (US) and Western Europe (WE). There are two possible actions: cooperation (the policy stance following the Second World War) and "finking" (the policy of continued aggression by nonmilitary means that so disastrously followed the First World War).

Cooperation in this game means that US gives aid to WE, and that WE stays democratic and trades with US. Finking means that US does not extend aid, and that WE goes communist. The hostile action of Europe is given in its 1940s context, not its 1920s version; we described the choices made after the First World War in Chapter 2. Although the game can describe choices after each war, the discussion in later chapters is about the aftermath of the Second World War and current choices. In the formal representation of the game, let US be the column player and WE be the row player. The rewards to each player are shown in Tables A.1 and A.2, where US chooses a column and WE chooses a row.

Consider US first in Table A.1. Assume that aid consists of US giving and loaning $13 billion to WE. In the language of the game, aid transfers $13 billion—roughly the size of total transfers under the Marshall Plan—from US to WE. If Europe goes communist, US suffers damages equal to the loss of $20 billion. These two events reflect choices by different players; in the worst case, US suffers a combined loss of $13 billion in aid and $20 billion in damages for a total of $33 billion.

The payoffs to WE appear in Table A.2. Assume that by going communist, WE gains somewhere around $7 billion dollars and in addition receives $13 billion dollars from US if the latter gives aid, for a total gain of $20 billion. The gain should be understood as the monetary equivalent of the

TABLE A.1 US Gains and Losses

		United States	
		Aid	No Aid
Europe	Democratic	−13	0
	Communist	−33	−20

TABLE A.2 WE Gains and Losses

		United States	
		Aid	No Aid
Europe	Democratic	13	0
	Communist	20	7

expected gain to WE. (We do not deal here with the now-apparent fact that WE workers would have been grievously disappointed in this expectation.)

To make this game a Prisoner's Dilemma, we assume that the Marshall Plan cost less to America than a communist takeover of Western Europe would have. In other words, the expected cost to US of WE going communist (finking) is larger than the cost of aid. If not—if there were no fear in the postwar United States of the consequence of communist expansion—then the Marshall Plan is inexplicable in terms of the self-interest of the United States. It could be explained only by altruism.

It should be noted that the gain to Europeans from going communist has to be positive and reasonably small to make this a Prisoner's Dilemma. If the Europeans expect to lose from going communist, then WE stays democratic no matter what US does. If the gain from going communist is larger than the size of the Marshall Plan, then the Europeans anticipate such a marvelous transformation from going communist that WE goes communist independent of US actions. In these other cases, the Marshall Plan again was altruistic. Only if the gain is positive and reasonably small does American action make a difference.

Assuming the gain to Western Europe from going communist is positive but small captures the perception in the United States after the Second World War that there was a chance that Western Europe would go communist, but that the pull toward communism was weak enough to be influenced by American aid. It reflects the deep divisions in the parliaments in France and Italy, the sense that Western Europe was balanced on a knife edge and could go either way. If the United States thought that Western Europe had no reason to go communist with or without aid, or would go communist despite aid from the United States, there was no self-interested motive for extending aid.

Thus, this game is a Prisoner's Dilemma for appropriate values of the parameters. Both parties prefer giving and receiving aid to the alternative of having no aid and having communism in WE, but there is a problem in achieving this optimal outcome. Each party has an incentive to cheat in this position—the upper left-hand cell of the matrix. US is even better off if WE stays democratic without aid. And WE would prefer to receive aid and still go communist. In the language of game theory, this solution is not a Nash equilibrium. US gains from not giving aid, holding constant what WE does, and WE gains from going communist, holding constant what US does.

It is well known that if this Prisoner's Dilemma game is played only once, then the Nash equilibrium is no aid and the presence of communists—the lower right-hand cells of Tables A.1 and A.2. This is worse for both players than the upper left-hand cell of the figures. In contrast, if the game is played many times, a tit-for-tat strategy will enable the parties to get to the upper left-hand cell of the figures, the better position of aid and democracy. Both parties in this strategy choose aid and democracy as long as the other does the same, but they threaten to go to the one-shot Nash equilibrium forever if the other player once finks. This threat promotes cooperation. Each player sees that if it chooses to fink once, it gets a gain in the next period and then has to settle for the less-desirable Nash solution forever after. Conditions can be derived under which repeated players will opt for this policy and outcome. Economists like the apparent rationality of the Nash equilibrium, but people and politicians are not condemned to stay there.[4]

The Modern Macroeconomic Framework

Here we briefly describes modern macroeconomic models and the way these models underpin the arguments in the text. Because this book is intended for noneconomists as well as economists, references to these more formal models were not made explicitly in the chapters. Instead, a brief exposition is provided here, to expose the common elements of these models to those economists who might wish to think about the issues discussed in this book in a more formal manner.

Modern macroeconomic theories include New Keynesian macroeconomic models, modern theories of economic growth, and models in the dynamic stochastic general equilibrium (DSGE) tradition. These modern macroeconomic theories of the economy are embodied in mathematical models that are based on the maximization of utility by rational consumers and the maximization of profits by firms. Both consumers and firms are assumed to form views about what will happen to the economy in the future.[5]

Our book deals with conditions that do not fit easily into these kinds of models for two reasons. The first reason is that we are dealing primarily with crises of the international economy. A crisis occurs when people change their minds about whether assets they hold will pay the contracted return and change their behavior as a result. These are not long-run decisions of optimizing individuals; they are the result of rapid changes of expectations about what will happen in the future. They typically come when countries or regions are out of internal or external balance, as we describe in the text, and their debts turn from good debts to bad ones. A crisis happens when a country or region, like an old-fashioned bank, runs out of resources to redeem its promises. These resources may be gold, foreign exchange, or guarantees from other institutions with stellar reputations. As the models of exchange crises shows, economies typically do not go to the boundary; instead, investors who anticipate such a collapse precipitate a crisis by scrambling to be first in line to sell the troublesome assets.

The second reason is that we are concerned with government policy to prevent such crises. Some modern macroeconomic theories aim to discuss optimal government policy in normal times, for example, the way in which it may be advantageous to introduce fiscal policy rules in a monetary union, as we discuss in Chapter 5. But such policies are only optimal if consumers and firms do not change their minds about the future prospects for the economy and then suddenly change their behavior. Our story of government policy would become even more complex if we attempted to discuss optimal government policy in the face of such changes in behavior by firms and consumers.

Nevertheless, there is much in modern macroeconomics that we have followed in this book. New Keynesian macroeconomics has shown how policymakers can and should stabilize the overall level of demand in the economy to prevent inflation and keep the economy close to full employment in the apparently normal times that ruled during the Great Moderation. Our approach is related to that work. Contrary to the ideas of Milton Friedman and the monetarist school of macroeconomics, policy as actually practiced by inflation-targeting central banks—by the US Federal Reserve, the ECB, and the Bank of England, among others—has been highly interventionist, designed to stabilize demand in the economy. The Greenspan put is an example of such a policy—interest rates were cut by whatever was necessary to keep demand high and the economy growing. We describe this aspect of policy as the government having a target for internal balance. This aspect of policy is central in many discussions in this book.

Modern macroeconomics has also sought to understand reasons for economic growth. Growth models display the outcomes for growing economies as and when demand is kept close to full employment, as in the quiet times of the Great Moderation. The essential framework deployed for this has been the Solow growth model, in which the growth of the supply side of the economy depends on how much of its output the economy saves and devotes to capital accumulation, and on the rate of technical progress.[6] Our approach is related to that work. We describe technical progress coming from the crucial innovations during the period of hegemonic leadership of Britain and the United States. We also describe the process of catch-up, as these technical developments were copied, first in continental Europe and then in East Asia.

A central task of modern macroeconomics has been to bring these two strands of analysis together. Models that did this can be thought of as coming from the modern DSGE tradition of New Keynesian macroeconomics. DSGE, again, stands for "dynamic stochastic general equilibrium." This mouthful reflects the fact that most modern macroeconomics concerns dynamics—the movement of the economy over time and into the future—rather than being about the kind of static changes studied in simple IS-LM systems. The term "stochastic" implies that these models study the effects of shocks. The "general equilibrium" reflects the idea that everything depends on everything else in macroeconomics. We discuss in Chapter 3 how important this insight is to the analysis in the present book.

These DSGE models explicitly brought together models describing short-run macroeconomics (of the kind practiced by inflation-targeting central banks) with models analyzing long-run growth (in which the growth of the supply side of the economy depends on how much of its output the economy saves and devotes the capital accumulation, and on the rate of technical progress). This DSGE tradition, which united the two older traditions, became the dominant way of thinking about macroeconomics in the period of the Great Moderation before the Global Financial Crisis.

A central feature of the period of the Great Moderation, at least up to 2004, was the high level of world savings relative to world investment, which led, ex post, to a low level of the riskless worldwide interest rate to encourage investment to make use of the savings. To understand why this happened, New Keynesian macroeconomics examined the kind of decisions that underpin the IS curve in the IS-LM model. This New Keynesian analysis suggested that forward-looking consumers and firms will go behind the kind of static features identified in the IS curve: they will relate their decisions to a longer term set of economic forces. At any point in time, the riskless rate of interest depends on the longer term forces that determine the demand for investment. If firms are pessimistic about the long-run growth prospect of the economy—and their expected rate of technical advance falters—then they will wish to invest less, which will tend to drive down the rate of interest. Similarly, if savings are high, this will tend to drive down the rate of interest. We show in Chapter 6 why these features led to a low rate of interest in the period after the East Asian crisis. DSGE models were helpful in understanding this process.[7]

During the Great Moderation, it appeared that this set of economic models was useful in guiding policymakers. At that time, many applications of the theory came to reflect this self-confidence. For example, Kapadia showed how, after any supply-side shock hits the economy, the more the private sector believed that the inflation target will be achieved, the easier it would be for monetary policymakers to achieve it. And there was some hubris. Blanchard wrote that "the state of macro is good . . . . The battles of yesteryear . . . are over, and there has been . . . a broad convergence of vision."[8]

But these DSGE models entirely abstracted from difficulties in the financial sector. This abstraction turns out to have been extremely misleading. Financial intermediation in DSGE models is essentially costless and can provide no impediment to the functioning of the economy. A competitive financial system—the banking system—drives risk premiums down to low levels, so that effectively, all short-term interest rates, including those on private debt, are set by the central bank. In versions of these DSGE models containing long-dated assets, the price of these assets is set by an intertemporal arbitrage condition, so that the return on them is equal to the return that would be earned by holding a succession of short-term assets. As a result, the policymaker who sets the short-term interest rate effectively sets the long-term interest rate as well.[9]

Reality proved to be very different. During the Great Moderation, forces related to the high levels of savings led to low interest rates and large amounts of borrowing by the private sector. These low interest rates then triggered a search for improved yields by financial institutions and resulted in high levels of leverage. Models of the DSGE kind assumed that these borrowings would be repaid and that leverage would be gradually unwound. Even models that included financial frictions and contained financial-accelerator features saw little disturbance coming from this quarter. We now know that this leverage undermined the hard-won stability of the Great Moderation. Suddenly, leverage came to seem very risky; interest rates on long-term borrowing rose, and leveraged financial institutions were unable to borrow from one another. The crisis that ensued was not predicted by DSGE models and is hard to display in such models.[10]

In international versions of these DSGE models, the exchange rate is either fixed or floating. In the latter case, it is determined by an international arbitrage condition. Exchange rates move to ensure that expected returns across countries come to be equalized; in particular, exchange rates move to bring about international levels of competitiveness that ensure that international borrowing will be repaid. In the former case, these models assume that wage and price adjustments will bring about the required changes in competitiveness. We now know that in the part of the world with fixed exchange rates—within Europe and between East Asia and the rest of the world—difficulties of adjusting international competitiveness and correcting international indebtedness have undermined the stability of the Great Moderation. We focus on these difficulties in Chapters 5 and 6. DSGE models have not been greatly helpful in understanding the resulting problems.

Attempts to apply DSGE models to the analysis of major depressions have led typically to the conclusion that falls in output come about from unexplained negative technology shocks. In this book, we instead focus on shocks to the international economy that lead to falls in aggregate demand, rather than on changes in underlying technology. This view has received support from an examination of local spending in recent years.[11]

The difficulty with the DSGE tradition stems from the assumption in these models that what is likely to happen in the future is properly understood in the present, that consumers and firms act optimally in light of this understanding, and that governments can devise optimal policies based on this understanding of what is happening. The possibility of crisis renders this assumption unsatisfactory. In particular, consumers and firms may add risk premiums into the price of financial assets, and they may hold back from decisions to spend, if it appears that crisis is possible. They may thereby precipitate crises through self-perpetuating falls in demand in ways that DSGE models find hard to capture.

In this book, we focus on features of the international economy that are likely to give rise to crisis—in particular, the accumulation of foreign debt—in situations where the repayment of that debt may become difficult. We focus on policies that are designed to make the possibility of crisis less likely. The DSGE framework is not yet able to help greatly with that analysis.

ONE The World Economy Is Broken

1. Kindleberger (1986) first popularized the term "hegemon" as applied to economic events. It has been taken up by many others, including Eichengreen (1992), Berenskoetter and Williams (2007), Ahrari (2012), and Williams et al. (2012).

2. Orwell (1958), p. 59.

3. Wolf (2011).

4. Hume (1752), part II, "Of the Balance of Trade."

5. Meade (1951); Swan (1955).

6. Reinhart and Rogoff (2009).

7. Koo (2008).

8. Keynes (1930), vol. 6, pp. 306–307.

9. Marx (1852), p. 1.

TWO The British Century and the Great Depression

1. Dickson (1967); Brewer (1989); O'Brien (2003).

2. Allen (2009).

3. Mokyr (2009), p. 15.

4. Keynes (1930), pp. 306–307.

5. Imlah (1958), p. 75.

6. Kindleberger (1964).

7. Ferguson (1999).

8. Carr (1966), p. 53.

9. Harrod (1972), chapter 6; Skidelsky (1983), chapter 15.

10. Keynes (1919), p. 118.

11. Ibid., p. 142.

12. Ibid., p. 157.

13. Berger (2004), pp. 118–124; Kitchen (2006), p. 223.

14. Great Britain (1918), p. 5.

15. Forsyth (1993), p. 238.

16. Schuker (1976).
17. Feldman (1997); Widdig (2001).
18. Feinstein et al. (2008), pp. 60–63.
19. Crafts et al. (1989).
20. Clark (1987); Saxonhouse and Wright (2010).
21. Temin (1989); Eichengreen and Temin (2000).
22. Mouré (1991), pp. 55–56.
23. Nurkse (1944), pp. 73–75.
24. Irwin (2010).
25. Lewis (1949); Temin (1971); Falkus (1975); Balderston (1983); McNeil (1986); Sommariva and Tullio (1986).
26. Borchardt (1979); Balderston (1983).
27. Kindleberger (1986), pp. 295–297; Eichengreen (1992).
28. Ferguson and Temin (2003).
29. Young Plan bonds were traded widely, but the most complete series is for Paris.
30. Temin (2008a).
31. Eichengreen and Temin (2000, 2010).
32. Accominotti (2012).
33. Sayers (1976), pp. 390–391.
34. Hawtrey (1938), p. 145.
35. Hoover (1951–52), vol. 3, p. 30.
36. Mouré (1991), p. 33.
37. Friedman and Schwartz (1963), p. 317.
38. Warren (1959), p. 280.
39. Blackett (1932), p. 71.
40. Grossman (1994).
41. Orwell (1958), p. 95; Feinstein et al. (2008), pp. 115–116
42. Rothermund (1996).
43. Temin and Wigmore (1990); Eggertsson (2008).
44. League of Nations (1933), p. 193–194.
45. Hamilton (1982); Childers (1983).
46. Tooze (2006).
47. Larson (2011).
48. Temin (1989, 2010).
49. Irwin (2011).

THREE Keynes from the Macmillan Committee to Bretton Woods

1. Quoted in Howson and Moggridge (1990), p. 158.
2. Keynes (1936), p. 383.
3. Keynes (1922).
4. Keynes (1923); *The Economic Consequences of Mr Churchill* and *Can Lloyd George Do It?* can be found in Keynes (1972); Harrod (1972), pp. 445–453.

5. Harrod (1972); Moggridge (1976, 1992); Skidelsky (1983, 1992, 2000).

6. Skidelsky (2000), chapter 13, pp. 498–507. See Harrod (1960), p. 68, who supports this view, and Vines (2003).

7. Keynes (1981), p. 17.

8. H. M. Treasury (1931).

9. Hayek (1952), p. 196.

10. Russell (1967), p. 72.

11. Keynes (1981).

12. Schumpeter (1946), p. 501.

13. Keynes (1919), pp. 15, 143.

14. Keynes (1981), p. 39.

15. Keynes (1981), pp. 39–42, 49, 53.

16. Ibid., pp. 50–66.

17. H. M. Treasury (1931), p. 3339.

18. Boyle (1967), p. 258.

19. This quotation and the ones from Keynes that follow are from Keynes (1981), Chapter 2, pp. 76, 77.

20. Keynes (1981), p. 93.

21. Harrod (1972), p. 495.

22. Skidelsky (1992), p. 358.

23. Harrod (1972), p. 497.

24. Skidelsky (1992), p. 361.

25. Keynes (1973), p. 338.

26. Ibid., p. 339.

27. Keynes (1973), p. 340.

28. Kahn (1931).

29. Vines (2008).

30. Kahn (1984).

31. Keynes (1973), pp. 527–562.

32. Ibid.

33. Vines (2008).

34. Skidelsky (2000), p. 20.

35. Keynes (1940); Harrod (1972), chapter 12; Skidelsky (2000), part 1.

36. Lukacs (2000), p. 100; Skidelsky (2000).

37. Williamson (1983); Skidelsky (2000); Harrod (1972); Vines (2003); House et al. (2008).

38. Keynes (1980a), pp. 41–67; Keynes (1980b); van Dormael (1978); Gardner (1956); Skidelsky (2000); Harrod (1972); Vines (2003).

39. Nurkse (1947).

40. Keynes (1980a), pp. 1–67.

41. Skidelsky (2000), chapter 4, especially p. 133.

42. Keynes (1980a); Skidelsky (2000), part 2; Harrod (1972), chapters 12 and 13.

43. Keynes (1980a), chapter 1, especially pp. 31, 98.
44. Ibid., pp. 23, 32.
45. Skidelsky (2000), especially pp. 236–238.
46. Vines (2008).
47. Swan (1955); Meade (1951); Buiter and Marsten (1984); Cooper (1985); Howson and Moggridge (1990); Vines (2008).
48. Vines (2003).
49. Ibid.; House et al. (2008).
50. Keynes (1980a), p. 216; Harrod (1972), pp. 747–749.

FOUR The American Century and the Global Financial Crisis

1. McCullough (1992), pp. 564–565.
2. Davis (1983); Axelrod (2006).
3. Keynes (1919), section 7.3; quote on p. 180.
4. House et al. (2008); Machlup (1964a,b).
5. Harrod (1972), p. 639.
6. Matthews et al. (1982); Matthews and Bowen (1988); Temin (2002); Eichengreen (1995); Eichengreen (2007).
7. Maddison (2007), p. 381.
8. Temin (1969).
9. Kazin (2006), p. 61; Friedman and Schwartz (1963), pp. 7, 58–61; Officer (1981).
10. Chandler (1977).
11. Carter et al. (2006), series Ee12; Engerman and Gallman (1996).
12. Nelson and Wright (1992).
13. Bordo et al. (1999); Temin (1989); Obstfeld and Taylor (2004).
14. Feinstein et al. (2008), p. 10.
15. Temin (1966).
16. Irwin (1998).
17. Denison (1967). See also Broadberry (1997).
18. Eichengreen and Ritschl (2009).
19. Gordon (2000); Field (2011).
20. Atkinson and Piketty (2007).
21. Eichengreen (2006).
22. Temin and Wigmore (1990); Eggertsson (2008).
23. Gross (1974).
24. Freeman (1998).
25. Koistinen (2004).
26. Lichtenstein (1995).
27. United Auto Workers press release, quoted in Lichtenstein (1995), p. 279.
28. Lichtenstein (1995), p. 279. See also Amberg (1994); Lichtenstein (1987).
29. Brody (1980); Kochan (1980); Weinstein and Kochan (1995).
30. Stein (2010).
31. Carter (1978); Cowan (1978); Stein (2010).

32. Haskel et al. (2012).

33. Blair (1989); Jensen (1997); Blair and Shary (1993); Holmström and Kaplan (2001); Philippon (2008); Wigmore 1997; Levy and Temin (2007); Stiglitz (2012).

34. Lewis (1989), p. 126.

35. Jensen (1997).

36. Friedman and Friedman (1980).

37. Levy and Temin (2007).

38. Autor et al. (2012).

39. See the Appendix for more details.

40. Friedman and Friedman (1980); Brewer (1989).

41. Kane (1989); White (1991).

42. Morris (2008).

43. Fisher (1933).

44. Goldin (2001); Goldin and Katz (2008).

45. Darling-Hammond (2010), chapter 1.

46. Blanchard and Milesi-Ferretti (2009).

47. Chinn and Frieden (2011).

48. Coval et al. (2009); Benmelech and Dlugosz (2009).

49. Reinhart (2011).

50. Morgenson (2012a,b); Stiglitz (2012), pp. 191–202.

51. Koppell (2003).

52. Hall (2010); Krugman (2012).

FIVE Restoring International Balance in Europe

1. EUROPA (1950).

2. Temin (2002).

3. These features were identified by Corden (1993).

4. Williamson (1977).

5. Fleming (1962); Mundell (1963).

6. European Commission (2011).

7. Alesina et al. (2001).

8. European Commission (1992).

9. European Commission (1997).

10. Issing (2002). See also Issing (2006).

11. This criticism of the Stability and Growth Pact was elaborated in Britain; see H. M. Treasury (2003); Westaway (2003); Allsopp and Vines (2007, 2010).

12. European Commission (2008), p. 6; Sapir (2011).

13. European Commission (2006).

14. Krugman (2011c).

15. This criticism is developed in Allsopp and Vines (2007, 2010).

16. Miller and Sutherland (1990); Allsop and Vines (2007, 2010).

17. Mundell (1961); Kenen (1969).

18. Jaeger and Schuhknecht (2004); Martinez-Mongay et al. (2007).

19. Keynes (1980a); Soros (2012).
20. Kirsanova et al. (2007); Allsopp and Vines (2007, 2010); Vines (2011a).
21. Soros (2012).
22. Vines (2011a).

SIX Restoring International Balance in the World

1. Bluestein (2001); Corbett and Vines (1999a,b); Corbett et al. (1999); Vines and Warr (2003).
2. Chung and Eichengreen (2003).
3. Irwin and Vines (2003).
4. House et al. (2008); Lane et al. (1999); IMF (2003); Fischer (2004); Boorman et al. (2000); Corden (2007).
5. Stiglitz (2002).
6. IMF (2003), p. 115.
7. Krueger (2002).
8. House et al. (2008).
9. Lin (2004).
10. Adam and Vines (2009); Eichengreen (2004); Portes (2009); Prasad (2009); Wei and Zhang (2009); Caballero et al. (2008); Mendoza et al. (2007); Aizenman et al. (2004); Dooley et al. (2004a,b).
11. The difference actually is a bit more subtle. The ECB can set the interest rate, but it also has another policy aim, as noted in Chapter 5. The interest rate cannot be used to allocate spending within EMU.
12. Blanchard and Milesi-Ferretti (2011). We follow their approach in the following paragraphs. For simplicity, they assume that interest rates are the same everywhere, but we do not need to do this.
13. Taylor (2008).
14. The reasoning is an extension of the Mundell-Fleming model of the 1960s discussed in Chapter 5, for which Robert Mundell won the Nobel Prize in 1999. Fleming (1962); Mundell (1963); Dornbusch (1976).
15. Corden (1994).
16. Oudiz and Sachs (1984) is the most famous paper from that brief interlude.
17. Kane (forthcoming).
18. Eichengreen (2011).
19. Eichengreen and O'Rourke (2010); Adam and Vines (2009).
20. Blanchard and Milesi-Ferretti (2011).
21. Koo (2008); *The Economist* (2012).
22. Altshuler and Bosworth (2010).
23. IMF (2010a).
24. Krugman (2010).
25. Yu (2009, 2011).
26. Huang and Wang (2010).
27. Blanchard and Milesi-Ferretti (2009); IMF (2012).

28. Ma et al. (2012); Yu (2009, 2011).
29. Obstfeld and Rogoff (2009).
30. Rabinovitch (2012).
31. Spence (2011).
32. Vines (2011b).
33. IMF (2010b, 2011c, 2012).

SEVEN Using Theory to Learn from History

1. IMF (2011a); G24 (2011); Qureshi (2011); Brown (2010).
2. IMF (2011a,b).
3. Erlanger and Kulish (2011).
4. Fischer (2011).
5. Garnaut and Llewellyn Smith (2009), pp. 182–183; Garnaut (2010); Ma et al. (2012).

APPENDIX

1. Keynes (1973), p. 342; Meade (1937); Hicks (1937); Young (1987); Vines (2008).
2. Vines (2008, 2011b).
3. Swan (1955).
4. Davis (1983); Axelrod (2006).
5. Woodford (2003).
6. Solow (1956).
7. Bernanke (2005).
8. Kapadia (2005); Blanchard (2008), p. 1.
9. Blanchard et al. (2010).
10. Bernanke et al. (1999).
11. Kehoe and Prescott (2007); Temin (2008b); Mian and Sufi (2012).

REFERENCES

All citations to Keynes are from *The Collected Writings of John Maynard Keynes*, edited by Donald E. Moggridge (London: Macmillan, 1971–86). The original date of publication is given, and the references supply the volume numbers.

Accominotti, Olivier (2012) "London Merchant Banks, the Central European Panic, and the Sterling Crisis of 1931," *Journal of Economic History*, Vol. 72, No. 1, pp. 1–43.

Adam, Christopher, and David Vines (2009) "Remaking Macroeconomic Policy after the Global Financial Crisis: A Balance-Sheet Approach," *Oxford Review of Economic Policy*, Vol. 25, No. 4, pp. 507–552.

Ahrari, Mohammed (2012) *The Great Powers versus the Hegemon*. New York: Palgrave Macmillan.

Aizenman, J., B. Pinto, and A. Radziwill (2004) "Sources for Financing Domestic Capital—Is Foreign Saving a Viable Option for Developing Countries?" NBER Working Paper 10624. Cambridge, MA: National Bureau of Economic Research.

Alesina, A., O. Blanchard, J. Gali, F. Giavazzi, and H. Uhlig (2001) *Defining a Macroeconomic Framework for the Euro Area*. London: Centre for Economic Policy Research.

Allen, Robert C. (2009) *The British Industrialization in Global Perspective*. Cambridge: Cambridge University Press.

Allsopp, Christopher, and David Vines (2007) "Fiscal Policy, Labour Markets, and the Difficulties of Intercountry Adjustment within EMU," in David Cobham (ed.), *The Travails of the Eurozone*. London: Palgrave-Macmillan, pp. 95–119.

——— (2010) "Fiscal Policy, Intercountry Adjustment and the Real Exchange Rate," in Marco Buti, Servaas Deroose, Vitor Gaspar, and João Nogueira Martins (eds.), *The Euro: The First Decade*. Cambridge: Cambridge University Press, pp. 511–551. Initially published in European Commission (2008) "EMU@10: Successes and Challenges after Ten Years of Economic and Monetary Union," *European Economy*. Available at http://ec.europa.eu/economy_finance/publications/publication12682_en.pdf.

Altshuler, Rosanne, and Barry Bosworth (2010) "Fiscal Consolidation in America: The Policy Options," paper presented at the Macro Economy Research Conference on Fiscal Policy in the Post-Crisis World, Tokyo, November 16.

Amberg, Stephen (1994) *The Union Inspiration in American Politics*. Philadelphia: Temple University Press.

Atkinson, Anthony B., and Thomas Piketty (2007) *Top Incomes over the Twentieth Century: A Contrast between Continental European and English-Speaking Countries*. Oxford: Oxford University Press.

Autor, David H., David Dorn, and Gordon H. Hanson (2012) "The China Syndrome: Local Labor Effects of Import Competition in the United States," Massachusetts Institute of Technology, Economics Department working paper, May.

Axelrod, Robert (2006) *The Evolution of Cooperation*. New York: Basic Books.

Balderston, Theodore (1983) "The Beginning of the Depression in Germany, 1927–30: Investment and the Capital Market," *Economic History Review*, Vol. 36, pp. 395–415.

Benmelech, Efriam, and Jennifer Dlugosz (2009) "The Alchemy of CDOs' Credit Ratings," *Journal of Monetary Economics*, Vol. 56, No. 5, pp. 617–634.

Berenskoetter, Felix, and M. J. Williams (eds.) (2007) *Power in World Politics*. London: Routledge.

Berger, Stefan (2004) *Germany*. London: Arnold.

Bernanke, Ben S. (2005)"The Global Saving Glut and the U.S. Current Account Deficit," Sandridge Lecture to the Association of Economics, Richmond, Virginia, March 10. Available at http://www.federalreserve.gov/boarddocs/speeches/2005/200503102/.

Bernanke, Ben S., Mark Gertler, and Simon Gilchrist (1999) "The Financial Accelerator in a Quantitative Business Cycle Framework," J. B. Taylor and M. Woodford (eds.), *Handbook of Macroeconomics*, Vol. 1. Amsterdam: Elsevier, pp. 1341–1393.

Blackett, Basil P. (1932) *Planned Money*. London: Constable.

Blair, Margaret M. (1989) "Theory and Evidence on the Causes of Merger Waves," PhD dissertation, Yale University, New Haven, CT.

Blair, Margaret M., and Martha A. Shary (1993) "Industry-Level Pressures to Restructure," in Margaret M. Blair (ed.), *The Deal Decade*. Washington, DC: Brookings Institution Press, pp. 149–191.

Blanchard, Olivier (2008) "The State of Macro," NBER Working Paper 14259. Cambridge, MA: National Bureau of Economic Research.

Blanchard, Olivier, and Gian Maria Milesi-Ferretti (2009) "Global Imbalances—in Midstream?" IMF Staff Position Note SPN/09/29. Washington, DC: International Monetary Fund.

——— (2011) "(Why) Should Current Account Imbalances be Reduced?" IMF Staff Discussion Note SDN/11/03. Washington, DC: International Monetary Fund.

Blanchard, Olivier, Giovanni Dell'Ariccia, and Paolo Mauro (2010) "Rethinking Macroeconomic Policy," IMF Staff Position Note SPN/10/03. Washington, DC: International Monetary Fund.

Bluestein, Paul (2001) *The Chastening: Inside the Crisis That Rocked the Global Financial System and Humbled the IMF*. Cambridge, MA: Public Affairs.

Boorman, Jack, Timothy Lane, Marianne Schulze-Ghattas, Ales Bulir, Atish Ghosh, Javier Hamann, Alex Mourmouras, and Steven Phillips (2000) "Managing Financial Crises:

The Experience in East Asia," IMF Working Paper 00/107. Washington, DC: International Monetary Fund.

Borchardt, Knut (1979, English translation 1991) "Constraints and Room for Manoeuvre in the Great Depression of the Early Thirties: Towards a Revision of the Received Historical Picture," in Knut Borchardt, *Perspectives on Modern German Economic History and Policy.* Cambridge: Cambridge University Press, pp. 143–160.

Bordo, Michael, Barry Eichengreen, and Douglas Irwin (1999) "Is Globalization Today Really Different from Globalization a Hundred Years Ago?" *Brookings Trade Forum.* Washington, DC: Brookings Institution, pp. 1–50.

Boyle, Andrew (1967) *Montagu Norman.* London: Cassell.

Brewer, John (1989) *The Sinews of Power: Money and the English State, 1688–1783.* London: Unwin Hyman.

Broadberry, Stephen N. (1997) "Anglo-German Productivity Differences, 1870–1990," *European Review of Economic History,* Vol. 1, pp. 247–267.

Brody, David (1980) *Workers in Industrial America.* Oxford: Oxford University Press.

Brown, Gordon (2010) *Beyond the Crash: Overcoming the First Crisis of Globalisation,* London: Simon and Schuster.

Buiter, Willem, and Richard Marsten (1984) *International Policy Coordination.* Cambridge: Cambridge University Press.

Caballero, Ricardo, Emmanuel Farhi, and Pierre-Olivier Gourinchas (2008) "An Equilibrium Model of 'Global Imbalances' and Low Interest Rates," *American Economic Review,* Vol. 98, No. 1, pp. 358–393.

Carr, Edward H. (1966) *International Relations between the Two World Wars, 1919–39.* London: Macmillan. First published in 1937 under the title *International Relations since the Peace Treaties.*

Carter, Jimmy (1978) "Transcript of the President's Address on Inflation," *New York Times,* April 12, 1978.

Carter, Susan B., Scott Gartner, Michael Haines, Alan Olmstead, Richard Sutch, and Gavin Wright (2006) *Historical Statistics of the United States: Earliest Times to the Present.* New York: Cambridge University Press.

Cecchetti, Stephen G. (2009) "Crisis and Responses: The Federal Reserve in the Early Stages of the Financial Crisis," *Journal of Economic Perspectives,* Vol. 23, No. 1, pp. 51–75.

Chandler, Alfred (1977) *The Visible Hand.* Cambridge, MA: Harvard University Press.

Childers, Thomas (1983) *The Nazi Voter: The Social Foundations of Fascism in Germany, 1919–1933.* Chapel Hill: University of North Carolina Press.

Chinn, Menzie D., and Jeffrey A. Frieden (2011) *Lost Decades: The Making of America's Debt Crisis and the Long Recovery.* New York: W. W. Norton.

Chung, Duck-Koo, and Barry Eichengreen (eds.) (2003) *The Korean Economy beyond the Crisis.* Cheltenham: Edward Elgar.

Clark, Gregory (1987) "Why Isn't the Whole World Developed? Lessons from the Cotton Mills," *Journal of Economic History,* Vol. 47, No. 1, pp. 141–173.

Congressional Budget Office (2011) "Trends in the Distribution of Household Income between 1979 and 2007." Washington, DC. Available at http://www.cbo.gov/sites/default/files/cbofiles/attachments/10-25-HouseholdIncome.pdf.

Cooper, Richard (1985) "Economic Interdependence and Coordination of Economic Policies," in R. Jones and P. Kenen (eds.), *Handbook of International Economics*, Vol. 2. Amsterdam: North-Holland, pp. 1195–1234.

Corbett, Jenny, and David Vines (1999a) "Asian Currency and Financial Crises: Lessons from Vulnerability, Crisis, and Collapse," *World Economy*, Vol. 22, No. 2, pp. 155–177.

—— (1999b) "The Asian Financial Crisis: Lessons from the Collapse of Financial Systems, Currencies, and Macroeconomic Policy," in Pierre-Richard Agénor, Marcus Miller, David Vines, and Axel Weber (eds.), *The Asian Financial Crisis. Causes, Contagion and Consequences*. Cambridge: Cambridge University Press, pp. 67–110.

Corbett, Jenny, Gregor Irwin, and David Vines (1999) "From Asian Miracle to Asian Crisis: Why Vulnerability, Why Collapse?" in David Gruen and Luke Gower (eds.), *Capital Flows and the International Financial System*. Sydney: Reserve Bank of Australia, pp. 190–213.

Corden, W. Max (1993) "Why Did the Bretton Woods System Break Down?" in Michael Bordo and Barry Eichengreen (eds.), *A Retrospective on the Bretton Woods System*. Chicago: University of Chicago Press, pp. 504–509.

—— (1994) *Economic Policy, Exchange Rates, and the International System*. Oxford: Oxford University Press.

—— (2007) "The Asian Crisis: a Perspective after Ten Years," *Asian Pacific Economic Literature*, Vol. 21, No. 2, pp. 1–12.

Coval, Joshua, Jakob Jurek, and Erik Stafford (2009) "The Economics of Structured Finance," *Journal of Economic Perspectives*, Vol. 23, No. 1, pp. 3–25.

Cowan, Edward (1978) "Can Kahn Contain Wage-Price Spiral?" *New York Times*, November 12.

Crafts, N.F.R., S. J. Leybourne, and T. C. Mills (1989) "The Climacteric in Late Victorian Britain and France: A Reappraisal of the Evidence," *Journal of Applied Econometrics*, Vol. 4, No. 2, pp. 103–117.

Darling-Hammond, Linda. 2010. *The Flat World and Education: How America's Commitment to Equity Will Determine Our Future*. New York: Teachers College Press.

Davis, Morton (1983) *Game Theory: A Non-Technical Introduction*. New York: Basic Books.

Denison, Edward (1967) *Why Growth Rates Differ*. Washington, DC: Brookings Institution.

Dickson, P.G.M. (1967) *The Financial Revolution in England: A Study in the Development of Public Credit, 1688–1756*. New York: Macmillan, St. Martin's Press.

Dooley, Michael, David Folkerts-Landau, and Peter Garber (2004a) "The Revised Bretton Woods System," *International Journal of Finance and Economics*, Vol. 9, No. 4, pp. 307–313.

—— (2004b) "Direct Investment, Rising Real Wages and the Absorption of Excess Labor in the Periphery," NBER Working Paper 10626. Cambridge, MA: National Bureau of Economic Research.

Dornbusch, Rudiger (1976) "Expectations and Exchange Rate Dynamics," *Journal of Political Economy,* Vol. 84, No. 6, pp. l161–1176.

The Economist (2012). "QE or Not QE?" July 14.

Eggertsson, Gaudi B. (2008) "Great Expectations and the End of the Depression," *American Economic Review,* Vol. 98, No. 4, pp. 1476–1516.

Eichengreen, Barry (1992) *Golden Fetters: The Gold Standard and the Great Depression, 1919–1939.* New York: Oxford University Press.

—— (ed.) (1995) *Europe's Postwar Growth.* New York: Cambridge University Press.

—— (2004) "The Dollar and the New Bretton Woods System," Henry Thornton Lecture, London, December 15. Available at http://emlab.berkeley.edu/~eichengr/policy/cityuniversitylecture2jan3-05.pdf.

—— (2006) "Institutions and Economic Growth in Europe after World War II," in Nicholas Crafts and Gianni Toniolo (eds.), *Economic Growth in Europe since 1945.* Cambridge: Cambridge University Press, pp. 38–72.

—— (2007) *The European Economy since 1945: Coordinated Capitalism and Beyond.* Princeton, NJ: Princeton University Press.

—— (2011) *Exorbitant Privilege: The Rise and Fall of the Dollar and the Future of the International Monetary System.* New York: Oxford University Press.

Eichengreen, Barry, and Kevin O'Rourke (2010) "What Do the New Data Tell Us?" *VoxEU.* Available at http://www.voxeu.org/article/tale-two-depressions-what-do-new-data-tell-us-february-2010-update.

Eichengreen, Barry, and Albrecht Ritschl (2009) "Understanding West German Economic Growth in the 1950s," *Cliometrica,* Vol. 3, No. 3, pp. 191–219.

Eichengreen, Barry, and Peter Temin (2000) "The Gold Standard and the Great Depression," *Contemporary European History,* Vol. 9, No. 2, pp. 183–207.

—— (2010) "Fetters of Gold and Paper," *Oxford Review of Economic Policy,* Vol. 26, No. 3, pp. 370–384.

Engerman, Stanley L., and Robert E. Gallman (eds.). 1996. *The Cambridge Economic History of the United States.* Cambridge: Cambridge University Press.

Erlanger, Steven, and Nicholas Kulish (2011) "German Leader Rules out Rapid Action on the Euro," *New York Times,* November 24.

EUROPA (1950) *The Declaration of 9 May 1950.* Available at http://europa.eu/abc/symbols/9-may/decl_en.htm.

European Commission (1992) Treaty on Monetary Union. Available at http://eur-lex.europa.eu/en/treaties/dat/11992M/htm/11992M.html.

—— (1997) Stability and Growth Pact. Available at http://europa.eu/legislation_summaries/economic_and_monetary_affairs/stability_and_growth_pact/l25021_en.htm.

—— (2006). *The EU Economy: 2006 Review: Adjustment Dynamics in the Euro Area—Experiences and Challenges.* Available at http://ec.europa.eu/economy_finance/publications/publication425_en.pdf.

—— (2008) "EMU@10: Successes and Challenges after Ten Years of Economic and

Monetary Union," *European Economy.* Available at http://ec.europa.eu/economy_finance/publications/publication12682_en.pdf.

European Commission (2011) "European Semester: A New Architecture for the New EU Economic Governance." Available at http://europa.eu/rapid/pressReleasesAction.do?reference=MEMO/11/14.

Falkus, Malcolm E. (1975) "The German Business Cycle in the 1920s," *Economic History Review,* Vol. 28, No. 3, pp. 451–465.

Feinstein, Charles, and Katherine Watson (1995) "Private International Capital Flows in the Inter-War Period," in Charles Feinstein (ed.), *Banking, Currency, and Finance in Europe between the Wars.* Oxford: Oxford University Press, pp. 94–130.

Feinstein, Charles, Peter Temin, and Gianni Toniolo (2008) *The World Economy between the Wars.* Oxford: Oxford University Press.

Feldman, Gerald (1997) *The Great Disorder: Politics, Economics and Society in the German Hyperinflation, 1914–1924.* New York: Oxford University Press.

Ferguson, Niall (1999) *The Pity of War.* New York: Basic Books.

Ferguson, Thomas, and Peter Temin (2003) "Made in Germany: The German Currency Crisis of 1931," *Research in Economic History,* Vol. 21, pp. 1–53.

——— (2004) "Comment on the 'The German Twin Crisis of 1931,'" *Journal of Economic History,* Vol. 64, No. 3, pp. 872–876.

Field, Alexander J. (2011) *A Great Leap Forward: 1930s Depression and U.S. Economic Growth.* New Haven, CT: Yale University Press.

Fischer, Joschka (2011) "The Threat of German Amnesia," *Project Syndicate.* Available at http://www.project-syndicate.org/commentary/the-threat-of-german-amnesia.

Fischer, Stanley (2004) *IMF Essays from a Time of Crisis: The International Financial System, Stabilization, and Development.* Cambridge, MA: MIT Press.

Fisher, Irving (1933) "The Debt-Deflation Theory of Great Depressions," *Econometrica,* Vol. 1, No. 4, pp. 337–357.

Fleming, J. M. (1962) "Domestic Financial Policy under Fixed and Floating Exchange Rates," *IMF Staff Papers,* Vol. 9, pp. 369–379.

Forsyth, Douglas J. (1993) *The Crisis of Liberal Italy: Monetary and Financial Policy, 1914–1922.* Cambridge: Cambridge University Press.

Freeman, Richard B. (1998) "Spurts in Union Growth: Defining Moments and Social Processes," in Michael D. Bordo, Claudia Goldin, and Eugene N. White (eds.), *The Defining Moment: The Great Depression and the American Economy in the Twentieth Century.* Chicago: University of Chicago Press, pp. 265–295.

Friedman, Milton, and Rose Friedman (1980) *Free to Choose.* New York: Harcourt Brace Jovanovich.

Friedman, Milton, and Anna Schwartz (1963) *A Monetary History of the United States, 1860–1963.* Princeton, NJ: Princeton University Press.

G24 (2011) "Issues for Discussion," G24 Technical Group Meeting, Pretoria, South Africa, March 17–18. Available at http://www.g24.org/ino311.pdf.

Gardner, Richard (1956) *Sterling Dollar Diplomacy.* Oxford: Oxford University Press.

Garnaut, Ross (2010) "Macro-economic Implications of the Turning Point," *China Economic Journal*, Vol. 3, No. 2, pp. 181–190.

Garnaut, Ross, and David Llewellyn Smith (2009) *The Great Crash of 2008*. Melbourne: Melbourne University Publishing.

Goldin, Claudia (2001) "The Human-Capital Century and American Leadership Virtues of the Past," *Journal of Economic History*, Vol. 61, No. 2, pp. 263–292.

Goldin, Claudia, and Lawrence F. Katz (2008) *The Race between Education and Technology*. Cambridge, MA: Harvard University Press.

Gordon, Robert J. (2000) "Interpreting the 'One Big Wave' in U.S. Long-Term Productivity Growth," in Bart van Ark, Simon Kuipers, and Gerard Kuper (eds.), *Productivity, Technology, and Economic Growth*. Boston: Kluwer, pp. 19–65.

Great Britain (1918) *First Interim Report of the Commission on Currency and Foreign Exchanges After the War*. Cd. 9182: 1918, Vol. VII, p. 853.

Gross, James A. (1974) *The Making of the National Labor Relations Board*. Albany: State University of New York Press.

Grossman, Richard (1994) "The Shoe That Didn't Drop: Explaining Banking Stability during the Great Depression," *Journal of Economic History*, Vol. 54, No. 3, pp. 654–682.

Hall, Robert E. (2010) "Fiscal Stimulus," *Daedalus*, Vol. 139, No. 4, pp. 83–94.

Hamilton, Richard (1982) *Who Voted for Hitler?* Princeton, NJ: Princeton University Press.

Harrod, Roy (1960) "Keynes, the Economist," in S. Harris (ed.), *The New Economics: Keynes' Influence on Theory and Public Policy*. London: Denis Dobson, pp. 65–72.

—— (1972) *The Life of John Maynard Keynes*. London: Penguin. First published by Macmillan in 1951.

Haskel, Jonathan, Robert Z. Lawrence, Edward E. Leamer, and Matthew J. Slaughter (2012) "Globalization and U.S. Wages: Modifying Classic Theory to Explain Recent Facts," *Journal of Economic Perspectives*, Vol. 26, No. 2, pp. 119–139.

Hawtrey, Ralph G. (1938) *A Century of Bank Rate*. London: Longmans, Green.

Hayek, Friedrich (1952) "Review of R. F. Harrod, *The Life of John Maynard Keynes*," *Journal of Modern History*, Vol. 24, No. 2, pp. 195–198.

H. M. Treasury (1931) *Report of the Committee on Finance and Industry* [Macmillan Committee]. Cmd 2897. Minutes of Evidence, 2 vols.

—— (2003) "Fiscal Stabilisation and EMU: A Discussion Paper." London. Available at http://www4.fe.uc.pt/jasa/m_i_2010_2011/fiscalstabilizationandemu_section234_and_567.pdf.

Hicks, John (1937) "Mr. Keynes and the 'Classics'; A Suggested Interpretation," *Econometrica*, Vol. 5, No. 2, pp. 147–159.

Holmström, Bengt, and Steven N. Kaplan (2001) "Corporate Governance and Merger Activity in the United States: Making Sense of the 1980s and 1990s," *Journal of Economic Perspectives*, Vol. 15, No. 2, pp. 121–144.

Hoover, Herbert (1951–52) *The Memoirs of Herbert Hoover: The Great Depression, 1929–1941*. New York: Macmillan.

House, Brett, David Vines, and W. Max Corden (2008) "The International Monetary Fund," in Steven Durlauf and Lawrence Blume (eds.), *New Palgrave Dictionary of Economics,* Second Edition, Vol. 4. London: Macmillan, pp. 463–479.

Howson, Sue, and Donald Moggridge (1990) *The Wartime Diaries of Lionel Robbins and James Meade, 1943–1945.* London: Macmillan.

Huang, Yiping, and Bijun Wang (2010) "Cost Distortions and Structural Imbalances in China," *China and the World Economy,* Vol. 18, No. 4, pp. 1–17.

Hume, David (1752) *Essays Moral, Political and Literary.* London.

Imlah, Albert H. (1958) *Economic Elements in the Pax Britannica: Studies in British Foreign Trade in the Nineteenth Century.* Cambridge: Harvard University Press.

IMF (International Monetary Fund) (2003) "The IMF and Recent Capital Account Crises: Indonesia, Korea, Brazil," Report of the Independent Evaluation Office of the IMF. Washington, DC. Available at http://www.imf.org/external/np/ieo/2003/cac/pdf/main.pdf.

—— (2010a) "Strategies for Fiscal Consolidation in the Post-Crisis World," paper prepared by the Fiscal Affairs Department. Washington, DC. Available at http://www .imf.org/external/np/pp/eng/2010/020410a.pdf.

—— (2010b) "World Economic Outlook." Washington, DC. Available at http://www .imf.org/external/pubs/ft/weo/2010/01/index.htm.

—— (2011a) "The G-20 Mutual Assessment Process (MAP)," International Monetary Fund Factsheet. Washington, DC. Available at http://www.imf.org/external/np/exr/ facts/g20map.htm.

—— (2011b) *IMF Staff Reports for the G-20 Mutual Assessment Process.* Washington, DC. Available at http://www.imf.org/external/np/g20/pdf/110411.pdf.

—— (2011c) "World Economic Outlook." Washington, DC. Available at http://www .imf.org/external/pubs/ft/weo/2011/01/index.htm.

—— (2012) "World Economic Outlook." Washington, DC. Available at http://www.imf .org/external/pubs/ft/weo/2012/01/index.htm.

Irwin, Douglas (1998) "From Smoot-Hawley to Reciprocal Trade Agreements: Changing the Course of U.S. Trade Policy in the 1930s," in Michael Bordo, Claudia Goldin, and Eugene White (eds.), *The Defining Moment: The Great Depression and the American Economy.* Chicago: University of Chicago Press, pp. 325–352.

—— (2010) "Did France Cause the Great Depression?" NBER Working Paper 16350. Cambridge, MA: National Bureau of Economic Research.

—— (2011) "Gold Sterilization and the Recession of 1937–38," NBER Working Paper 17595. Cambridge, MA: National Bureau of Economic Research.

Irwin, Gregor, and David Vines (2003) "Government Guarantees, Investment, and Vulnerability to Financial Crises," *Review of International Economics,* Vol. 11, No. 5, pp. 860–874.

Issing, Otmar (2002) "On Macroeconomic Policy Coordination in EMU," *Journal of Common Market Studies,* Vol. 40, No 2, pp. 345–358.

—— (2006) "The Euro: A Currency without a State," BIS Review 23/2006. Basel: Bank for International Settlement.

Jaeger, Albert, and Ludger Schuhknecht (2004) "Boom-Bust Phases in Asset Prices and Fiscal Policy Behavior," Working Paper 04/54. Washington, DC: International Monetary Fund.

Jensen, Michael C. (1997) "Eclipse of the Public Corporation" (revised version). Available at http://papers.ssrn.com/abstract=146149. Paper originally published in *Harvard Business Review*, September–October 1989.

Kahn, Richard (1931) "The Relation of Home Investment to Unemployment," *Economic Journal*, Vol. 41, No. 162, pp. 173–198.

—— (1984) *The Making of Keynes' General Theory*. Cambridge: Cambridge University Press.

Kane, Edward J. (1989) *The S&L Mess: How Did It Happen?* Washington, DC: Urban Institute.

—— (forthcoming) "Bankers and Brokers First: Loose Ends in the Theory of Central Bank Policy Making," in Doug Evanoff (ed.), *The Role of Central Banks in Financial Stability: How Has It Changed?* Singapore: World Scientific.

Kapadia, Sujit (2005) "Inflation-Target Expectations and Optimal Monetary Policy," Economics Series Working Paper 227. Oxford: University of Oxford, Department of Economics.

Kazin, Michael (2006) *A Godly Hero: The Life of William Jennings Bryan*. New York: Knopf.

Kehoe, Timothy J., and Edward C. Prescott (2007) *Great Depressions of the Twentieth Century*. Minneapolis, MN: Federal Reserve Bank of Minneapolis, Research Department.

Kenen, Peter (1969) "The Theory of Optimum Currency Areas: An Eclectic View," in Robert Mundell and Alexander Swoboda (eds.), *Monetary Problems in the International Economy*. University of Chicago Press, Chicago, pp. 41–60.

Keynes, John Maynard (1919) *The Economic Consequences of the Peace. Collected Writings of J. M. Keynes*, Vol. II.

—— (1922) *A Revision of the Treaty. Collected Writings of J. M. Keynes*, Vol. III.

—— (1923) *A Tract on Monetary Reform. Collected Writings of J. M. Keynes*, Vol. IV.

—— (1930) *A Treatise on Money, Volumes 1 and 2. Collected Writings of J. M. Keynes*, Vols. V and VI.

—— (1936) *The General Theory of Employment, Interest and Money Collected Writings of J. M. Keynes*, Vol. VII.

—— (1940) *How to Pay for the War. Collected Writings of J. M. Keynes*, Vol. IX.

—— (1972) *Essays in Persuasion. Collected Writings of J. M. Keynes*, Vol. IX.

—— (1973) *The General Theory and After: Part I, Preparation, Collected Writings of J. M. Keynes*, Vol. XIII.

—— (1980a) *Activities 1940–1944 Shaping the Post War World: The Clearing Union. Collected Writings of J. M. Keynes*, Vol. XXV.

—— (1980b) *Activities 1941–1946 Shaping the Post War World: The Clearing Union. Collected Writings of J. M. Keynes*, Vol. XXVI.

—— (1981) *Activities 1929–1931: Rethinking Employment and Unemployment Policy. Collected Writings of J. M. Keynes*, Vol. XX.

Kindleberger, Charles P. (1964) *Economic Growth in France and Britain.* Cambridge, MA: Harvard University Press.

—— (1986) *The World in Depression, 1919–1939,* Second Edition. London: Allen Lane. First edition published in 1973.

Kirsanova, T., M. Satchi, D. Vines, and S. Wren-Lewis (2007) "Optimal Fiscal Policy Rules in a Monetary Union," *Journal of Money, Credit and Banking,* Vol. 39, No. 7, pp. 1759–1784.

Kitchen, Martin. 2006. *A History of Modern Germany.* Oxford: Blackwell.

Kochan, Thomas A. (1980) *Collective Bargaining and Industrial Relations.* Homewood, IL: Irwin.

Koistinen, Paul A. C. (2004) *Arsenal of World War II: The Political Economy of American Warfare, 1940–1945.* Lawrence: University Press of Kansas.

Koo, Richard (2008) *The Holy Grail of Macroeconomics: Lessons from Japan's Great Recession.* Singapore: Wiley.

Koppell, Jonathan (2003) *The Politics of Quasi-Government: Hybrid Organizations and the Dynamics of Bureaucratic Control.* Cambridge: Cambridge University Press.

Krueger, Anne (2002) A *New Approach to Sovereign Debt Restructuring.* Washington, DC: International Monetary Fund. Available at www.imf.orghttp://www.imf.org/external/pubs/ft/exrp/sdrm/eng/sdrm.pdf.

Krugman, Paul (2010) "1938 in 2010," *New York Times,* September 5.

—— (2011a) "Inequality Trends in One Picture," *The Conscience of a Liberal,* November 3. Available at krugman.blogs.nytimes.com.

—— (2011b) "Wishful Thinking and the Road to Eurogeddon," *The Conscience of a Liberal,* November 7. Available at krugman.blogs.nytimes.com.

—— (2011c) "Mysterious Europe," *New York Times,* November 26.

—— (2012) *End This Depression Now!* New York: W. W. Norton.

Lane, Timothy, Atish Ghosh, Javier Hamann, Steven Phillips, Marianne Schulze-Ghattas, and Tsidi Tsikata (1999) "IMF-Supported Programs in Indonesia, Korea and Thailand: A Preliminary Assessment," IMF Occasional Paper 178. Washington, DC: International Monetary Fund.

Larson, Eric (2011) *In the Garden of Beasts: Love, Terror, and an American Family in Hitler's Berlin.* New York: Crown.

League of Nations (1933) *World Economic Survey 1932/33.* Geneva: League of Nations.

Levy, Frank, and Peter Temin (2007) "Inequality and Institutions in 20th Century America," NBER Working Paper 13106. Cambridge, MA: National Bureau of Economic Research.

Lewis, Michael (1989) *Liar's Poker: Rising through the Wreckage on Wall Street.* New York: W. W. Norton.

Lewis, W. Arthur (1949) *Economic Survey.* London: Allen and Unwin.

Lichtenstein, Nelson (1987) "Reutherism on the Shop Floor: Union Strategy and Shop-Floor Conflict in the USA 1946–1970," in Steven Tolliday and Jonathan Zeitlin (eds.), *The Automobile Industry and Its Workers: Between Fordism and Flexibility.* New York: St. Martin's Press, pp. 121–143.

———— (1995) *Walter Reuther: The Most Dangerous Man in Detroit.* Urbana and Chicago: University of Illinois Press.

Lin, Justin (2004) "Is China's Growth Real and Sustainable?" mimeo, China Centre for Economics Research, Peking University. Available at http://en.ccer.edu.cn/download/3024-1.pdf.

Lukacs, John (2000) *Five Days in London, May 1940.* New Haven, CT: Yale University Press.

Ma, Guonan, Robert McCauley, and Lillie Lam (2012) "Narrowing China's Current Account Surplus: The Role of Saving, Investment and the Renminbi," in Huw McKay and Ligang Song (eds.), *Rebalancing and Sustaining Growth in China.* Canberra and Beijing: Australian National University E Press and Social Sciences Academic Press, pp. 65–91.

Machlup, Fritz (1964a) *International Monetary Arrangements: The Problem of Choice.* Princeton, NJ: Princeton University, International Finance Section.

———— (1964b) "Plans for Reform of the International Monetary System," Special Papers in International Economics No. 3. Princeton, NJ: Princeton University, International Finance Section.

Maddison, Angus (2007) *Contours of the World Economy, 1–2003 AD.* Oxford: Oxford University Press.

Martinez-Mongay, Carlos, Luis-Angel Maza Lasierra, and Javier Yaniz Igal (2007) "Asset Booms and Tax Receipts: The Case of Spain, 1995–2006," Occasional Papers 293. Brussels: European Commission Directorate General for Economics and Financial Affairs.

Marx, Karl (1852) *The Eighteenth Brumaire of Louis Bonaparte.* New York: International.

Matthews, R.C.O., and A. Bowen (1988) "Keynesian and Other Explanations of Postwar Macroeconomic Trends," in W. A. Eltis and P.J.N. Sinclair (eds.), *Keynes and Economic Policy.* London: National Economic Development Office, pp. 354–388.

Matthews, Robin, Charles Feinstein, and John Odling-Smee (1982) *British Economic Growth, 1856–1973.* Oxford: Oxford University Press.

McCullough, David G. 1992. *Truman.* New York: Simon and Schuster.

McNeil, William C. (1986) *American Money and the Weimar Republic.* New York: Columbia University Press.

Meade, J. E. (1937) "A Simplified Model of Mr. Keynes' System," *Review of Economic Studies,* Vol. 4, No. 2, pp. 98–107.

———— (1951) *The Theory of International Economic Policy,* Vol. 1: *The Balance of Payments.* London and New York: Oxford University Press.

Mendoza, Enrique, Vincenzo Quadrini, and José Ríos-Rull (2007) "Financial Integration, Financial Deepness, and Global Imbalances," CEPR Discussion Paper 6149. London: Centre for Economic Policy Research.

Mian, Atif R., and Amir Sufi (2012) "What Explains High Unemployment? The Aggregate Demand Channel," NBER Working Paper 17830. Cambridge, MA: National Bureau of Economic Research.

Miller, Marcus, and Alan Sutherland (1990) "The 'Walters Critique' of the EMS: A Case of Inconsistent Expectations," CEPR Discussion Paper 480. London: Centre for Economic Policy Research.

Moggridge, Donald (1976) *Keynes*. London: Fontana.

——— (1992) *Maynard Keynes: An Economist's Biography.* London: Routledge

Mokyr, Joel (2009) *The Enlightened Economy: An Economic History of Britain, 1700–1850.* New Haven, CT: Yale University Press.

Morgenson, Gretchen (2012a) "Company Faces Forgery Charges in Mo. Foreclosures," *New York Times*, February 6.

——— (2012b) "Audit Uncovers Extensive Flaws in Foreclosures," *New York Times*, February 15.

Morris, Charles R. (2008) *Two Trillion Dollar Meltdown*. New York: Public Affairs.

Mouré, Kenneth (1991) *Managing the franc Poincaré: Economic Understanding and Political Constraint in French Monetary Policy, 1928–1936.* Cambridge: Cambridge University Press.

Mundell, Robert (1961) "A Theory of Optimum Currency Areas," *American Economic Review*, Vol. 51, No. 4, pp. 657–665.

——— (1963) "Capital Mobility and Stabilization Policy under Fixed and Flexible Exchange Rates," *Canadian Journal of Economics and Political Science*, Vol. 29, No. 4, pp. 475–485.

Nelson, Richard R., and Gavin Wright (1992) "The Rise and Fall of American Technological Leadership: The Postwar Era in Historical Perspective," *Journal of Economic Literature*, Vol. 30, No. 4, pp. 1931–1964.

Nurkse, Ragnar (1944) *International Currency Experience: Lessons of the Inter-war Period.* Geneva: League of Nations.

——— (1947) "Conditions of International Monetary Equilibrium." Princeton Essays in International Finance No. 4. Princeton NJ: Princeton University, International Finance Section. Reprinted in S. Harris (ed.) (1947) *The New Economics: Keynes' Influence on Theory and Public Policy.* New York: Knopf, pp. 264–292.

O'Brien, Patrick (2003) "Political Structures and Grand Strategies for the Growth of the British Economy, 1688–1815," in Alice Teichova and H. Matis (eds.), *Nation, State and the Economy in History.* Cambridge: Cambridge University Press, pp. 11–33.

Obstfeld, Maurice, and Kenneth Rogoff (2009) "Global Imbalances and the Financial Crisis: Products of Common Causes." Available at http://elsa.berkeley.edu/~obstfeld/santabarbara.pdf.

Obstfeld, Maurice, and Alan M. Taylor. 2004. *Global Capital Markets: Integration, Crisis, and Growth.* Cambridge: Cambridge University Press.

Officer, Lawrence H. 1981. "A Test of Theories of Exchange-Rate Determination," *Journal of Economic History*, Vol. 41, No. 3, pp. 629–650.

Orwell, George (1958) *The Road to Wigan Pier.* San Diego: Harcourt Brace. First published in 1937.

Oudiz, Gilles, and Jeffrey Sachs (1984) "Macroeconomic Policy Coordination among the Industrial Economies," *Brookings Papers on Economic Activity*, No. 1, pp. 1–64.

Oxford Economics / Haver Analytics, *Haver Analytics*. Available at http://www.haver.com/databaseprofiles.html.

Philippon, Thomas (2008) "Why Has the Financial Sector Grown So Much? The Role of Corporate Finance," working paper. New York: New York University, Stern School of Business.

Portes, Richard (2009) "Global Imbalances," mimeo. London: London Business School.

Prasad, Eswar (2009) "Rebalancing Growth in Asia," NBER Working Paper 15169. Cambridge, MA: National Bureau of Economic Research.

Qureshi, Zia (2011) "G20 MAP: Growth, Rebalancing, and Development," presentation to the G24 meeting, Pretoria, March 17. Available at http://www.g24.org/zqu0311.pdf.

Rabinovitch, Simon (2012) "China's FX Reserves: The Coming Peak," *Financial Times*, June 1.

Reinhart, Carmen M., and Kenneth S. Rogoff (2009) *This Time Is Different: Eight Centuries of Financial Folly*. Princeton, NJ: Princeton University Press.

Reinhart, Vincent (2011) "A Year of Living Dangerously: The Management of Financial Crisis in 2008," *Journal of Economic Perspectives*, Vol. 25, No. 1, pp. 71–90.

Rothermund, Dieter (1996) *The Global Impact of the Great Depression, 1929–1939*. London: Routledge.

Russell, B. (1967) *The Autobiography of Bertrand Russell: 1872–1914*. London: George Allen and Unwin.

Sapir, A. (2011) "Europe after the Crisis: Less or More Role for Nation States in Money and Finance?" *Oxford Review of Economic Policy*, Vol. 27, No. 4, pp. 608–619.

Saxonhouse, Gary R., and Gavin Wright (2010) "National Leadership and Competing Paradigms: The Globalization of Cotton Spinning, 1878–1933," *Journal of Economic History*, Vol. 70, No. 3, pp. 535–566.

Sayers, Richard S. (1976) *The Bank of England, 1891–1944*. Cambridge: Cambridge University Press.

Schuker, Stephen A. (1976) *The End of French Predominance in Europe: The Financial Crisis of 1924 and the Adoption of the Dawes Plan*. Chapel Hill: University of North Carolina Press.

Schumpeter, Joseph (1946) "John Maynard Keynes 1883–1946," *American Economic Review*, Vol. 36, No. 4, pp. 495–518. Reprinted as "Keynes the Economist," in S. Harris (ed.) (1947) *The New Economics: Keynes' Influence on Theory and Public Policy*. New York: Knopf, pp. 73–101.

Skidelsky, Robert (1983) *John Maynard Keynes: Hopes Betrayed: 1883–1920*. London: Macmillan.

—— (1992) *John Maynard Keynes: The Economist as Saviour, 1920–1937*. London: Macmillan.

—— (2000) *John Maynard Keynes: Fighting for Britain, 1937–1946*. London: Macmillan.

Solow, Robert (1956) "A Contribution to the Theory of Economic Growth," *Quarterly Journal of Economics*, Vol. 70, No. 1, pp. 65–94.

Sommariva, Andrea, and Giuseppe Tullio (1986) *German Macroeconomic History, 1880–1979*. London: Macmillan.

Soros, George (2012) "How to Save the Euro," *New York Review of Books,* February.

Spence, Michael (2011) *The Next Convergence: The Future of Economic Growth in a Multi-speed World.* New York: Farrar, Straus and Giroux.

Stein, Judith (2010) *Pivotal Decade.* New Haven, CT: Yale University Press.

Stiglitz, Joseph (2002) *Globalization and Its Discontents.* New York: W. W. Norton.

—— (2012) *The Price of Inequality.* New York: W. W. Norton.

Swan, Trevor (1955) "Longer Run Problems of the Balance of Payments," paper presented to the Annual Conference of the Australian and New Zealand Association for the Advancement of Science. Published in H. W. Arndt and W. M. Corden (eds.) (1963) *The Australian Economy.* Melbourne: Cheshire Press, pp. 384–395. Reprinted in R. Caves and H. Johnson (eds.) (1968) *Readings in International Economics.* Homewood, IL: Irwin, pp. 455–464.

Taylor, John (2008) "The Financial Crisis and the Policy Responses: An Empirical Analysis of What Went Wrong." Available at http://www.stanford.edu/~johntayl/~johntayl/.

Temin, Peter (1966) "The Relative Decline of the British Steel Industry, 1880–1913," in H. Rosovsky (ed.), *Industrialization in Two Systems: Essays in Honor of Alexander Gerschenkron.* New York: John Wiley and Sons, pp. 140–155.

—— (1969) *The Jacksonian Economy.* New York: W. W. Norton.

—— (1971) "The Beginning of the Depression in Germany," *Economic History Review,* Vol. 24, No. 2, pp. 240–248.

—— (1989) *Lessons from the Great Depression.* Cambridge, MA: MIT Press.

—— (2002) "The Golden Age of Economic Growth Reconsidered," *European Review of Economic History*, Vol. 6, No. 1, pp. 3–22.

—— (2008a) "The German Crisis of 1931: Evidence and Tradition," *Cliometrica*, Vol. 2, No. 1, pp. 5–17.

—— (2008b) "Real Business Cycle Views of the Great Depression and Recent Events: A Review of Timothy J. Kehoe and Edward C. Prescott's *Great Depressions of the Twentieth Century*," *Journal of Economic Literature*, Vol. 46 (September), pp. 669–684; "Corrigendum," *Journal of Economic Literature*, Vol. 47 (March 2009), p. 3.

—— (2010) "The Great Recession and the Great Depression," *Daedalus*, Vol. 139, No. 4, pp. 115–124.

Temin, Peter, and Barrie A. Wigmore (1990) "The End of One Big Deflation," *Explorations in Economic History,* Vol. 27, No. 4, pp. 483–502.

Tooze, J. Adam (2006) *The Wages of Destruction: The Making and Breaking of the German Economy.* New York: Allen Lane.

van Dormael, Armand (1978) *Bretton Woods: Birth of an International Monetary System.* Basingstoke, UK: Macmillan.

Vines, David (2003) "John Maynard Keynes 1937–1946: The Creation of International Macroeconomics." Review of *John Maynard Keynes 1937–1946: Fighting for Britain,* by Robert Skidelsky. *Economic Journal,* Vol. 113, pp. F338–F360.

—— (2008) "Meade, J. E." in Steven Durlauf and Lawrence Blume (eds.), *New Palgrave Dictionary of Economics,* Second Edition, Vol. 5. London: Macmillan, pp. 485–503.

—— (2011a) "Recasting the Macroeconomic Policymaking System in Europe," *Zeitschrift für Staats- und Europeawissenschaften,* November.

—— (2011b) "After Cannes: The G20MAP, Global Rebalancing, and Sustaining Global Economic Growth." Available at http://www.bruegel.org/fileadmin/bruegel_files/Events/Event_materials/AEEF_Dec_2011/David_Vines_PRESENTATION_UPDATE.pdf.

Vines, David, and Peter Warr (2003) "Thailand's Investment-Driven Boom and Crisis," *Oxford Economic Papers*, Vol. 55, No. 3, pp. 440–446.

Warren, Harris G. (1959) *Herbert Hoover and the Great Depression.* New York: Oxford University Press.

Wei, S.-J., and X. Zhang (2009) "The Competitive Saving Motive: Evidence from Rising Sex Ratios and Savings Rates in China," NBER Working Paper 15093. Cambridge, MA: National Bureau of Economic Research.

Weinstein, Marc, and Thomas Kochan (1995) "The Limits of Diffusion: Recent Developments in Industrial Relations and Human Resource Practices in the United States," in Richard Locke, Thomas Kochan, and Michael Piore (eds.), *Employment Relations in a Changing World Economy.* Cambridge, MA: MIT Press, pp. 1–31.

Westaway, Peter (2003) *Modelling the Transition to EMU.* London: H. M. Treasury. Available at http://www.hm-treasury.gov.uk/d/adwiltshire03_123_452.pdf.

White, Lawrence J. (1991) *The S&L Debacle: Public Lessons for Bank and Thrift Regulation.* New York: Oxford University Press.

Widdig, Bernd (2001) *Culture and Inflation in Weimar Germany.* Berkeley: University of California Press.

Wigmore, Barrie. 1997. *Securities Markets in the 1980s: The New Regime, 1979–1984.* New York: Oxford University Press.

Williams, Kristen P., Steven E. Lobell, and Neal G. Jesse. 2012. *Beyond Great Powers and Hegemons.* Stanford, CA: Stanford University Press.

Williamson, John (1977) *The Failure of World Monetary Reform 1971–1974.* New York: New York University Press.

—— (1983) "Keynes and the International Economic Order," in G.D.N. Worswick and J. Trevithic (eds.), *Keynes and the Modern World.* Cambridge: Cambridge University Press, pp. 87–113.

Wolf, Martin (2011) "Creditors Can Huff But They Need Debtors," *Financial Times,* November 2.

Woodford, Michael (2003) *Interest and Prices: Foundations of a Theory of Monetary Policy.* Princeton, NJ: Princeton University Press.

Young, Warren (1987) *Interpreting Mr. Keynes: The IS-LM Enigma.* Cambridge: Policy Press.

Yu, Yongding (2009) "China's Policy Responses to the Global Financial Crisis," Richard Snape Lecture, Melbourne, November 25. Available at http://www.relooney.info/0_New_6189.pdf.

—— (2011) "Rebalancing the Chinese Economy," Exim Bank Annual Commencement Day Lecture, Mumbai, India, July 27. Available at http://www.eximbankindia.in/lecture11.pdf.

Page numbers for entries occurring in figures are followed by an *f;* those for entries in notes, by an *n;* and those for entries in tables, by a *t.*

Volcker, Paul, 125, 128, 208
voters, unemployed, 6. *See also* elections

wages: in British coal industry, 33; in EMU,
    181–82; evolution of Keynes' understanding
    of, 88–89, 96; in Keynes' explanation of gold-
    standard mechanism, 68–76; minimum, 121
wages, US: in auto industry, 122–23; in
    financial sector, 128–29, 130f, 131; impact of
    international trade on, 127–28. *See also*
    income distribution
Wagner, Robert, 121
Wagner Act. *See* National Labor Relations Act
Walters, Sir Alan, 190
Walters critique, 190–96
Washington Consensus: and Asian financial
    crises of 1997, 136; in Global Financial Crisis
    of 2008, 147, 148; and income distribution,
    131; and military budget, 133; origins of, 128,
    131. *See also* deregulation
Wassenaar agreement, 182
Waterloo, Battle of (1815), 22
Watt, James, 22
Weidmann, Jens, 252
Weimar Republic (Germany), 27–44;
    anti-Semitism in, 27; balance of payments of,
    36–37, 37t; budgetary problems of 1930s in,
    41; deflationary policies of, 38–39, 48, 52–53;
    Dolchstosslegende in, 27–28, 37, 54; economic
    slump in, 38–40; expansionary policies in,
    53–54; financial crisis of 1931 in, 41–44, 42t,
    43f, 48; foreign investment in, 37–39; gold
    standard in, end of, 43–44; internal politics
    in, 27–28, 53; recession of 1925–26 in, 38–39;
    recovery of 1932 in, 53–54; reparations in
    (*See* reparations); social reforms in, 30

West Germany: in European Coal and Steel
    Community, 153; in origins of European
    integration, 161–62, 163–64; reunification of,
    165–66, 168
White, Harry Dexter: at Bretton Woods, 104;
    in development of international monetary
    system, 95, 96, 103, 104; on need for inter-
    national cooperation, 250
Wilson, Charles, 122
Wilson, Woodrow, 24
Wittgenstein, Ludwig, 61
Woolf, Virginia, 62
working class, impact of First World War on,
    29–30
World Bank: limitations of, 108; origins of,
    103–4, 105; purpose of, 112; in Second World
    War recovery, 111, 112, 113, 151
world depression, definition of, 12
world economy: collapse of 2008 in (*See* Global
    Financial Crisis of 2008); contraction of
    2007–9 in, 1; downturn of 2008–9, 1, 229; as
    Keynes' primary interest, 245; need for
    hegemonic power in, 2, 18, 105, 147, 244; in
    recovery of national economies, 2; after
    Second World War, 206–9; three-body
    problem of, 206, 226–29, 247; universal
    participation in, 3
World Trade Organization (WTO), origins of,
    100, 103–4, 151
World War I. *See* First World War
World War II. *See* Second World War
WTO. *See* World Trade Organization

Young Plan, 39, 42, 43f, 113–14, 276n29

zombie banks, 135